REVISED THIRD EDITION

Introduction to Logic
Propositional Logic

Howard Pospesel

University of Miami

With an Appendix on Metatheory by

William G. Lycan

University of North Carolina at Chapel Hill

Prentice Hall
Upper Saddle River, New Jersey 07458

Library of Congress Cataloging-in-Publication Data

Pospesel, Howard
    Introduction to logic : propositional logic / Howard Pospesel ; with an appendix on
metatheory by William G. Lycan. – Rev. 3rd ed.
        p.   cm.
    Includes bibliographical references and index.
    ISBN 0-13-025849-0
        1. Proposition (Logic)   2. Logic, Symbolic and mathematical. 3. Reasoning.   I. Lycan,
    William G.   II. Title.
    BC181.P64   1999
    160–dc21   99-047648

Acquisitions editor: Karita France
Production editor: Pine Tree Composition, Inc.
Cover design: Pat Wosczyk
Buyer: Tricia Kenny
Marketing: Sheryl Adams
Editorial assistant: Jennifer Ackerman

This book was set in 10/12 Baskerville by Pine Tree Composition, Inc.
and was printed and bound by Courier Companies, Inc. The cover was
printed by Phoenix Color Corp.

Printed in the United States of America

10   9   8   7   6   5   4

ISBN   0-13-025849-0

Prentice-Hall International (UK) Limited, *London*
Prentice-Hall of Australia Pty. Limited, *Sydney*
Prentice-Hall Canada Inc., *Toronto*
Prentice-Hall Hispanoamericana, S.A., *Mexico*
Prentice-Hall of India Private Limited, *New Delhi*
Prentice-Hall of Japan, Inc., *Tokyo*
Pearson Education Asia Pte. Ltd., *Singapore*
Editora Prentice-Hall do Brasil, Ltda., *Rio de Janeiro*

For Carmen

Contents

Student's Preface

I intend this book to accomplish three ends. The *first goal* is to introduce you to an exciting branch of knowledge: contemporary symbolic logic. I shall do this by explaining in detail the elements of propositional logic, the fundamental part of symbolic logic. The *second goal* I have set for the book is to increase your awareness of the arguments you read and hear every day. Being aware of arguments is a precondition for assessing them. The means I have chosen to increase your awareness of arguments is to fill the following pages with actual examples of arguments that are very like the arguments you encounter. These examples have been drawn from newspapers, magazines, books, term papers, posters, television programs, films, records, and conversations. The *third goal* of the book is to sharpen your native ability to evaluate arguments. This is a goal of utmost consequence; one of the marks of a well-educated person is the ability to assess correctly the worth of arguments. I hope to achieve this goal by providing you with three important logical instruments: the methods of formal proofs (in Chapters Two through Nine), truth tables (Chapter Ten), and truth trees (Chapter Eleven).

I enjoyed writing this book; I hope you enjoy reading it.

Teacher's Preface

Any logic text written in English today should give some account of why it deserves to be added to the mountain of available material. The most important feature of this book is its *application*–from first example to final exercise–of the techniques of symbolic logic to arguments of the sort students encounter in their reading, conversing, and televiewing. In this respect the present volume differs from all other logic texts with which I am acquainted. The book was written in the belief that a study of propositional logic can improve one's rational skills, and it has been designed to help college students achieve such improvement.

The book is organized around natural-deduction formal-proof procedures. I am convinced that these procedures, because of their similarity to native patterns of inference and their emphasis upon plotting strategy, are well suited as instruments for accomplishing the end described above. Truth-table and truth-tree techniques are also presented, but only after an extensive treatment of formal proofs.

Statement connectives are introduced gradually, one per chapter. Students are afforded an opportunity to master both symbolization and proof moves involving a given connective, before adding more connectives to their logical vocabulary. This approach has proved successful in my own logic classes.

For several years I used E. J. Lemmon's outstanding text, *Beginning Logic,* in my introductory logic course. Those familiar with Lemmon's book will recognize the extent to which I have been influenced by it.

The (revised) third edition differs from the second edition chiefly in these ways:

1. Many of the exercises and examples have been replaced by better and more current ones.
2. I have added a chapter on truth trees.
3. The book is packaged with a computer tutorial program written by Mark Pospesel and me.
4. William G. Lycan has provided a much-needed appendix on metatheory.
5. For improved pedagogy the presentation of derived rules has been divided into two sections separated by an exercise set.
6. The brief-truth-table technique has been extended to make it a decision procedure.
7. I have replaced the tilde with the dash, primarily because the dash is easier to use in computer programs.
8. The distinction between an argument expressed in natural language and its representation in logical notation has been sharpened, in part through the introduction of the concept of a "sequent."

Acknowledgments

David Marans read and criticized each of the several drafts of the first edition; many pages have been improved by his suggestions. David created the crossword puzzles in Chapters Five, Nine, and Thirteen, and supplied twenty-five additional exercises.

The book has benefited from critical reading by Samuel Gorovitz, Gene James, Tom O'Kelley, Mark Woodhouse, and Greg Young. The following friends contributed exercises: Raymond Beck, Arnold Burr, Don Carignan, Debby Conrad, David Cooper, Laurie Dimun, Barbara Hecht, Barbara Irwin, Joan Kilpatrick, William King, Ernest Kloock, Hon-Fai Lee, Jeffrey Marcus, Robert McCleskey, Jorge Mederos, Jorge Morales, Denise Oehmig, Jon Ruse, Yolanda Sánchez, Alan Simpson, Linda Sumarlidason, Maria Valdez, Maria Vidaña, Edith Watson-Schipper, Fred Westphal, and Harold Zellner.

The second edition has been improved by suggestions from Ila Eisenberg, William Hanson, David Harrah, Owen Herring, David Randall Luce, Wayne MacVey, David Marans, and David Sanford. Howard Goldberg supplied elegant proofs for the "superchallenges" (exercise 18 in Chapter Eight and exercise 22 in Chapter Nine). Each of the following friends contributed several examples new to this edition: Juan Aldea, Carol Casey, David Marans, Denise Oehmig, Carmen and Michael Pospesel, and James Rachels. Other new exercises were supplied by Kaoru Abbey, Fabio Arber, Rondus Bennett, Nancy Cain, Marika Christ, Nancy Day, Bill Finlay, Noel Gianelli, Owen Herring, James Humble, Sharon Klein, Steve Klimacek, Scott Morrison, John Murray, Leo de la Peña, Jon Reynard, Jesús Rodríguez, Charles Rogers, Catherine Schmitt, Richard Talda, Bill Webber, Todd Williams, Michael Young, and Harold Zellner.

The third edition has benefitted from useful suggestions, and criticisms of the second edition, made by Carol Caraway, Owen Herring, Tony Hill, William G. Lycan, David Marans, and the publisher's four reviewers. Owen Herring, Tony Hill, and Carmen Pospesel read the manuscript for the third edition and caught numerous errors. Owen suggested a nice refinement for the truth-tree test, and Tony devised the "gonzo challenge" (exercise 23 in Chapter Nine). Risto Hilpinen reviewed Chapter Eleven. Stephen Satris provided an elegant proof for exercise 20(a) in Chapter Nine, and Jackie Schoonover did the same for problem (d) in the same exercise. Maxwell Nachlinger and Carmen Pospesel checked the page proofs.

Each of the following friends supplied two or more examples new to the third edition: Mariela Alvarez, Tony Hill, Miriam Mount, and Daisy Rosen. Other new exercises were provided by Ali Akhtar, Susan Alwell, John Clarke, Tanya Coll, Cyndi Cutler, Ed Erwin, James Hall, Robert Kelley, Fabienne Leconte, Carmen and Mark Pospesel, Supryia Ray, Zach Shelomith, Carl Snyder, Chris Tollefson, Jason Vida, and Fernando Vilela.

William Hanson, Owen Herring, David Marans, and Alan Soble were kind enough to class test beta versions of the computer program *PropLogic*. They, and their students, made useful suggestions for its improvement. Heidi Grasswick, Les Hammer, Tony Hill, Aman Mehan, Robert Rodes, and Jose Soberon reviewed the program and made many helpful comments. Harold Zellner and David Marans were most generous with their time and their suggestions were particularly helpful. *PropLogic* would not exist but for the creative talent and computer skills of its lead author, Mark Pospesel. He contributed much to the overall design and did all of the programming. Whoever examines the program will recognize his exceptional accomplishment.

1

Logic

1.1 Introduction

Blanche and Irwin Block died in their bed of gunshot wounds, and the weapon used was discovered clutched in Blanche's hand.[1] It *appeared* to be a murder-suicide, but according to the medical examiner, it was in fact a double murder. The medical examiner had a number of reasons for rejecting the murder-suicide theory. One of them was that Blanche had three incapacitating wounds to the head. This reason is expressed by the following argument:

> If Blanche committed suicide, then she would not have more than one incapacitating head wound.
> She did have more than one such wound.
> Therefore, Blanche did not commit suicide.

Every day, each of us advances arguments and encounters arguments put forward by others. Of course, few are as dramatic as the example above. Here is a more commonplace example. As you approach your bank you see that the parking lot is completely empty, and you reason as follows:

> If the bank is open, the parking lot won't be empty.
> But it is empty.
> Therefore, the bank is not open.

Arguments can be assessed in two quite different ways. On the one hand, we may determine the truth or falsity of the premises occurring in an argu-

---

[1]"Autopsies Point to Son in Death of His Parents," *Miami Herald* (April 11, 1996), pp. 1B, 5B. (I use a fictitious last name.)

ment. This may be called assessing the argument's *content*. On the other hand, we may determine whether the conclusion follows from the premises. When we evaluate an argument on this score we are assessing its *form* or *structure*. In general, *logic* is concerned with evaluating the form rather than the content of arguments. For example, it is not the business of logic to determine the truth (or falsity) of the premises in the above argument about murder; this job falls within the province of forensic medicine. The logician is interested in identifying and assessing the form of the argument. When we remove the content from the "Murder" argument, this form remains:

> If P then not Q
> Q
> Therefore not P

The "Bank" argument also has this form. The form is a good one; if an argument exhibits it, its conclusion follows from its premises.

This distinction between form and content may be further illustrated with the help of these examples:

Argument One	Argument Two
If Atlanta is the capital of Florida, then Atlanta is in Florida.	If Atlanta is in Florida, then Atlanta is south of Detroit.
Atlanta is the capital of Florida.	Atlanta is south of Detroit.
Therefore, Atlanta is in Florida.	Therefore, Atlanta is in Florida.

Because these two arguments have false conclusions, each must incorporate some error. The mistake in Argument One is obvious: its second premise is false (a mistake of content). The premises of Argument Two are true. However, it has a different type of defect: its conclusion does not follow from its premises. The argument exhibits the following defective form:

> If P then Q
> Q
> Therefore P

What is the form of Argument One?

Occasionally you come across a really rotten argument that has faulty content *and* faulty form. The smooth dude in the "Sylvia" comic strip on page 159 employs such an argument.[2]

As stated above, logic focuses on evaluating the form of arguments. Here is the approach to be used in the following chapters: I provide a system for representing arguments in symbols and then present several techniques for

---

[2]The argument's *content* is faulty because many girls play team sports. The *formal* mistake committed by the argument is discussed in Section 5.2.

evaluating these symbolizations. We will evaluate the form of arguments indirectly by assessing their symbolic representations.[3]

An argument does not establish the truth of its conclusion unless it has *both* correct content *and* a good form. One purpose of education is to prepare people for the job of evaluating the content of the arguments they encounter. One purpose of a logic course (and perhaps the main purpose) is to enhance people's native ability to evaluate the form of the arguments they meet. Another purpose of a logic course is to impress upon the student the importance of identifying arguments and assessing them in both of these ways (in terms of content and form).

But why should we assess the arguments that come our way? Because we want (as far as possible) to believe only what is true. The best way to establish the truth or falsity of many of our beliefs is to assess the arguments that can be advanced for or against those beliefs. And why do we want to believe only truths? Because actions based upon false beliefs are often unsuccessful; and because—practical considerations aside—people find distasteful the idea of believing to be true what is actually false.

1.2   Key Terms

Before proceeding further, it will be helpful to clarify some of the terms that have occurred above and to introduce additional ones. Each term in this list requires comment:

> argument
> conclusion
> premise
> statement
> deductive logic
> valid
> invalid
> true
> false
> inductive logic

The meanings that logic assigns these terms will not necessarily match the meanings they have in ordinary discourse.

---

[3]This approach traces back to the first systematic logician, Aristotle (384–322 B.C.). Modern symbolic logic was developed by several nineteenth-century mathematician-logicians, chiefly George Boole, Augustus De Morgan, Charles Peirce, and Gottlob Frege. Their work was greatly expanded in the twentieth century by scholars too numerous to mention here.

Argument is a fundamental logical concept. An *argument* is a set of statements, one of which (the *conclusion*) supposedly follows from the others (the *premises*). (Including the word 'supposedly' broadens the definition so that it covers bad arguments as well as good ones.) Arguments are the expressions in language of pieces of reasoning. The constituents of arguments are statements. The question of the nature of statements is an unresolved philosophical issue. Fortunately, this working definition suffices for our purposes: a *statement* is a sentence that is true or false. The class of statements is roughly the class of declarative sentences. Some examples:

Statements	Nonstatements
Al Gore is a Democrat.	Do you have the time?
All acoustic neuromas are benign.	Don't cross the street.
Some Egyptians are blonds.	Please help me find my brother.
	Look out!
	Bless this food.

The two main branches of logic are deductive and inductive logic. In *deductive logic* we are concerned with dividing arguments into two classes: (1) those whose conclusions follow with necessity from their premises; and (2) all other arguments. Arguments in the first class are called *valid;* those in the second class are called *invalid.* Here are two equivalent definitions of 'validity':

A valid argument is one having a form such that *if* all its premises are true, *then* its conclusion must also be true.

A valid argument is one having a form such that it is impossible that its premises are all true and its conclusion false.

Because "validity" is such an important concept in deductive logic there are several equivalent ways of saying that an argument is valid, for example:

The premises of the argument *entail* its conclusion.
The conclusion of the argument *follows with necessity* from its premises.
The conclusion of the argument *follows logically* from its premises.

Note that *validity* as we have defined it is a matter of form, not content. A valid argument may contain false statements, and an invalid one may be composed exclusively of truths. These examples illustrate:

Valid	Invalid
Boris Yeltsin is an American and he is also a poet. Therefore, he is a poet.	Gwendolyn Brooks is an American. Therefore, she is an American and she is also a poet.

Both statements in the "Yeltsin" argument are false. In spite of this defect, it exhibits impeccable form. If the premise of the "Yeltsin" argument *were* true, then the conclusion *would also be* true. Both statements in the "Brooks" argument are true. But in spite of this virtue, its form is poor. The conclusion of the "Brooks" inference simply does not follow from its premises. The two arguments have these forms:

"Yeltsin"	P and Q Therefore P	*valid form*
"Brooks"	P Therefore P and Q	*invalid form*

Within the class of invalid arguments one can find all the possible combinations of the truth and falsity of constituent statements. Here are several examples:

false premise and
  false conclusion
	Sandra O'Connor is a Cuban.
	Therefore, she is a Cuban and she is also
	  a brickmason.

false premise and *true conclusion*	All Protestants are Lutherans. Therefore, all Lutherans are Protestants.

true premise and
  false conclusion
	Al Gore is either a Protestant or he is a
	  Catholic.
	Therefore, he is a Catholic.

In the class of valid arguments one can find all combinations except one. Here are some examples:

true premise and *true conclusion*	Some Lutherans are Democrats. Therefore, some Democrats are Lutherans.

false premise and
  true conclusion
	Al Gore is a Catholic.
	Therefore, he is either a Protestant or he is
	  a Catholic.

Among deductive arguments one combination—namely, "(all) true premises and a false conclusion"—is excluded by the definition of 'validity'. The virtue of validity lies in this feature—that it is *truth preserving*. A valid argument can never take you from truth to falsity.

The term 'valid' as we have defined it does not exactly correspond to the term 'valid' of ordinary discourse. (As the technical term has a precise meaning and the ordinary term does not, their meanings could not correspond completely.) The principal difference is that the ordinary term encompasses both form and content while the technical term is restricted to form alone. When we assess a piece of reasoning as "valid" in nontechnical discourse, we mean to praise both its structure and its substance. The 'valid' of everyday language would not be applied to arguments that are defective in either respect.

To avoid confusion, let's agree (while we are engaged in logic) to apply the adjectives 'valid' and 'invalid' only to arguments and to assess statements, but not arguments, as 'true' or 'false'. According to this proposal, nothing will be called both *valid* and *true,* as the following argument proves.

> Only arguments are valid.
> No arguments are true.
> Therefore, nothing is both valid and true.

And, of course, nothing will be called both *invalid* and *false.* A statement is *true* when it accords with the actual state of affairs, and one that does not is *false.*

In *inductive logic* we are concerned with locating arguments on a continuum that has at one pole arguments whose premises provide no support whatever for their conclusions, and that has at the other pole arguments whose premises provide the maximum support for their conclusions. (The deductive logician would label arguments at the latter pole *valid.*) The inductive logician is not primarily concerned with the arguments falling at either extreme but with those falling between the poles; that is, arguments whose premises provide some—but not absolutely conclusive—support for their conclusions. The seventh scene of Tennessee Williams's *The Glass Menagerie* provides a nice example:

> AMANDA: . . . *What is the young man's name?*
>
> TOM: *His name is O'Connor.*
>
> AMANDA: *That, of course, means fish—tomorrow is Friday! I'll have that salmon loaf—with Durkee's dressing!*[4]

Under one possible analysis Amanda's reasoning may be expressed as two linked arguments:

> The Gentleman Caller is a man named "O'Connor."
> All men named "O'Connor" are Irish.
> Therefore, the Gentleman Caller is Irish.

> The Gentleman Caller is Irish.
> Most Irish people are Catholic.
> Most Catholics do not eat meat on Fridays.[5]
> Therefore, the Gentleman Caller does not eat meat on Fridays.

---

[4] *The Glass Menagerie* (New York: New Directions, 1949), p. 61.

[5] This dietary prohibition was dropped in 1966 following the Second Vatican Council.

The conclusion of the first argument follows from its premises with necessity. The premises of the second argument provide some support for their conclusion, but that conclusion does not follow with necessity.

A major difference between the two branches of logic lies in the standards used in assessing argument forms. Deductive logic employs all-or-nothing standards; each argument is valid or invalid. The second argument displayed above is judged invalid in deductive logic. Inductive logic employs standards that permit graded assessments. Because the form of the second "Gentleman Caller" argument has some merit, but not maximum merit, that argument is more usefully evaluated in inductive logic.

Both branches of logic are important. Unfortunately, inductive logic is not as well developed as its older sibling. The remainder of this volume is devoted exclusively to deductive logic.[6] Actually, its scope is further restricted to a branch of deductive logic called *propositional logic.* Many of the preceding examples fall within the scope of propositional logic; others belong to another branch of deductive logic called *predicate logic.*[7] What distinguishes propositional logic from the rest of deductive logic is explained in the next chapter.

EXERCISES

1. Consider this valid argument form:

   P and Q
   Therefore P

   ('P' and 'Q' mark gaps to be filled by statements.) Invent an English argument with a true premise and a true conclusion that exhibits this form. Here is an example:

   Newt Gingrich is a Republican and he is a Protestant.
   Therefore, Newt Gingrich is a Republican.

   Devise a second English argument exhibiting this form that has a false premise and a true conclusion, and a third with a false premise and false conclusion. Can you invent a fourth argument having this form that has a true premise and a false conclusion?

2. Consider this invalid argument form:

   P and Q
   Therefore P and R

   ('P', 'Q', and 'R' mark gaps to be filled by statements.) Invent four English arguments exhibiting this form such that the first has a true premise and a true conclusion, the second has a false premise and a true conclusion,

---

[6]If you want to learn some inductive logic, begin with Brian Skyrms, *Choice and Chance: An Introduction to Inductive Logic* (Belmont, Calif.: Dickenson, 1966).

[7]See my *Introduction to Logic: Predicate Logic* (Englewood Cliffs, N.J.: Prentice-Hall, 1976). This book presupposes familiarity with propositional logic.

the third has a false premise and a false conclusion, and the fourth has a true premise and a false conclusion.

3. This logic puzzle appeared on the Internet as the focus of a contest:

> Many years from now, two guys are sitting in the county park. The following is part of their discussion:
>
> MAN 1: *Yes, I'm married and have three fine sons.*
> MAN 2: *That's wonderful! How old are they?*
> MAN 1: *Well, The product of their ages is equal to 36.*
> MAN 2: *Hmm. That doesn't tell me enough. Give me another clue.*
> MAN 1: *O.K. The sum of their ages is the number on that building across the street.*
> MAN 2: *Ah ha! I've almost got the answer, but I still need another clue.*
> MAN 1: *Very well. The oldest one has red hair.*
> MAN 2: *I've got it!*
>
> What were the ages of the three sons of Man 1? (Hint: all ages are integers.)

Solve this puzzle if you can. The solution calls for deductive reasoning. Provide not only the answer, but also the reasoning (the argument) that supports your answer. Later in the book you will evaluate an argument that contains my solution to this puzzle.

9, 2, 2

2

If

2.1 Compound Statements

We will call a statement that has no parts that are themselves statements *simple*. Some examples:

> Some Lutherans are Democrats.
> The bank is open.

Any statement that is not simple we will call *compound*.[1] Some sample compound statements:

> *If* the fan belt breaks *then* the alternator stops turning.
> Gwendolyn Brooks is an American *and* she is a poet.
> *Either* one of the children is up *or* there is an intruder in the house.
> Active euthanasia is justified *if and only if* passive euthanasia is.

Each of these four statements consists of two simple statements and an expression that connects the simple statements. These connecting expressions (which are italicized in the above examples) are called, naturally enough, *statement connectives*. The following statement is also compound:

> It is not the case that Blanche committed suicide.

---

[1]Grammarians use the term 'compound' (also 'simple') in a different sense. A number of expressions employed in this book have other meanings in grammar.

It consists of the locution 'it is not the case that' and a simple statement. The locution is called a *statement connective* in spite of the fact that it attaches to one statement instead of connecting two.

There are many statement connectives in English (or in any natural language), but these five are of special importance in logic:

> if . . . then
> and
> it is not the case that
> if and only if
> either . . . or

The remainder of this book is a study of these five connectives, the compound statements that can be constructed with their help, and especially the arguments that involve these compound statements. The study of the forms of arguments whose validity or invalidity rests on the pattern of compound statements composing them is called *the logic of statements* or, more commonly, *propositional logic*. Now you can see why some of the arguments considered in Chapter One belong to propositional logic, while others do not.

In this chapter (and Chapter Four) we devote our attention to the statement connective 'if . . . then'. In Chapters Three, Five, Six, and Seven we concentrate on the other four connectives listed above.

2.2   Symbolizing Conditionals

PEANUTS © United Feature Syndicate. Reprinted by permission.

A statement composed of two constituent statements and the connective 'if . . . then' is called a *conditional*. The component statement that precedes 'then' is called the *antecedent* (meaning "that which precedes"), and the component following 'then' is termed the *consequent* ("that which follows"). The antecedent and the consequent may be either simple or compound. A sample conditional:

(S1) If the fan belt BREAKS, then the alternator STOPS turning.

We facilitate our work by employing symbols. Three kinds of symbols will suffice for the present. (1) *Capital letters* are used to abbreviate simple statements. Any letter could be used, of course, but I will adopt the convention of choosing the first letter of a prominent word in the statement. In this text the words I have selected to supply statement abbreviations are printed entirely in capital letters–this will help us keep track of the symbols chosen. An example: The antecedent of S1 will be symbolized by the letter B. Although the convention I have chosen for indicating letters involves printing *words* in capital letters, do not think that an abbreviating letter represents a word or any linguistic expression shorter than a statement. For example, in S1 B abbreviates 'The fan belt breaks'–not 'breaks'. Simple statements (occurring in one problem) that convey the same information or have the same content are abbreviated by the same letter. For example, these three statements would be symbolized with the same letter:

> Marvin struck Norton.
> Marvin hit Norton.
> Norton was struck by Marvin.

Simple statements (occurring in one problem) with different content are abbreviated by different letters.

(2) The statement connective 'if ... then' is abbreviated by the *arrow* symbol ($\rightarrow$). The arrow is preceded by a capital letter (or letters) representing the antecedent statement and followed by a letter (or letters) representing the consequent. S1 is symbolized by the formula F1.

(F1) $B \rightarrow S$

This formula is read "If B then S" or "B arrow S." We defined 'conditional' in terms of *statements*; now let's extend that concept so that it applies also to *formulas* like F1, which are the symbolizations of conditional statements.

(3) A formula containing three or more letters requires *grouping symbols* in order to avoid ambiguity. For example, it isn't clear whether F2X (below) symbolizes a conditional with a simple antecedent and a compound (conditional) consequent or one with a compound antecedent and a simple consequent.

(F2X) $A \rightarrow B \rightarrow C$

Our primary grouping symbols are the *parentheses*: '(' and ')'. These can be used in an entirely natural fashion to eliminate the ambiguity present in F2X.

(F3) $A \rightarrow (B \rightarrow C)$
(F4) $(A \rightarrow B) \rightarrow C$

F3 represents a conditional with a simple antecedent; the conditional represented by F4 has a compound antecedent. Speaking metaphorically, the parentheses in F3 are fences that limit the range of the second arrow. This indicates that the first arrow, which is not similarly limited, is the primary connective in F3. We say that the first arrow has greater *scope* than the second. Its scope is the entire formula, while the scope of the second arrow is the string of symbols lying between the parentheses. This emphasis on the use of grouping symbols is not (as it might seem) academic nitpicking, for, as we shall prove later (in Section 13.2), F3 and F4 are not equivalent. Our policy will be to avoid ambiguous formulas such as F2X.

In the punctuation of some formulas we will need *brackets* ('[' and ']') in addition to parentheses; in a few instances we will even require *braces* ('{' and '}'). F5 illustrates the use of all six grouping symbols.

$$(F5) \quad D \to \{ \, [E \to (F \to G)] \to H \, \}$$
$$\qquad\quad 1 \qquad 3 \quad\ \ 4 \qquad 2$$

The grouping symbols in F5 assign varying scopes to the four arrows. The numbers beneath the arrows show their rank in terms of scope. If we employed all the grouping symbols in punctuating a formula and needed still more, we could start over again with parentheses.

English provides many ways of expressing S6.

(S6)   *If* MARVIN stays, *then* NANCY leaves.

We can describe S6 as a conditional expressed in *standard form.* The sentences in the following list are equivalent to S6:

> *If* Marvin stays Nancy leaves.
> Nancy leaves *if* Marvin stays.
> *Provided that* Marvin stays Nancy leaves.
> Nancy leaves *provided that* Marvin stays.
> *Should* Marvin stay, Nancy will leave.
> Marvin's staying will *result in (bring about, lead to,* etc.) Nancy's leaving.

Each of these statements is correctly symbolized by F6.

(F6) $M \to N$

It is particularly important to realize that not one of these statements is correctly rendered by F6X.

(F6X) $N \to M$

The order given to the components of a conditional is critical. We may employ this symbolization guide:

> **The statement following the word 'if' (or its synonym 'provided that') is the antecedent; accordingly, its abbreviation is placed before the arrow.**

If you apply this guide to the above statements that contain 'if' or 'provided that', you will arrive at F6 (not F6X) in each case. (Unfortunately, the guide breaks down when applied to the locution 'only if'; however, we will not encounter any "only if" statements until Chapter Four.)

We can analyze into several steps the procedure for symbolizing a conditional (or any other type of statement that may be analyzed in propositional logic):

1. Put the sentence into standard form ("If . . . then . . . " in the case of conditionals).
2. Substitute capital letters for simple statements.
3. Replace English connective expressions with connective symbols.
4. Add grouping symbols if necessary.
5. Check the adequacy of your symbolization by translating it back into English and comparing the result with the original sentence.

As you gain practice in symbolizing you will compress the first four steps into one. Let's illustrate the procedure with a more complex problem. This sentence is quoted from a logic textbook:

> *If the RULES are valid, then if the AXIOMS are true, all the THEOREMS must be true.*

The sentence is nearly in standard form as it stands; all we need do is insert a 'then' after the second comma. Substituting capital letters we reach:

> If R, then if A, then T.

We can substitute arrows for the two English connectives in two steps, beginning with the connective having greater scope:

> R → (if A, then T)
> R → (A → T)

As a final example I will symbolize this statement from a newspaper column:

> *. . . He [Newt Gingrich] may be TEMPTED to run—if the CONTRACT [with America] rolls roughshod through Congress, if Newt's POPULARITY rises, and if Bill Clinton SINKS into Bushlike vulnerability.*

It is not really obvious how to put this into standard form, but we can make a reasonable attempt as follows:

If C, then if P, then if S, then T.
$C \rightarrow [P \rightarrow (S \rightarrow T)]$

If we compare the English equivalent of this triple-arrow formula with the original English we will probably conclude that they make the same claim. One peculiarity of this treatment is that it ignores the 'and' in the original sentence. For a different symbolization that does not ignore the 'and' (but does ignore two of the 'if's), see exercise 17 at the end of Chapter Four.

2.3   Arrow Out

The most basic and most frequently employed pattern of valid inference is this:

If $\mathcal{P}$ then $\mathcal{Q}$
$\mathcal{P}$
Therefore $\mathcal{Q}$

('$\mathcal{P}$' and '$\mathcal{Q}$' mark gaps that may be filled by statements. I use script letters to represent the generality of this inference form. *Any* statements may fill the gaps marked by '$\mathcal{P}$' and '$\mathcal{Q}$'.) Observe that the second premise of an argument exhibiting this form is identical to the *antecedent* of the first premise, and that the conclusion is identical to the *consequent* of the first premise. This pattern of inference is employed by every human who reasons and has been recognized since antiquity. It bears the Latin label *modus ponens,* meaning "in the mood of affirming" (the second premise affirms the antecedent of the first premise). *Modus ponens* is so basic that its validity does not require justification. In fact, it is so fundamental that any argument that might be advanced in its behalf would be at least as questionable as (and very probably, more questionable than) *modus ponens* itself. Nevertheless, we shall suggest a justification in Section 10.1.

Supreme Court Chief Justice Earl Warren summed up his opinion in the historic *Brown* v. *Board of Education* case[2] as follows:

> *We conclude that, in the field of public education, the doctrine of "separate but equal" has no place. Separate educational facilities are inherently unequal. Therefore, we hold that the plaintiffs and others similarly situated for whom the actions*

[2]347 U.S. 483 (1954).

have been brought are, by reason of the segregation complained of, deprived of the equal protection of the laws guaranteed by the Fourteenth Amendment.

This argument is an *enthymeme*; that is, one of its elements (the conditional premise) is missing. When we supply that statement a *modus ponens* argument emerges:

> If segregated public schools are inherently UNEQUAL, then they VIO-LATE the Fourteenth Amendment. And they are inherently unequal. It follows that segregated public schools violate the Fourteenth Amendment.

This argument may be symbolized:

$$U \rightarrow V, U \vdash V$$

The premises are separated by a comma. We adopt the *turnstile* symbol, '$\vdash$', as shorthand for the word 'therefore': the turnstile is placed between the last premise and the conclusion.

Let's call a sequence of two or more formulas where the last formula follows a turnstile a "sequent." Most of the sequents that we will consider in this book will be symbolizations of arguments expressed in English. We need to extend the concepts of "validity" and "invalidity" to sequents. What will it mean to call a "sequent" valid? That it has a form such that if its premise formulas symbolize true statements, then the statement that its conclusion formula symbolizes must also be true. We will call a sequent "invalid" if it is not valid. It is clear that if we can show that the sequent symbolizing some argument is valid, that will demonstrate the validity of the argument as well.

It is important to distinguish *modus ponens* from the following invalid inference pattern:

> If P then Q
> Q
> Therefore P

The second premise of an argument having this form is identical to the *consequent* of the first premise. This pattern is appropriately labelled *the fallacy of affirming the consequent*. The contrast between the two argument patterns is shown clearly in the following:

> *modus ponens*: $\quad P \rightarrow Q, P \vdash Q$ *(valid)*
> affirming the consequent: $\quad P \rightarrow Q, Q \vdash P$ *(invalid)*

Consider an example of an argument that commits the fallacy of affirming the consequent:

> If Jesse Jackson is PRESIDENT, then he is FAMOUS. He is famous.
> So, he is president.

Symbolized:

$$P \rightarrow F, F \vdash P$$

The first premise of the argument asserts that Jackson's attaining the presidency would imply his being famous; it does *not* assert that his achieving fame implies his being president. Thus, when the first premise is coupled with the second, it does not follow that Jackson is president.

The deficiency of the "Jackson" argument is especially noticeable because its premises are obviously true and its conclusion is plainly false. Some arguments that commit the same fallacy have conclusions that are true or at least not clearly false. Such arguments can seduce the unwary. The following passage from a book by Hillyer Straton provides an example:

> *Never has a book been subjected to such pitiless search for error as the Holy Bible. Both reverent and agnostic critics have ploughed and harrowed its passages; but through it all God's word has stood supreme, and appears even more vital because of the violent attacks made upon it. This is proof to Baptists that here we have a revelation from God; for we believe that if God reveals himself to man for purposes of blessing, he will preserve a record of that revelation in order that men who follow may know his way and will.*[3]

Straton appears to be advancing this argument:

> If the Bible is God's REVELATION, then it will WITHSTAND critical attack. It does withstand such attack. Hence, it is revelation.

In symbols:

$$R \rightarrow W, W \vdash R$$

Some may fail to see the formal defect in the "Revelation" argument (despite the fact that it has the same form as the "Jackson" argument). The first premise of the "Revelation" argument does *not* assert that the Bible's withstanding attack implies its being revelation. This fact constitutes the basis of the argument's invalidity. A formal demonstration of its invalidity is given in Section 10.1.

The first step in determining the form of an argument is identifying its premises and conclusion. How do you do this? Of course, there is no substitute for understanding the passage that contains the argument. However, certain key terms are fairly reliable indicators. These expressions follow premises and introduce conclusions:

---

[3] *Baptists: Their Message and Missions* (Philadelphia: Judson Press, 1941), p. 49.

therefore
so
hence
thus
consequently
it follows that
. . . proves that
. . . shows that

And these expressions regularly follow conclusions and introduce premises:

since
because
for

Neither of these lists is exhaustive. The quotation from Hillyer Straton above illustrates the usefulness of these indicator expressions. The phrase 'This is proof to Baptists that' precedes the conclusion, and follows a premise, and the word 'for' (on line five of the quotation) introduces another premise.

It often helps to first identify the conclusion of an argument. As there is only *one* conclusion per argument, the remaining statements (assuming they all belong to the argument) will be premises. The conclusion may appear at the beginning, in the middle, or at the end of an English argument. When we symbolize the argument, we place the (symbolized) conclusion last. The order given to the symbolized premises is not critical, but I follow the practice of symbolizing premises in the order in which they occur in the English formulation of the argument.

Let's return to our discussion of the argument pattern *modus ponens*. It can be used to establish the validity of certain other more complex arguments. An argument advanced by *Star Trek's* Mr. Spock provides an example.

In one episode he addresses the following to Assistant Commander Matt Decker (paraphrased):

> *Continuing to attack the enemy ship would be suicide. Anybody who attempts suicide is psychologically unfit to command the* Enterprise. *Therefore, I will have to relieve you of your duty.*

With a little tinkering we can formalize Spock's argument as follows:

> Decker is ATTACKING the enemy ship. If so, then he is attempting SUICIDE. Decker is psychologically UNFIT to command the *Enterprise* if he is trying to commit suicide. If Decker is psychologically unfit to command the *Enterprise,* then he must be RELIEVED of duty. Therefore, Decker must be removed.

This argument is symbolized:

$$A, A \rightarrow S, S \rightarrow U, U \rightarrow R \vdash R$$

One way of showing this sequent to be valid is to note that one can infer S from the first two premises and then, by combining S with the third premise, infer U, and finally, by combining U with the fourth premise, infer the conclusion, R. All three inferences are instances of *modus ponens*.

We have in the above reasoning implicitly assumed a principle that should be brought to the surface—namely, that if one can proceed from the premises of a sequent to its conclusion by a series of valid inferences, then the sequent is valid. This principle underlies a logical technique called the method of *formal proof*, which we shall introduce now and develop in the next seven chapters. A formal proof of the validity of a sequent is a list of formulas that satisfies two conditions: (1) each item in the list is either a premise of the sequent or a formula derived by means of a valid inference rule from formulas above it in the list; and (2) the last item in the list is the conclusion of the sequent. (This explanation of "formal proof" will be tightened in Section 8.3.)

The first rule of inference we adopt sanctions *modus ponens* inferences. We call it the *Arrow Out Rule* because it licenses the passage from a formula containing an arrow (and a second formula) to one lacking the arrow.

The Arrow Out Rule ($\rightarrow$O): From a conditional formula and a formula identical to its antecedent derive a formula identical to its consequent.

We can state this rule more simply if we let '$\mathcal{A} \rightarrow \mathcal{B}$' represent any conditional formula (no matter how complex), '$\mathcal{A}$', a formula identical to the antecedent of that conditional, and '$\mathcal{B}$', a formula identical to the consequent of the conditional. The rule restated:

From $\mathcal{A} \rightarrow \mathcal{B}$ and $\mathcal{A}$ derive $\mathcal{B}$.

We are now in a position to construct this formal proof (or simply "proof") for the *Star Trek* sequent:

A
A $\rightarrow$ S
S $\rightarrow$ U
U $\rightarrow$ R
S
U
R

To facilitate the checking of proofs and to render one person's proofs more intelligible to another, we shall include two additional columns. (Later, we will add a fourth column.) In the column on the left we number the items; in the one on the right (called the *justification* column) we give for each item a reason or justification for including it in the list. With these conventions adopted, the proof of the *Star Trek* sequent becomes:

(1)	A	A
(2)	A → S	A
(3)	S → U	A
(4)	U → R	A
(5)	S	2,1 →O
(6)	U	3,5 →O
(7)	R	4,6 →O

We adopt *A* as an abbreviation for 'Introduced as an assumption'. (For the time being, all assumptions in a proof will be premises of the sequent being validated.) We adopt, for example, '2, 1 →O' as shorthand for 'Derived from lines 2 and 1 by the Arrow Out Rule'. In justifying a step made in accordance with the Arrow Out Rule, I cite the conditional premise first.

Thor Heyerdahl, the Norwegian ethnologist and explorer, claimed that logic led him to sail from Peru to Polynesia in a balsa raft, "Kon-Tiki." He knew that some Polynesian plants had come from South America before the first Europeans had arrived in South America, and he knew that the pre-Columbian Peruvian boats were made of balsa:

> *If experts said this boat or that could not sail in the open sea, I had the evidence of earlier voyages—the plants, say—and if they clearly had made these voyages centuries ago and if they had only one kind of possible boat to make them in, then the logic is clear—they sailed in those boats, no matter what the experts might say about their seaworthiness.*[4]

Heyerdahl's reasoning is expressed in this argument:

> Peruvians sailed to Polynesia BEFORE Columbus. If so, then they must have TRAVELLED to Polynesia in balsa boats if the boats available at that time were ALL made of balsa. The boats available at that time were all constructed of balsa. Conclusion: the Peruvians travelled to Polynesia in boats made of balsa.

In symbols:

$$B, B \rightarrow (A \rightarrow T), A \vdash T$$

[4]Henry Mitchell, "Author's Voyage through History," *Miami Herald* (May 30, 1986), p. 1B.

A proof of validity:

(1)	B	A
(2)	B → (A → T)	A
(3)	A	A
(4)	A → T	2,1 →O
(5)	T	4,3 →O

Line 2 in this proof is a conditional whose consequent is also a conditional. The inference of line 4 from lines 2 and 1 illustrates the point noted above that the Arrow Out Rule applies to conditionals having compound parts.

As a final example I construct a proof for this sequent:

$$(I \rightarrow J) \rightarrow K, K \rightarrow I, I \rightarrow J \vdash J$$

(1)	(I → J) → K	A
(2)	K → I	A
(3)	I → J	A
(4)	K	1,3 →O
(5)	I	2,4 →O
(6)	J	3,5 →O

Note that the conditional on line 1 of this proof has a compound antecedent ('I → J') that is matched by the conditional on line 3. Also note that line 3 serves as a premise in the deduction of *two* lines (4 and 6). This is permissible; any line in a proof can be used as a premise as often as needed.

This logical technique is called the method of *formal* proof for at least two reasons. First, every step in a proof must be sanctioned *explicitly* by some rule. There is no room for informal sanctions such as "Well, I see that this follows." Second, each inference rule employed refers only to the *forms* of the lines to which it is applied.

EXERCISES[5]

1. Symbolize each statement using the suggested abbreviations.
    (a) *(Hezbollah guerrilla)* "If I die for ISLAM, then I go to PARADISE."
   *(b) *(oceanographer Sylvia Earle)* "If the OCEANS die, WE die."
    (c) *(Florida Turnpike toll card)* "If ticket is LOST regular toll from farthest point will be COLLECTED."

---

[5]You can check your symbolizations and proofs with the computer program *PropLogic.*
*Solutions (or partial solutions) to starred problems are provided in Appendix Six.

(d) *(Newspaper)* "Some 7,000 employees of Southern Bell in Dade County would be AFFECTED if a nationwide STRIKE of Bell System workers goes into effect."

(e) *(Margaret Thatcher)* "I am extraordinarily PATIENT provided I get my own WAY in the end."

*(f) *(Newspaper)* "Should the Dolphins QUALIFY as a runnerup team, they will PLAY at Cleveland Christmas weekend."

(g) *(Newspaper)* "San Diego can CLINCH the AFC West crown by BEATING Denver in their final game." $C \to (B \to A)$

(h) *(Science fiction)* "Had the stowaway REFUSED to obey, the pilot would have used the BLASTER."

(i) *(quarterback Ryan Collins on competition for the starting assignment)* "As long as it's FAIR, I'm going to WIN the job."

*(j) *(logician James Carney)* "If the AXIOMS could be so selected that they were necessarily true, then, if the DEDUCTIONS were valid, the truth of the THEOREMS would be guaranteed."

(k) *(newspaper)* "If you have a specific QUESTION, we will RELAY it to him, if he CALLS in." $Q \to (C \to R)$ If Q, Then R, if C. $Q \to (C \to R)$

(l) *(newspaper)* "If U.S. Shipyard's own bid to acquire the property FAILS, the company would be interested in a LEASE so long as the payments are REASONABLE." $F \to (R \to L)$

2. Translate each formula into an English sentence using this "dictionary":

A = Salt is added to the solution
D = The solution's boiling point drops
M = The manual is correct
S = The solution boils sooner

(a) $A \to D$
*(b) $M \to (A \to S)$
(c) $(A \to D) \to (A \to S)$

3. Complete the following proofs. Every assumption has been identified in the justification column.

(a)
(1) $A \to B$ — A
(2) $B \to (C \to D)$ — A
(3) A — A
(4) — 1,3 →O
(5) — 2,4 →O

*(b)
(1) $E \to F$ — A
(2) $(E \to F) \to E$ — A
(3) E — 2,1 →O
(4) F — 1,3 →O

(c)
(1) $(G \to H) \to (I \to J)$ — A
(2) $G \to H$ — A
(3) I — A
(4) $I \to J$
(5) J

(d) (1)   K → L   A
    (2)   M   A
    (3)   L → N   A
    (4)   M → K   A
    (5)   K   1 4→0
    (6)   L   5,3 →0
    (7)   N   3, 4→0

Instructions for exercises 4 through 11: Symbolize each argument on one horizontal line. Construct a proof for each sequent. These exercises are arranged so that the simplest problems occur first. This practice is followed throughout the book.

4. From a television ad:

> *Papa John's uses better ingredients, and better ingredients make a better pizza.*

We can formalize the argument like this:

> Papa John's uses better INGREDIENTS. If so, then Papa John's makes a better PIZZA. Therefore, Papa John's makes a better pizza.

5. Dad reasons:

> My NAME is on the lease. If so, then the apartment is MINE. If the apartment is mine, then I have the RIGHT to tell Curtis to turn down the music. It follows that I have the right to tell Curtis to lower the volume.

$N,\ N \to M,\ M \to R, \vdash R$

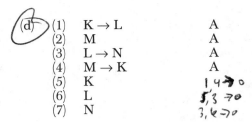

Reprinted with special permission of King Features Syndicate.

6. Two arguments displayed on page 40 deal with the problem of symbolizing sentences that contain the expression 'only if'. The first of these arguments is symbolized:

A, B, A → (B → C) ⊢ C

Prove its validity. (A = S̲1̲ is equivalent to S̲4̲, B = S̲4̲ is equivalent to S2, C = S̲1̲ is equivalent to S̲2̲)

7. A → (A → B), A ⊢ B

8. Stuffed animals can reason:

> *"Aha!" said Pooh.* (Rum-tum-tiddle-um-tum.) *"If I know anything about anything, that hole means Rabbit," he said, "and Rabbit means Company," he said, "and Company means Food. . . ."*[6]

Pooh's argument:

> There is a rabbit HOLE here. A rabbit hole means that there is a RABBIT nearby. If there is a rabbit nearby, then there is COMPANY around. If there is company around, then there is FOOD available. Thus, there is food available.   *H, H→R, R→C, C→F, ⊢F*

The second premise is a conditional.

(*9. If we buy a PIANO, then we'll go BROKE if we also install AIR conditioning. If we buy a piano, we'll have to have an air-conditioning system installed [because of the humidity problem].[7] We are buying a piano. So, we will be broke.   *P→(A→B), (P→A), P, ⊢B*

10. (C → D) → E, E → C, C → D ⊢ D

11. (F → G) → (G → H), F → G, F ⊢ H

[6]A. A. Milne, *Winnie the Pooh* (New York: Dutton, 1926), p. 22.

[7]The bracketed material supplies background information; do not symbolize it. (By the way, we learned later that the second premise is false; a small heater attached to the back of the piano solves the humidity problem.)

3

And

3.1 Symbolizing Conjunctions

A statement consisting of two constituent statements joined by the connective 'and' is called a *conjunction*. The component statements are termed *conjuncts*; they may be simple or compound statements. A sample conjunction:

Steve Forbes is a POLITICIAN and he is a MAGAZINE publisher.

We introduce the *ampersand* (&) as an abbreviation for the connective 'and'. The conjunction above is symbolized:

P & M

This formula is read "P and M" or "P ampersand M."

In Chapter Two we adopted a principle of avoiding ambiguity in the formulas we write. Hence, these formulas are objectionable:

A & B → C
D → E & F

It is impossible to determine whether they symbolize conjunctions or conditionals. We outlaw such formulas, replacing them with unambiguous formulas such as these:

(A & B) → C   A & (B → C)
D → (E & F)   (D → E) & F

The formulas on the left are conditionals; those on the right are conjunctions.

Several English connective expressions are equivalent (from the standpoint of logic) to the connective 'and'. Some appear (in italics) in the following list of statements:

MARVIN stays *but* NANCY leaves.

Marvin stays, *however* Nancy leaves.

Marvin stays, *moreover* Nancy leaves.

Marvin stays *although* Nancy leaves.

Marvin stays *yet* Nancy leaves.

Marvin stays *even though* Nancy leaves.

Each of these statements is symbolized 'M & N'. The italicized expressions are not completely synonymous; nevertheless, there is a common factor in their meanings that justifies our treating them in a group. (Did you notice that the preceding sentence is a conjunction?) The meaning of each term is such that a person who assents to a compound statement built around that term is logically committed to accepting both of the constituent statements.

I'll symbolize some more complex sentences, starting with this one from a newspaper sports story:

A Houston loss to Denver and a Miami victory over New England puts the playoff game in the Orange Bowl.

This is a conditional with a conjunctive antecedent:

If HOUSTON loses to Denver and MIAMI beats New England, then the playoff game will be in the ORANGE Bowl.

We symbolize it:

(H & M) → O

Two more sentences and their symbolizations:

(S1) *(newspaper)* "If the rule on school uniforms is to STAND, it must win support from the school board at its meetings of JANUARY 22 and FEBRUARY 19."

(F1) S → (J & F)

(S2) *(Miami politician)* "If the bond issue PASSES, all the citizens will WIN, and if it FAILS, this GENERATION and future ONES will lose."

(F2) (P → W) & [F → (G & O)]

Would it be wrong to symbolize S2 with the pair of formulas F3 and F4?

(F3) P → W
(F4) F → (G & O)

Since F2 has the same content as F3 and F4 taken together, it would not be a logical error to symbolize S2 with the latter two formulas. However, for the sake of uniform treatment, let's adopt the following convention:

One English sentence will be represented by one formula.[1]

In some contexts the word 'and' does not function as a statement connective, for example, in S5.

(S5) Marvin and Nancy are cousins.

S5 is not equivalent to the conjunction S6. (Why not?)[2]

(S6) Marvin is a cousin and Nancy is a cousin.

S5 is a simple statement; accordingly, it will be symbolized with a single capital letter (and no ampersand). In other contexts the word 'and' has a temporal implication, as in this sentence:

Fred lost his job and became depressed.

In propositional logic, the ampersand has no temporal significance whatever, so when we symbolize this sentence an aspect of its meaning disappears.

Occasionally one will find a sentence built around 'and' that is much closer to a conditional than to a conjunction. Thus, S7, from a labor union TV spot, seems equivalent in content to S7′ and definitely not to S7X:

(S7) "Buy American and Americans work."
(S7′) If Americans buy American products, then there are jobs for Americans.
(S7X) Americans [do] buy American products, and there are jobs for Americans.

The moral that should be drawn from these observations is that one should *think* while symbolizing, rather than proceeding by rote.

---

[1]An exception to this convention must be made when both a premise and the conclusion of an argument occur in the same English sentence. In such a case, of course, two formulas are required.

[2]If both Marvin and Nancy have cousins but are not related to each other, then S5 is false and S6 is true.

3.2 Ampersand In

Sigmund Freud writes about his patient, "Dora":

> ... *Herr K. spoke of her [Dora] with disparagement, and produced as his trump card the reflection that no girl who read such books and was interested in such things could have any title to a man's respect. Frau K., therefore, had betrayed her and had calumniated [maligned] her; for it had only been with her that she had read Mantegazza and discussed forbidden topics.*[3]

Freud's argument formalized and symbolized:

> Herr K. KNEW that Dora had discussed forbidden topics. Dora had discussed these topics ONLY with Frau K. Obviously, if Herr K. knew that Dora had discussed these topics and Dora had discussed them only with Frau K., then Frau K. betrayed her. Therefore, Frau K. BETRAYED Dora.
>
> K, O, (K & O) → B ⊢ B

The argument is obviously valid, but in order to construct a proof for it we need to adopt a rule that sanctions the deduction of conjunctions.

The Ampersand In Rule (&I): From two formulas derive a conjunction formed from them.

The rule restated:

From A and B derive A & B.

The inference pattern sanctioned by this rule is so simple that we rarely employ it consciously in ordinary contexts. Still, it is clearly sound and will frequently be needed in proof construction. A proof of the "Dora" argument:

(1)	K	A
(2)	O	A
(3)	(K & O) → B	A
(4)	K & O	1,2 &I
(5)	B	3,4 →O

The justification for line 4 ('1,2 &I') is short for 'Derived from lines 1 and 2 by the Ampersand In Rule'. (I cite first the premise identical to the left conjunct of the statement being derived.)

---

[3]"Dora" (1901), in *The Standard Edition of the Complete Psychological Works of Sigmund Freud*, tr. J. Strachey (London: Hogarth Press, 1953–74), VII: 62.

Next, we construct a proof for this sequent:

A, B, C ⊢ (B & A) & C

The proof involves a double application of the Ampersand In Rule.

(1)   A   A
(2)   B   A
(3)   C   A
(4)   B & A   2,1 &I
(5)   (B & A) & C 4,3 &I

A move sanctioned by the Ampersand In Rule involves *two* premises. Thus, the following "proof" is incorrect.

(1)   A   A
(2)   B   A
(3)   C   A
(4)   (B & A) & C 2,1,3 &I (ERROR!)

From a given pair of lines in a proof either one of two formulas may be deduced by means of the Ampersand In Rule. For example, on line 3 of the following partial proof one may deduce either 'D & E' or 'E & D'.

(1)   D   A
(2)   E   A

Let's call any rule that permits different formulas to be derived from a given formula or pair of formulas a "choice" rule. Obviously Ampersand In is a choice rule. Is Arrow Out?[4]

3.3   Ampersand Out

This simple argument is valid:

> Al Gore is an ENVIRONMENTALIST and a POLITICIAN. So, he is a politician and an environmentalist.

In symbols:

E & P ⊢ P & E

----

[4]No. From a pair of formulas, one formula at most may be derived by Arrow Out.

The order of the conjuncts in a conjunction is unimportant (from the standpoint of logic). In logicians' jargon, the ampersand is *commutative*. (Is the arrow commutative?) In order to construct a proof for the above sequent, we require another rule of inference.

> *The Ampersand Out Rule* (&O): **From a conjunction derive either conjunct.**

The rule restated:

> **From $\mathcal{A}$ & $\mathcal{B}$ derive either $\mathcal{A}$ or $\mathcal{B}$.**

It is obvious from its statement that Ampersand Out is a "choice" rule. Now we can construct a proof for the "Gore" sequent.

(1)	E & P	A
(2)	E	1 &O
(3)	P	1 &O
(4)	P & E	3,2 &I

Notice that a slightly different proof could have been constructed for the sequent:

(1)	E & P	A
(2)	P	1 &O
(3)	E	1 &O
(4)	P & E	2,3 &I

For most valid sequents (particularly the more complex ones) there will be several alternative correct proofs. A practical corollary of this fact: If a proof you construct for a starred exercise differs from the proof given in Appendix Five, it does not follow that your proof is mistaken. It would be a good policy in such a situation, though, to recheck your proof.

Where there are two or more alternative correct proofs for a sequent are there grounds for preferring one proof to another? A logician will prefer an organized proof to a disorganized one and a shorter, more "elegant" proof to a longer one. For our purposes, however, any error-free proof is wholly acceptable.

How shall we symbolize Jesse Jackson's statement "Our FLAG is red, white and blue, but our nation is a RAINBOW—red, yellow, brown, black and white—and we're all PRECIOUS in God's sight"? (Note that 'Our FLAG is red, white and blue' is a simple statement, not a conjunction.[5]) Three possibilities:

---

[5] 'Our flag is red, white and blue' is not equivalent to the conjunction 'Our flag contains red, and our flag contains white, and our flag contains blue'. Why not?

(F1X) F & R & P
 (F2) F & (R & P)
 (F3) (F & R) & P

It will facilitate the development of our proof procedure if we agree to re-
nounce formulas patterned like F1X. Which of the remaining two shall we
adopt as the proper symbolization?

Preliminary to answering this question, I note that F2 *entails* F3. (One
statement or formula entails a second when the argument or sequent that has
the first as sole premise and the second as conclusion is valid. When one statement or formula entails a second, the second *follows logically from* the first.) This
proof demonstrates that F2 entails F3.

(1)	F & (R & P)	A
(2)	F	1 &O
(3)	R & P	1 &O
(4)	R	3 &O
(5)	P	3 &O
(6)	F & R	2,4 &I
(7)	(F & R) & P	6,5 &I

Not only does F2 entail F3, F3 entails F2. (Exercise 9 at the end of the chapter
is concerned with this entailment.) Mutually entailing statements or formulas
are said to be <u>*logically equivalent*</u>. Logically equivalent statements (formulas)
have the same content. We can now answer the question about which formula
is the symbolization of Jackson's statement.

Because the two formulas have the same content (and both track the
English sentence reasonably well) either one will do. Generalizing on this
point: If two formulas are equivalent and track a given sentence adequately,
then either they are both satisfactory symbolizations of that sentence or neither
is. (A formula *tracks* a sentence when the formula and the sentence have the
same or comparable logical structures. The structures are shown by the connectives.) So, if your symbolization of a sentence in a starred exercise differs
from the solution in Appendix Five, it may still be correct. It *is* right if it is
equivalent to the solution provided and it tracks the English sentence adequately.

The logician describes the logical equivalence of F2 and F3 by saying
that the ampersand is *associative*. (Is the arrow associative?)

Consider this argument:

> If four is **LESS** than six and **EVERY** number less than six is prime, then
> four is **PRIME**. Therefore, if four is less than six it is a prime number.

In symbols:

$$(L \& E) \to P \vdash L \to P$$

It should be clear that the premise of this argument is true. (The premise does not maintain that four *is* prime.) The conclusion, on the other hand, is false; four is less than six but (being divisible by two) is not a prime. Because its premise is true and its conclusion false, the "Prime" argument must be invalid. If we can construct a "proof" for this invalid argument with the set of rules we are developing, then our proof procedure is useless as a method of establishing validity. It may seem that such a "proof" is possible:

(1) $(L \& E) \to P$ A
(2) $L \to P$ 1 &O (ERROR!)

Fortunately for the system we are developing, this is not an acceptable proof. Line 2 is incorrectly derived by applying the Ampersand Out Rule to a *part* of line 1 (namely, the antecedent of line 1). The Ampersand Out Rule *and all the other rules* introduced in Chapters Two through Nine apply to *whole* lines only. This restriction can be emphasized by providing a second instance of a violation.

(1) F & (R & P)   A
(2) R   1 &O (ERROR!)

The sequent that this "proof" treats is valid. A three-line proof will establish its validity.

We now have three inference rules at our disposal; some suggestions for developing strategies for constructing proofs may be useful at this point. When you are in the process of constructing a proof there will usually be two types of lines on your worksheet: (1) those set down at the top (which will be either premises of the sequent or lines derived from them), and (2) those set down at the bottom as goals. Let's call lines of the first type "premise lines" and those of the second "goal lines." The last goal line, of course, will be the conclusion of the sequent; but there may also be intermediate goal lines—lines that will help you reach the final goal. Here is a strategic suggestion for each of the rules we have covered so far:

ARROW OUT: **If one of the premise lines is a conditional, search the other premise lines for the antecedent. If you find it, apply Arrow Out. If you do not find the antecedent among the premise lines, add it as a goal line.**

AMPERSAND IN: **If one of the goal lines is a conjunction, search the premise lines for the two conjuncts. If you find both conjuncts,**

apply Ampersand In. If you find only one conjunct, add the other as a goal line. If you find neither conjunct among the premise lines, add both as goal lines.

AMPERSAND OUT: **If one of the premise lines is a conjunction, apply Ampersand Out (once or twice).**

Each intermediate goal line is placed above the goal lines already on the worksheet. Note that setting down a goal line must be distinguished from deriving a line in a proof. A line added as a goal must at some later stage be derived from higher lines or the proof will remain incomplete.

EXERCISES

1. Symbolize each statement using the suggested notation.
    (a) *(bumper sticker)* "Sometimes I Wake Up Grumpy, And Sometimes I Let Him Sleep." (W = Sometimes I wake up Grumpy, S = Sometimes I let Grumpy sleep)

   *(b) *(Shakespeare,* Macbeth) "Drink PROVOKES the desire, but it TAKES away the performance."

    (c) *(children's book)* "And although he was a very SMALL ghost, Georgie had a really BIG idea."

    (d) *(ad)* "Arthricare is WARMING yet ODOR-FREE."

    (e) *(Lincoln)* "Let the people KNOW the facts and the country will be SAVED." (Let *K* abbreviate 'The people are allowed to know the facts'.)

   *(f) *(bumper sticker)* "I May Be FAT, But You're UGLY–And I Can DIET!"

    (g) *(Joseph E. Levine)* "You can FOOL all the people all the time if the ADVERTISING is right and the BUDGET is big enough."

    (h) *(oldie goldie lyrics[6])* "It's my PARTY, and I'll CRY if I WANT to."

    (i) *(sign at Watson Island State Park)* "[Notice!] Should the Missouri River waters start FLOWING over the main road, campers will be required to LEAVE and the park will be CLOSED."

   *(j) *(oldtime ballplayer Goose Goslin)* "If I make an OUT I LOSE the batting championship, and if I get a HIT I WIN it."

    (k) *(newspaper)* "If he [Laurent Kabila] ARRIVES, and if he is the new BOSS, I [Jonas Mukamba] will OBEY him."

    (l) *(logician James Carney)* "If one can show that the axioms of system one can be INTERPRETED so as to be theorems of system two, [and] that system two has the same inference RULES as system one, then system ONE must be consistent if system TWO is consistent."

---

[6]By Herb Wiener, Wally Gold, and John Gluck, Jr.

(m) *(newspaper)* "While there is much DEBATE on whether the gains are temporary, and although wide gulfs in OPPORTUNITY, IN-COME and EDUCATION still exist between blacks and whites, SIGNS of improvement abound." (O = Wide gulfs in opportunity still exist between blacks and whites)

2. Translate each formula into an English sentence using this dictionary:

A = Miami wins its last regular-season game
B = Miami loses its last regular-season game
C = New York loses its last regular-season game
D = Miami wins the division championship
E = Miami is the "wild-card" team

   (a) A & D
  *(b) (A & C) → D
   (c) A & (C → D)
   (d) A → (C & D)
   (e) (A → D) & (B → E)

3. Complete the following proofs. Every assumption has been identified.

(a) (1) (A & B) & C   A   *(b) (1) A & C   A
    (2) A & B   (2) B   A
    (3) A   (3) A   1 &O
    (4) C   (4) C   1 &O
    (5) A & C   (5) A, & B   3,2 &I
                              (6) (A & B) & C 5, 4, & I

(c) (1) D & E   A   (d) (1) (H & I) → (J & K) A
    (2) (D → F) & (E → G) A   (2) I & H   A
    (3) D → F   (3) I
    (4) D   (4)
    (5)   3,4 →O   (5) H & I
    (6) E → G   (6)
    (7)   (7) J
    (8)
    (9) F & G

Instructions for exercises 4 through 13: Symbolize and construct proofs.

4. Mother–son conversation:

    MARK: *Did I feed my fish?*
    CARMEN: *You fed your big ones.*
    MARK: *If I fed the big ones, I fed the little ones.*

Mark reasoned:

    I fed the BIG fish. If I fed the big ones, I also fed the LITTLE fish. Thus, I fed both my big fish and my little ones.

*5. I fed the BIG fish, and if I fed them I fed all my fish. Hence, I fed ALL my fish.

6. W. T. Jones explains one of Aristotle's contentions about the "unmoved mover":

> *And what is the object of his thought? Clearly it can only be himself. This follows because the unmoved mover knows only the best, and the best is the unmoved mover.*[7]

Jones's argument:

> The unmoved mover KNOWS only the best. The unmoved mover IS the best. If the unmoved mover knows only the best and is the best, then he knows only himself. So, the unmoved mover knows only HIMSELF.

7. News story:

> *Fourteen Dade County jail prisoners were held in isolation today because one of them has hepatitis, a disease he apparently contracted in the jail.*
> *Jail officials did not say the ill prisoner got the disease in jail but the incubation period for it is from 10 to 50 days, and the prisoner has been in jail more than four months.*[8]

The reporter advances an argument in this passage. The conclusion is put forward (cautiously) at the end of the first paragraph; premises are supplied in the second paragraph. A formalization of his argument:

> The prisoner CONTRACTED hepatitis in jail. This is a consequence of the following facts: The INCUBATION period for the disease is from 10 to 50 days, yet the prisoner has been in jail more than FOUR months. Now if the incubation period is from 10 to 50 days, then providing the man has been jailed over four months, he must have contracted the illness in jail.

*8. When Manny Roman shot and killed a thief who broke into his warehouse, prosecutors charged him with murder.[9] One of the issues was whether Roman had reloaded his handgun. He denied it, but the prosecutor argued that he had reloaded (my paraphrase):

> Roman RELOADED. Here is the proof: his 9mm Beretta HOLDS 17 bullets, and there were five LIVE rounds in the weapon. But detectives found 13 spent CASINGS! Now if the handgun holds 17 bullets, and the police recovered 13 spent casings, and there were five live rounds still in the weapon, then Roman must have reloaded.

9. (F & R) & P ⊢ F & (R & P)

[7]W. T. Jones, *The Classical Mind: A History of Western Philosophy* (New York: Harcourt Brace, 1969), p. 231.

[8]Bill Gjebre, "Jail Inmate Has Hepatitis; Authorities Isolate Cell," *Miami News* (April 9, 1971), p. 1A.

[9]Manny Garcia, "To Kill a Thief: Was It Self-defense or Murder?" *Miami Herald* (April 23, 1995), pp. 1A, 11A.

10. Calvin reasons:

> Mom is taking a SHOWER. That means she is GOING out. She hasn't told me to get CLEANED up. That means I'm staying HOME. Mom's going out while I'm staying home means I'll have a BABY sitter. If I'll have a sitter, it will be ROSALYN. Ergo, Rosalyn will be my baby sitter.

$(C = \text{Mom hasn't told me to get cleaned up})^{10}$

Calvin and Hobbes   by Bill Watterson

11. The instruction manual for my lawnmower advised me to begin cutting my lawn with three clockwise swaths and then to finish with a counter-clockwise spiral; however, the booklet gives no rationale for these directions. I conjectured the following explanation (which is cast as an argument):

> Mowing clockwise blows clippings toward the CENTER of the lawn; and if this is so, beginning with three clockwise circuits will keep clippings off the SIDEWALK. Mowing counterclockwise blows clippings toward the PERIMETER; and if this is true, doing the rest of the lawn counterclockwise MINIMIZES mowing clippings. So, starting with three clockwise laps will keep the clippings off the sidewalk; moreover, doing the rest of the lawn in the other direction will minimize mowing clippings.

12. Newspaper story:

> *Dr. Howard Knuttgen, a Boston University biologist, is conducting a study on the harm professional football players can do to each other.*
>
> *In 1942, Knuttgen says, pro football players averaged 200 pounds a man, but last year that average was 222.*

---

[10]We treat this negative sentence as a simple statement; beginning in Chapter Five we will treat negative sentences as compounds.

"As momentum equals mass times velocity," Knuttgen says, "there can be no doubt that these men are hitting harder and injuring each other more seriously."[11]

Knuttgen's reasoning can be given this formal dress:

Momentum EQUALS mass times velocity. Today's players have more MASS than the players of 1942, but move with equal (or greater) VE-LOCITY. If momentum equals mass times velocity, then if players today have at least the same velocity as, and more mass than, players in '42, today's players are HITTING harder than those in '42. If football players today hit harder than players in '42, then they are INJURING each other more seriously than did the men playing in '42. All of this proves that the men playing now are injuring each other more seriously than did the players of '42.

*13. When an ice cube floats in a glass of water, some of it extends above the surface. One might expect, therefore, that as the cube melts the water level will rise slightly, but this does not happen. A scientific explanation of why the water level remains constant can be formulated as a deductive argument.[12]

[According to Archimedes' principle,] a solid body floating in a liquid DISPLACES a volume of liquid that has the same weight as the body it-self. If this is true, the chunk of ice has the SAME weight as the water displaced by its submerged portion. The weight of a substance remains CONSTANT through melting. If (i) the ice has the same weight as the water displaced by its submerged portion and (ii) the weight of a sub-stance is unaffected by melting, then the ice cube turns into a mass of water having the same WEIGHT as the water initially displaced by its submerged portion. Provided that the cube turns into a mass of water having the same weight as the water initially displaced by its submerged portion, it turns into a mass of water having the same VOLUME as the water initially displaced. The LEVEL of water in the glass will remain constant if the cube becomes a mass of water having the same volume as the water initially displaced. Hence, the water level remains constant.

Note: The next three exercises are more difficult than any of the preceding ones. These problems (16 in particular) require the employment of ingenuity. If you are developing a liking for logic or if you enjoy a challenge (or both), you will want to attempt these exercises. There are challenging problems in most of the exercise sets in the volume. To distinguish them from the other exercises, I have marked them with the word 'CHALLENGE'.

---

[11]Charlie Nobles, "Football Injuries Could Alter Rules," *Miami News* (July 14, 1971), p. 3C.

[12]This explanation is based on an example provided in Carl Hempel, *Aspects of Scientific Explanation* (New York: Free Press, 1965), p. 346.

14. (CHALLENGE) Symbolize each statement using the suggested notation.

    (a) *(tax instructions)* "If MARRIED filing a JOINT return and both spouses worked and had IRAs, figure each spouse's deduction SEPARATELY." (A = You worked, B = Your spouse worked, C = You had an IRA, D = Your spouse had an IRA, S = Each spouse's deduction should be figured separately)

    (b) *(author James Boswell writing to the philosopher David Hume)* "If you will agree to CORRESPOND with me, you shall have London NEWS, LIVELY fancies, HUMOROUS sallies, provided that you give me ELEGANT sentiments, JUST criticism, and INGENIOUS observations on human nature."

    (c) *(sports story)* "The winner of Saturday's Buffalo-Miami game wins the division title, with the loser getting a wild-card spot."

        B = Buffalo wins Saturday's game
        M = Miami wins Saturday's game
        C = Buffalo wins the division title
        D = Miami wins the division title
        E = Buffalo gets the wild-card spot
        F = Miami gets the wild-card spot

15. (CHALLENGE) A Bible reference work remarks:

> *The first three gospels are not the earliest Christian documents, for all the genuine epistles of St. Paul were almost certainly written before the Gospel of St. Mark, which in turn provided the foundation for St. Matthew and St. Luke.*[13]

The reasoning contained in this passage can be formulated as a propositional-logic argument:

> The Pauline epistles predate the Gospels of Matthew, Mark, and Luke. Proof: The Pauline epistles predate the Gospel of St. Mark. That gospel provides the foundation for those of St. Matthew and St. Luke. If Mark provides the foundation for Matthew it must precede Matthew, and similarly if Mark provides the foundation for Luke it must precede Luke as well. Now if St. Paul's letters antedate Mark, which in turn antedates both Matthew and Luke, then Paul's letters obviously antedate both Matthew and Luke. Q.E.D.

Symbolize the argument and prove it valid. Use these symbols:

    A = Paul's letters predate Matthew
    B = Paul's letters predate Mark
    C = Paul's letters predate Luke
    D = Mark provides the foundation for Matthew
    E = Mark provides the foundation for Luke
    F = Mark predates Matthew
    G = Mark predates Luke

[13]James Hastings, *Dictionary of the Bible,* rev. by Frederick C. Grant and H. H. Rowley (New York: Scribner's, 1963), p. 139.

16. (CHALLENGE)

(A & A) → B, A ⊢ B

A proof for this sequent:

(1)	(A & A) → B	A
(2)	A	A
(3)	A & A	2,2 &I
(4)	B	1,3 →O

In this proof, line 2 supplies both the left and the right conjuncts of line 3. I am willing to accept the "liberal" interpretation of the Ampersand In Rule that is presupposed in this proof. However, there are proofs for sequent 16 that do not employ the Ampersand In Rule in this unusual way. Can you construct such a proof?

4

If (Again)

4.1 Symbolizing Puzzling Conditionals

In this section we examine three perplexing expressions: 'only if', 'sufficient condition', and 'necessary condition'. We'll begin with 'only if'. S1 seems to be a conditional, but is it equivalent to S2 or S3?

(S1) Colin Powell is PRESIDENT of the United States only if he is a U.S. CITIZEN.

(S2) If Colin Powell is president of the United States, then he is a U.S. citizen.

(S3) If Colin Powell is a U.S. citizen, then he is president of the United States.

It is plain enough that S1 and S3 make different claims as one is true and the other false. So, if S1 is equivalent to one of the other two sentences—and it is—it must be equivalent to S2. (Did you notice that each of the preceding sentences conveys an argument?) Both S1 and S2 express the thought that Powell's being president would imply his being a citizen.

If S1 and S2 express the same thought, then we can use S2's symbolization, F2, to represent S1.

(F2) $P \to C$

We can adopt the following guide in symbolizing "only if" sentences:

The expression 'only if' introduces consequents.

A sentence having the form

$\mathcal{P}$ only if $\mathcal{Q}$

is properly symbolized

$\mathcal{P} \to \mathcal{Q}.$

The arrow replaces the words 'only if' without any change in the order of the constituent statements.

Well, that takes care of 'only if', right? Wrong! Years of experience teaching logic have convinced me that more has to be said. Why? Because many students have a strong inclination to mis-symbolize 'only if' sentences, and that inclination must be overcome. No doubt part of the inclination stems from the fact that in all other contexts the word 'if' introduces antecedents. When 'if' is preceded by 'only' the normal sequence is reversed, and some people find this hard to accept. At the risk of boring you, I provide two more arguments that prove that S1 is equivalent to S2 (and may therefore be symbolized with F2), rather than equivalent to S3. These arguments revolve around statements S1 through S3 displayed above and two more statements:

(S4) If Powell is not a U.S. citizen, then he is not president.
(S5) Powell is president if he is a U.S. citizen.

The arguments do double duty as exercises in other chapters.

> S1 is (logically) equivalent to S4. S4 is equivalent to S2.[1] If S1 is equivalent to S4, then provided that S4 is equivalent to S2, S1 must be equivalent to S2. It follows that S1 is equivalent to S2. (Chapter Two, exercise 6.)

> S3 is equivalent to S5. If S1 is equivalent to S3 and S3 to S5, then S1 is equivalent to S5. If S1 is equivalent to S5, then the word 'only' in S1 does not affect the meaning of S1. But since the word *does* affect S1's meaning, S1 is not equivalent to S3. (Chapter Five, exercise 11.)

These are valid arguments with true premises; thus, they establish the truth of their conclusions.

Following the translation guide explained above, we symbolize S6 with F6.

(S6) DAVID will go to the party only if AMY goes.
(F6) D $\to$ A

[1]This is established in Chapter Five.

Formula F6 claims that David's presence at the party is proof of Amy's presence; that is, that David will not attend in Amy's absence. It is clear that F6 expresses at least part of the content of S6, but isn't F7 also implied by S6?

(F7) $A \to D$

Formula F7 claims that Amy's presence is proof of David's presence. Is this claim part of the content of S6? Note that F7 may well be true and also that a person asserting S6 may mean to claim F7 (in addition to F6). However, neither of these observations shows that S6 entails F7. We should distinguish between what a *person* means to claim in uttering a sentence and what the uttered *sentence* actually means. Sentence S6, strictly construed, does not entail F7. Contrast S6 with the stronger statement S8:

(S8) David will go to the party *if and only if* Amy goes.

Sentence S8 is a stronger statement precisely because it entails F7 while S6 does not. Both statements, of course, entail F6. In Chapter Six we will study sentences like S8.

The word 'only' should be regarded as a caution sign in logic. It causes trouble for the unwary in propositional logic and in other branches of logic as well. A final note: Don't confuse 'only if' with 'if only'.

Let's turn now to an examination of the locutions 'sufficient condition' and 'necessary condition'. If event (or state of affairs) A is a sufficient condition for event (or state) B, then A's occurrence ensures B's occurrence. If event (or state) C is a necessary condition for event (or state) D, then D cannot occur in C's absence. Sufficient conditions need not be necessary conditions and necessary conditions need not be sufficient. Consider these sentences:

(S9) Marvin's being BUSTED for "pot" possession is a sufficient condition for his being DROPPED from the team.

(S10) Nancy's SCORING above 1,000 on the GRE is a necessary condition for her ADMISSION to graduate school.

S9 means approximately the same as S11 below and is, therefore, symbolized by F11. S10 means roughly the same as S12 below and, so, is symbolized by F12.[2]

(S11) If Marvin is busted for possessing "pot," he will be dropped from the team.

(F11) $B \to D$

---

[2]F11 (F12) is not a wholly satisfactory symbolization of S9 (S10), but it represents the best that can be done within standard propositional logic.

(S12) Nancy will be admitted to graduate school only if she scores above 1,000 on the GRE.

(F12) A → S

We can formulate these translation principles:

Sufficient conditions become antecedents.

Necessary conditions become consequents.

For example, Marvin's being busted is the sufficient condition in S9, and so *B* is the antecedent of F11. Nancy's scoring above 1,000 is the necessary condition in S10, and so *S* is the consequent of F12. Note that the translation principle 'Sufficient conditions *become* antecedents' does not mean "The *expression* 'is a sufficient condition for' *introduces* antecedents." A similar comment applies to the translation principle concerning statements of necessary condition.

Sentences S10 and S12 are incorrectly symbolized by F13.

(F13) S → A

S10 and S12 deal with possible or actual events: Nancy's taking the GRE and her being admitted to graduate school. In the normal case taking the GRE *precedes* admission to graduate school. This fact might persuade someone to choose F13 (instead of F12) as the symbolization of S10 or S12 on the grounds that in a conditional sentence dealing with events, the earlier event should be mentioned by the antecedent statement. In fact, the arrow symbol has no temporal significance. F12 does not mean "If A then *later* S." In many conditionals the later of two events is described in the antecedent; S14 is an example.

(S14) If the vase smashed on the floor, then Harry dropped it.

In sum, the antecedent statement need not describe the antecedent (earlier) event.

4.2   Arrow In

In the movie "Witness," John Book (Harrison Ford) is trying to protect a young Amish boy from corrupt police who intend to kill him. The boy's mother, Rachel (Kelly McGillis), finds Book after he has been shot. This conversation ensues:

RACHEL: *My God, why didn't you get to a hospital?*

JOHN: *No, no doctor. Gunshot wound—they have to make a report and if they make a report they find me and if they find me they find the boy.*

Part of John Book's reasoning may be rephrased as follows:

> If a doctor is CALLED, the gunshot wound will be REPORTED.
> If a report is made, the corrupt police will find ME.
> If the police find me, they will also find the BOY.
> So, calling a doctor will result in the corrupt police locating the boy.

In symbols:

$$C \rightarrow R, R \rightarrow M, M \rightarrow B \vdash C \rightarrow B$$

This is an instance of a pattern known as *chain argument*. A chain argument has at least two premises and possesses these features:

1. Every statement is a conditional.
2. The antecedent of the first premise is identical with the antecedent of the conclusion.
3. The consequent of each premise (except the last) is identical with the antecedent of the following premise. (In this way the premises are forged into a chain.)
4. The consequent of the last premise is identical with the consequent of the conclusion.

The "Witness" argument seems intuitively valid, but how can we *establish* its validity? Our formal-proof procedure as developed so far is inadequate to the task. However, we might give an informal demonstration along these lines:

> Look, *suppose* Rachel calls the doctor. It would follow from this supposition and premise one that the doctor will report John's gunshot wound. Then it would follow with help from premise two that the bad cops will find John. And with premise three it will follow that they will find the boy. To summarize: From the assumption of calling the doctor we can conclude the finding of the boy. So, we are warranted in asserting that *if* the doctor is called, *then* the boy will be found.

This is a legitimate way to reason, and we can strengthen our proof procedure by adding a rule of inference that sanctions inferences of just this sort.

The Arrow In Rule ($\rightarrow$I): **If from an assumed formula (and perhaps other assumptions) a second formula can be derived, then derive the conditional that has as antecedent the assumption and as consequent the second formula.**

The rule restated:

From the derivation of $\mathcal{B}$ from assumption $\mathcal{A}$ (and perhaps other assumptions) derive $\mathcal{A} \rightarrow \mathcal{B}$.

What is meant by "deriving $\mathcal{B}$ from assumption $\mathcal{A}$"? Is it required that the deductive passage from $\mathcal{A}$ to $\mathcal{B}$ be one step long? No; we may proceed by any number of steps from assumption $\mathcal{A}$ to $\mathcal{B}$, and we shall describe this as "a derivation of $\mathcal{B}$ from $\mathcal{A}$." A more exact account of this notion will be given later in the chapter.

Since Chapter Two, we have been justifying the introduction of premises into proofs by calling them "assumptions." It is necessary now to state formally a rule that covers the introduction of premises, as well as certain other formulas.

The Assumption Rule (A, PA): Any formula may be introduced as an assumption at any point in a proof.

This rule may seem inordinately liberal; I explain below why it is not.

With the aid of the two rules immediately above—plus the Arrow Out Rule—we construct a formal proof of the "Witness" sequent.

(1)	$C \to R$	A
(2)	$R \to M$	A
(3)	$M \to B$	A
(4)	C	PA
(5)	R	1,4 $\to$O
(6)	M	2,5 $\to$O
(7)	B	3,6 $\to$O
(8)	$C \to B$	4-7 $\to$I

The first four lines are justified by the Assumption Rule. The first three formulas are premises of the sequent; let's call them _original_ assumptions. The fourth line is a _provisional_ assumption made in order that the Arrow In step can be taken at line 8. We identify provisional assumptions with the abbreviation 'PA'. The entry on line 8 of the justification column ('4-7 $\to$I') is short for 'Derived by the Arrow In Rule from the derivation of line 7 from the assumption on line 4'. (The assumption line is always cited first.)

Notice that the Arrow In Rule differs in an important respect from the inference rules introduced previously. Each of the earlier rules sanctions a passage from a _formula_ (or formulas) to a formula. The Arrow In Rule sanctions the passage from a _derivation_ (or inference) to a formula. That is, it is because we were able to _derive_ line 7 from the assumption on line 4 that we are warranted in adding line 8. This difference is reflected in the justification entry for an Arrow In step by the use of a hyphen (rather than a comma) to separate line numbers.

When proofs were first explained in Chapter Two, a three-column format was provided—with a note that one more column would be added later;

we need that fourth column now. Many of the proofs that we shall construct will have assumptions of two kinds: original assumptions (premises of the sequent being evaluated) and provisional assumptions (the proof just completed is of this sort). If these proofs are to be successful, their last lines must depend only on original assumptions. As a means of keeping track of this matter we add an *assumption-dependence* column to our proof format.[3] The purpose of this column is to indicate for each formula in the proof which assumption(s) it depends upon. We locate this column to the left of the line-number column. For each rule, we will adopt a principle that determines the assumption dependence of any line introduced by that rule. The principle governing the Assumption Rule:

An assumption depends upon itself.

This principle applies to original and provisonal assumptions alike. The assumption-dependence principles for the other four rules presented so far:

→O   &I   &O : **The formula derived depends on all of the assumptions on which the premise(s) of the step depend(s). (We refer to this as the "standard assumption-dependence principle.")**

→I: **The conditional derived depends on all of the assumptions on which the formula corresponding to its consequent depends—less the assumption that corresponds to its antecedent.**

To illustrate these principles and the modified proof format, I rewrite the proof for the "Witness" sequent as follows:

1	(1)	$C \to R$	A
2	(2)	$R \to M$	A
3	(3)	$M \to B$	A
4	(4)	C	PA
1,4	(5)	R	1,4 →O
1,2,4	(6)	M	2,5 →O
1,2,3,4	(7)	B	3,6 →O
1,2,3	(8)	$C \to B$	4-7 →I

Each of the first four lines, being an assumption, depends only on itself. Line 5 depends on the assumptions its premises depend on—namely, 1 and 4. Line 6 is derived from line 2 (depending on assumption 2) and line 5 (depending on assumptions 1 and 4) and, thus, depends on assumptions 1, 2, and 4. A similar

[3]This proof format was devised by Patrick Suppes.

explanation applies to line 7. Line 8 depends on whatever assumptions line 7 depends on (1 through 4) less assumption 4; hence, it depends on 1 through 3. Only numbers of assumption lines can appear in the new column. In the above proof, lines 5 through 8 are *derived* lines, not assumption lines. Thus, none of the numbers 5 through 8 could appear in the assumption-dependence column of that proof.

The assumption-dependence column can be included in any proof; however, it is needed only in proofs that involve provisional assumptions. I will not include this column in other proofs. Note that when the column is included in a proof, the proof demonstrates the validity of a number of sequents—not just one. Consider the proof displayed above, for example. When you reach line 5 of that proof you have shown that the sequent whose conclusion is line 5 and whose premises are lines 1 and 4 (that is, the lines listed in the assumption-dependence column for line 5) is itself a valid sequent. In fact, that proof demonstrates the validity of eight separate sequents, because it has eight lines. The sequent associated with a given line has the formula on that line as conclusion and has as premises the formulas on the lines listed in the assumption-dependence column for the given line.[4] The first four sequents validated by the proof displayed above are pretty uninteresting. (The first sequent is 'C $\rightarrow$ R $\vdash$ C $\rightarrow$ R'.)

You will notice that an Arrow In step reduces assumption dependence (line 8 of the above proof depends on fewer assumptions than does 7). It is by the use of the Arrow In Rule (and other rules to be introduced later) that provisional assumptions are eliminated before the proof is concluded. If we had not been able to eliminate assumption 4 from the set of assumptions on which line 8 depends, we would not have succeeded in proving the validity of the "Witness" sequent, inasmuch as 4 was *not* a premise of that sequent. We can formulate this general rule:

A proof of a sequent is not complete if the last line depends on a provisional assumption.

It is because of this requirement that the Assumption Rule is not so lax as it might appear, for any provisional assumption introduced by this rule must be eliminated from the set of assumptions on which the final line depends.

Why does the Arrow In Rule bring about a reduction of assumption dependence? Specifically, how does line 8 in the above proof avoid depending on line 4? The key to understanding this matter is the realization that when you advance a conditional, you are not thereby committed to the antecedent. Suppose that you assert this conditional:

---

[4]As you will discover below, some proof lines have no assumption dependence. To accommodate this we should expand the notion of "sequent" to include sequents that have no premise formulas. Such a sequent will consist of a turnstile followed by a formula.

If the government drafts men, then they will also draft women.

In asserting this conditional, you have not claimed that the government *will* draft men. Similarly, the formula on line 8 of the proof for the "Witness" sequent–namely, 'C → B'–does not assume that its antecedent is true; that is, it is free of the assumption made on line 4. What the formula 'C → B' does assert is that there is a connection between its antecedent (true or false) and its consequent. This connection has been established by passing from line 4 to line 7. The existence of this connection is quite independent of whether the formula on line 4 is true or false.

Let's return to an interesting question about symbolization first raised (with a different example) on pages 13–14. We know how to symbolize S1 (with F1) and S2 (with F2), but how are we to symbolize S3?

(S1) If Chip is ADMITTED to college, then if he STAYS four years, it will COST us $100,000.

(S2) If Chip is admitted to college and stays there four years, it will cost us $100,000.

(S3) If Chip is admitted to college, and if he stays four years, it will cost us $100,000.

(F1) $A \rightarrow (S \rightarrow C)$
(F2) $(A \& S) \rightarrow C$

The content of S3 appears to be caught by at least one of these two formulas– but which one? If we can prove that F1 and F2 are logically equivalent, this will show that both formulas are acceptable symbolizations of S3.[5] And we *can* show that F1 and F2 are logically equivalent. (This is a *modus ponens* argument with an unstated conclusion. Did you notice it?) We prove the equivalence of these formulas by showing that each entails the other.

A proof that F1 entails F2:

1	(1)	$A \rightarrow (S \rightarrow C)$	A
2	(2)	$A \& S$	PA
2	(3)	A	2 &O
1,2	(4)	$S \rightarrow C$	1,3 →O
2	(5)	S	2 &O
1,2	(6)	C	4,5 →O
1	(7)	$(A \& S) \rightarrow C$	2-6 →I

[5]Both formulas track the English fairly well, but neither tracks completely. No formula tracks it perfectly.

In constructing this proof, I employed the *Arrow In strategy*. When we wish to derive a conditional, we make a provisional assumption of the antecedent of that conditional and attempt to derive the consequent. I restate the strategy using the terminology introduced at the end of Chapter Three:

If one of the goal lines is a conditional, add the antecedent as a premise line and the consequent as a goal line.

The Arrow In strategy is employed twice in this proof that F2 entails F1:

1	(1)	(A & S) → C	A	[1]
2	(2)	A	PA	[3]
3	(3)	S	PA	[5]
2,3	(4)	A & S	2,3 &I	[7]
1,2,3	(5)	C	1,4 →O	[6]
1,2	(6)	S → C	3-5 →I	[4]
1	(7)	A → (S → C)	2-6 →I	[2]

The column on the extreme right is not part of the proof; rather, it is a teaching device. The bracketed numbers indicate the order in which I wrote down the lines when I first created the proof, and this gives you insight into how I thought through the proof. Occasionally I will supply such a "proof-discovery" column for difficult proofs.

I will make some suggestions designed to simplify the task of constructing proofs and illustrate them by referring to this proof. When devising a proof, concentrate first on the principal column, which is the list of formulas; the other columns can always be added later. Very often, it is helpful to construct this main column by working from both the top and the bottom toward the middle. (When you write formulas at the bottom while there is a gap in the middle, you are of course *setting goals* rather than *making deductions*.) At the start I knew what would be the first and last lines in the proof. Noting that the last line is a conditional, I adopted the Arrow In strategy—that is, I made a provisional assumption of *A* on the second line and set down 'S → C' (as a secondary goal) on the next-to-last line. Realizing that the next-to-last line is itself a conditional, I employed the Arrow In strategy again, this time making a provisional assumption of *S* on the third line from the top and putting *C* (as a tertiary goal) on the third line from the bottom. At this point only a small gap remained in the middle. With a little thought I found that 'A & S' would plug that gap. Having connected the top set of formulas with the bottom group, I added the remaining three columns in this order: line number, justification, and assumption dependence. These three columns were by necessity built from top to bottom.

It may be helpful to view an Arrow In proof as involving a *subproof*, or proof-within-a-proof. The subproof begins with the provisional assumption and concludes with the formula that matches the consequent of the conditional that will be derived by the Arrow In Rule. I illustrate by repeating the proof of the "Witness" sequent.

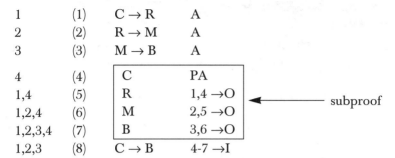

1	(1)	C → R	A
2	(2)	R → M	A
3	(3)	M → B	A
4	(4)	C	PA
1,4	(5)	R	1,4 →O
1,2,4	(6)	M	2,5 →O
1,2,3,4	(7)	B	3,6 →O
1,2,3	(8)	C → B	4-7 →I

Note that the first and last lines of the subproof are identified by the numbers in the justification entry on line 8. The subproof shows that (with the help of assumptions 1 through 3) one can derive line 7 from the assumption on line 4. Viewed in terms of this notion of "subproof," what justifies the Arrow In deduction on line 8 is the completion of the subproof on line 7.

Viewing Arrow In proofs in this way may help to make sense of proofs involving more than one Arrow In step. Consider again the proof that F2 entails F1.

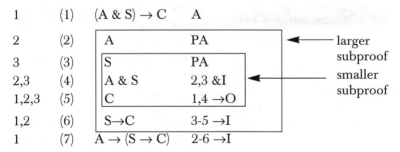

1	(1)	(A & S) → C	A
2	(2)	A	PA
3	(3)	S	PA
2,3	(4)	A & S	2,3 &I
1,2,3	(5)	C	1,4 →O
1,2	(6)	S→C	3-5 →I
1	(7)	A → (S → C)	2-6 →I

The smaller subproof occurs as part of the larger one; accordingly, it could be called a *subsubproof* of the main proof. The completion of the subsubproof on line 5 justifies the step taken on line 6. Line 6 completes the larger subproof, and that justifies the deduction of line 7.

I conclude the chapter by mentioning several matters pertaining to the Arrow In Rule. First, can this rule be applied to just any pair of lines in a proof? No; careful inspection of the rule reveals that these two conditions must be met:[6]

---

[6]These conditions are implied by the particular formulation of the Arrow In Rule presented in this book. There are other logically sound formulations of the rule that do not imply these conditions.

1. **The first line (which is identical to the antecedent of the conditional being derived) must be an *assumption*.**
2. **The other line (which is identical to the consequent of the conditional) must be *derived from* the first line (and perhaps other assumptions).**

The following "proof" of the invalid "Prime" argument (see Section 3.3) has a concluding step that violates both conditions. The argument symbolized:

$$(L \ \& \ E) \to P \vdash L \to P$$

The "proof":

1	(1)	$(L \ \& \ E) \to P$	A
2	(2)	L & E	PA
2	(3)	L	2 &O
1,2	(4)	P	1,2 →O
1	(5)	$L \to P$	3-4 →I (ERROR!)

The second of the two conditions stated in the preceding paragraph is that the consequent line must be *derived from* the antecedent line. I promised earlier in the chapter to give a more exact account of this notion.

A line *B* is derived from an assumption *A* (and perhaps other assumptions) if and only if (1) *B* is a derived line (not an assumption) and (2) *B* depends on *A*.

Of course, line *B* depends on assumption *A* if and only if the line number of *A* occurs in the assumption-dependence column opposite *B*.

It was stressed above that the last line in a proof cannot depend on any *provisional* assumptions. Must the last line depend on *all* of the *original* assumptions? In nearly every case it will; occasionally, however, you will encounter sequents with one or more superfluous premises (premises that could be deleted without destroying validity). An example:

$$A \to B, \ C, \ A \vdash B$$

The second premise of this sequent is superfluous. The last line of a proof for this sequent will probably not depend on this premise (the assumption-dependence entry will be '1, 3'). This is perfectly acceptable. If you prove that the conclusion of an argument or sequent follows from *some* of its premises, you have at the same time shown that it follows from the entire set of premises.

Consider these valid sequents involving the ampersand and the arrow:

$$A \to B, \ B \to C \vdash A \to C$$
$$(A \ \& \ B) \to C \vdash A \to (B \to C)$$

$$A \rightarrow (B \rightarrow C) \vdash (A \& B) \rightarrow C$$
$$A \rightarrow (B \rightarrow C) \vdash B \rightarrow (A \rightarrow C)$$
$$A \rightarrow (B \& C) \vdash A \rightarrow B$$
$$A \rightarrow B \vdash (A \& C) \rightarrow B$$
$$A \rightarrow B, A \rightarrow C \vdash A \rightarrow (B \& C)$$
$$A \rightarrow B, C \rightarrow D \vdash (A \& C) \rightarrow (B \& D)$$

All of these sequents can be validated by our method of formal proof.

From this point on, proofs will be more challenging and, hence, more fun to tackle.

EXERCISES

1. Symbolize each statement using the suggested notation.
    (a) *(newspaper)* "The Heat MAKES it [to the playoffs] only if the Hawks LOSE to the Cavs."
    *(b) Your having a QUIZ average over 90 is a sufficient condition for being EXCUSED from the final.
    (c) *(junk mail)* "Only if we can ATTRACT readers of your caliber in these early days of *Saturday Review/Education,* can we PUBLISH the magazine we have in mind."
    (d) *(philosopher Linda Zagzebski)* "[Aquinas . . . thought that] the fact that the intellect is under the CONTROL of the will is a necessary condition for the existence of intellectual VIRTUES." (C = The will controls the intellect, V = There are intellectual virtues)
    (e) *(Winston Churchill)* "The SETTLEMENT of the West could only take place if the Indian barrier were REMOVED." (S = The West is settled)
    *(f) Hannah could SAVE the company if only the president would PROMOTE her.
    (g) *(Snoopy)* "The commanding officer only offers me a ROOT beer when there's a DANGEROUS mission to be flown." (R = The commanding officer offers me a root beer)
    (h) If he really is DETERMINED not to run, and if he wants to see the nomination go to someone who shares his VIEWPOINT, then he should ANNOUNCE now that he is not a candidate.
    (i) *(newspaper)* "Should the Dolphins WIN their division and DEFEAT the Western champion, the American Conference title game will be held in MIAMI Jan. 2 only if the RUNNERUP team beats Cleveland."
    *(j) *(columnist Bob Herbert)* "The tobacco companies . . . could not SURVIVE without ENTICING adolescents into using their products." (S = The tobacco companies survive)

(k) *(General Lüttwitz to General McAuliffe in Bastogne, 1944)* "There is only one possibility to SAVE the encircled U.S.A. troops from total annihilation: that is the HONORABLE surrender of the encircled town."[7]

(l) *(newspaper column)* "A PROSPEROUS, DEMOCRATIC Latin America is essential to hemispheric WELL-BEING." (P = Latin America prospers, D = Latin America is democratic, W = The hemisphere enjoys well-being)

(m) *(TV sportscaster)* "The only way the BILLS and the CHARGERS can get to the playoffs is if JACKSONVILLE loses."

*(n) *(newspaper)* "If the Chiefs beat the 49ers and Buffalo (their final opponent) and should the Raiders beat their last opponent, Denver, and play to a tie against Kansas City, then the Dolphins would be eliminated by losses to the Colts and Packers."

$$
\begin{array}{rcl}
F &=& \text{The Chiefs beat the 49ers} \\
B &=& \text{The Chiefs beat Buffalo} \\
D &=& \text{The Raiders beat Denver} \\
K &=& \text{The Raiders tie Kansas City} \\
E &=& \text{The Dolphins are eliminated} \\
C &=& \text{The Dolphins lose to the Colts} \\
P &=& \text{The Dolphins lose to the Packers}
\end{array}
$$

2. (a) Is Garfield's thought better captured by S1 or by S2? Why?

(S1) I will release your HAND if you release the BURGER.
(F1) B → H

(S2) I will release your hand only if you release the burger.
(F2) H → B

*(b) Is Edmund Burke's maxim, "The only thing necessary for the triumph of evil is for good men to do nothing," better captured by S3 or S4? Why?

[7]McAuliffe's reply: "Nuts!"

(S3) Evil TRIUMPHS if good men do NOTHING.
(F3) N → T

(S4) Evil triumphs only if good men do nothing.
(F4) T → N

3. Which of the following sentences could be *naturally* symbolized as conditionals? (The qualifier 'naturally' is added because *every* statement is logically equivalent to some—perhaps quite involved—conditional.) You need not symbolize the sentences.

(a) *(Aesop)* "He [the fox] crouched down, then took a run and a jump."

*(b) *(tennis shoe advertisement)* "Tretorn on your heel means more comfort on the court."

(c) *(Mark Twain)* "Often a hen who has merely laid an egg cackles as if she had laid an asteroid."

(d) *(Dickens character)* "Stand on your head again, and I'll cut one of your feet off."

(e) *(newspaper)* "American journalists have traditionally refused to reveal sources even if it means jail for contempt of court."

*(f) *(ad for brochure on South Carolina)* "With a copy of our new book, you can do a little sightseeing before you go on vacation."

(g) *(Oscar Wilde)* "The sick do not ask if the hand that smoothes their pillow is pure. . . . "

(h) *(lyrics by Kim Gannon and Walter Kent)* "I'll be home for Christmas if only in my dreams."

4. Complete the following proofs (including assumption-dependence columns). Every assumption has been identified.

(a)
1	(1)	A → B	A
2	(2)	A	PA
1,2	(3)	B	1,2 →o
1,2	(4)	A & B	2,3 &I
1	(5)	A → (A & B)	2-4 →I

*(b)
	(1)	C → D	A
	(2)	C → E	A
	(3)	C	PA
	(4)	D	1,3 →o
	(5)	E	2,3 →o
	(6)	D & E	4,5 ·I
1,2	(7)	C → (D & E)	3-6 →I

(c)
1	(1)	F → (G → H)	A
2	(2)	G & F	PA
2	(3)	F	2 ·o
1,2	(4)	G → H	1,3 →o
2	(5)	G	PA
1,2	(6)	H	4,5 →o
1	(7)	(G & F) → H	2-6 →I

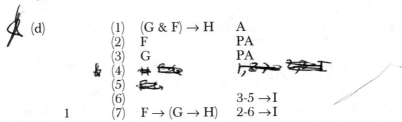

Instructions for exercises 5 though 20: Symbolize and construct proofs.

5. In the first two panels Charlie Brown reasons:

> If we GET this last guy out, we WIN the game. We will get the guy out if Snoopy CATCHES the fly ball. Thus, if Snoopy catches it, we win!!

PEANUTS © United Feature Syndicate. Reprinted by permission.

*6. In Section 3.3, it was pointed out that S1 does *not* entail S2.

(S1) If four is LESS than six and EVERY number less than six is prime, then four is PRIME.

(S2) If four is less than six it is a prime number.

Prove that S2 *does* entail S1; that is, prove the validity of the argument whose premise is S2 and whose conclusion is S1.

7. When Injun Joe tells his accomplice about his plan to disfigure the Widow Douglas, his partner recoils. Injun Joe responds:

> *"My friend, you'll help in this thing—for my sake—that's why you're here—I mightn't be able alone. If you flinch, I'll kill you. Do you understand that? And if I have to kill you, I'll kill her—and then I reckon nobody'll ever know much about who done this business."*[8]

An argument lurks in Injun Joe's speech:

> If you FLINCH, I'll kill YOU. And if I have to kill you, I'll kill HER. There-fore, I'll kill both of you, if you flinch.

8. A newspaper story about high-school football contains this sentence:

> *According to the NCHSAA, Littlejohn will be eligible if two things happen: If he lives in the Asheville school district, which he does; and if the person he lives with—his uncle William Ruff—gets sole court-ordered custody of him.*[9]

[8]Mark Twain, *The Adventures of Tom Sawyer* (New York: Grosset & Dunlap, 1946), p. 259.

The reporter concludes that if Ruff is awarded custody, Littlejohn will be eligible. The argument:

> Littlejohn will be ELIGIBLE if (1) he lives in the ASHEVILLE district and (2) his uncle is awarded CUSTODY; and Littlejohn does live in the Asheville district. It follows that he will be eligible if the uncle is awarded custody.

9. (a) News story:

> *PHILADELPHIA—Police attempts to stamp out heroin by attacking the suppliers of the drug may be counterproductive and lead to an increase in crime by addicts, two scientists believe.*
>
> *The two said that . . . by aiming at the supply of the drug, police succeed in forcing the price of heroin up. Addicts have no choice but to pay the increase and if necessary turn more and more to crime in order to get enough money for the heroin.*[10]

A formalization of their argument:

> Reduction by police of the heroin SUPPLY is a sufficient condition for rising heroin PRICES. Addicts will NEED more money for heroin purchases if the price rises, and if they need more money they will commit more CRIMES. Thus, if the police reduce the supply of heroin, crimes committed by addicts will increase. $S \to P, \ \mathord{\not}P \to N, \ N \to C, S \to C$

(b) Excerpt from an opinion column:

> *[Drug] treatment reduces demand, which reduces drug spending, which reduces the rewards for drug dealing. That leads to less violence over drug-dealing turf and fewer property crimes committed to pay for drugs.*[11]

Formalize and symbolize the argument. The unstated conclusion is:

> If drug TREATMENT programs are expanded, then there will be less drug-related VIOLENCE and fewer PROPERTY crimes committed by addicts. $T \to (V \cdot P)$

(D = Demand for drugs is reduced, S = Drug spending is reduced, R = The rewards for drug dealing are reduced)

*10. Abraham Lincoln had the following to say on the importance of keeping Kentucky in the Union:

> *I think to lose Kentucky is nearly the same as to lose the whole game. Kentucky gone, we can not hold Missouri nor, as I think, Maryland. These all against us, and the job on our hands is too large for us.*[12]

[9]Sean Coughlin, "Littlejohn's Eligibility Delayed," *Asheville Citizen-Times* (August 21, 1996), p. D2.

[10]"Another Look at Heroin," *Miami News* (January 5, 1972), p. 10A.

[11]Joanne Jacobs, "Gingrich: If you sell drugs, we'll kill you," *Miami Herald* (May 14, 1997), p. 11A.

[12]Frank B. Latham, *Lincoln and the Emancipation Proclamation* (New York: Franklin Watts, 1969), p. 31.

President Lincoln's reasoning restated:

> Should KENTUCKY join the Confederacy the Union will lose the Civil WAR, for the following reasons: If we lose Kentucky, then we will also lose Missouri and Maryland to the Confederacy. And we will lose the war if all of these states join the Confederacy.

(A = Missouri joins the Confederacy, B = Maryland joins the Confederacy)

11. Consider this sentence from a newspaper story (exercise 1(k) in Chapter Two):

    > *If you have a specific QUESTION, we will RELAY it to him, if he CALLS in.*

    It is not clear which of the two occurrences of 'if' is to predominate. The two possibilities may be expressed by inserting parentheses and italicizing the main 'if'.

    > (S1) *If* you have a specific question (we will relay it to him if he calls in).
    >
    > (S2) (If you have a specific question we will relay it to him) *if* he calls in.

    Prove that S1 entails S2. A formally identical proof would show that S2 also entails S1; hence, the two statements are logically equivalent. This establishes that in a conditional whose consequent is a conditional [such as 'Q → (C → R)'], the two antecedents ('Q' and 'C') may trade places without affecting the logical content of the statement or formula.

12. The main argument against running the air conditioner in a classroom with the windows wide open is that it wastes energy, but there is also this reason:

    > If the windows are OPEN we get HOT air. If the air CONDITIONER is on we get NOISE [noisy units]. It follows that if the windows are open and the air conditioner is on, we get both hot air and noise.

13. The philosopher Ernest Nagel writes:

    > *The current claim that the principle of causality is inapplicable to the subject matter of quantum mechanics is TENABLE only if it is construed to LEGISLATE the use of special types of state-descriptions, and only if the use of statistical state variables by a theory is taken to MARK the theory as lacking a deterministic structure.*[13]

    F1 and F2 are two possible symbolizations of this sentence.

    > (F1) (T → L) & (T → M)
    > (F2) T → (L & M)

    Prove that F1 entails F2.

---

[13] *The Structure of Science* (New York: Harcourt Brace Jovanovich, 1961), p. 323.

*14. Prove that F2 entails F1 (see preceding exercise). This establishes that both are correct symbolizations of Ernest Nagel's sentence, if either is (since both formulas track the sentence reasonably well).

15. In *Brave New World*, Mustapha Mond makes this reply to the Savage's defense of chastity:

> But chastity means passion, chastity means neurasthenia. And passion and neurasthenia mean instability. And instability means the end of civilization.[14]

Supply the unstated conclusion. Use these abbreviations:

C = People are chaste
P = People are passionate
N = People are neurasthenic
U = People are unstable
E = Civilization ends

Let's interpret the second sentence in Mond's speech as expressing this claim: If people are passionate and neurasthenic, then they are unstable.

16. When the circus owner threatens to fire Dr. Dolittle, the strong man stands up for him:

> "If the Doctor goes, I go too. And if I go, my nephews, the trapeze acrobats, will come with me. And I've a notion that Hop the clown will join us. Now how about it?"
> Mr. Alexander Blossom, proprietor of "The Greatest Show on Earth," hesitated, chewing his moustache in dismay and perplexity. . . . Deserted by the strong man, the trapeze brothers, [and] his best clown . . . , his circus would be sadly reduced.[15]

The strong man's argument:

> If the DOCTOR goes, I go too. And if I go, the TRAPEZE acrobats will leave. The exodus of the trapeze acrobats and me will cause Hop the CLOWN to leave. Our leaving (the strong man, the trapeze brothers, and Hop the clown) would result in a sadly REDUCED circus. So, if Dr. Dolittle leaves, the circus will be greatly reduced.

(S = The strong man leaves)

17. (SEMICHALLENGE) The statement about Newt Gingrich discussed on pages 13–14 can be symbolized by either of the following formulas.

$$C \rightarrow [P \rightarrow (S \rightarrow T)]$$
$$[(C \ \& \ P) \ \& \ S] \rightarrow T$$

Demonstrate their equivalence by constructing proofs that show that each formula entails the other.

18. (CHALLENGE)

$$[(A \rightarrow B) \rightarrow (A \rightarrow C)] \rightarrow D, B \rightarrow C \vdash D$$

---

[14] Aldous Huxley, *Brave New World* (New York: Bantam, 1953), p. 161.
[15] Hugh Lofting, *Doctor Dolittle's Circus* (Philadelphia: Lippincott, 1952), p. 244.

19. (CHALLENGE)

     M ⊢ T → M

A five-line proof is possible. But remember the second restriction on the use of the Arrow In Rule.

     Sequent 19 is demonstrably valid, but it is not clear that all English arguments that seem to have this form are valid. Consider, for example, the following:

> Tipper Gore is monogamous. Hence, if she has two husbands she is monogamous.

This problem is discussed in Appendix Two.

20. (CHALLENGE)

     G ⊢ G

Every statement entails itself. (Why is this so?) Therefore, sequent 20 is valid. There is a *one-line* formal proof for 20:

     (1)   G   A

You might check the account of "proof" given in Section 2.3 (or stated more precisely in 8.3) to satisfy yourself that this does constitute a proof of sequent 20. One can also devise a more ordinary proof that involves deriving the conclusion from the premise. To make this suitably challenging, don't employ the Ampersand In Rule in the liberal way discussed in exercise 16 (end of Chapter Three). My proof has six lines; can you improve on that?

5

Not

5.1 Symbolizing Negations

A statement composed of the expression 'It is not the case that' and a constituent statement is called a *negation* (or *negative statement*). The constituent statement may be either simple or compound. A sample negation:

(S1) It is not the case that Al Gore is a DENTIST.

We introduce the *dash* (–) as an abbreviation for the connective 'It is not the case that'. (We call this expression a "connective" even though it attaches to one statement rather than joining two statements. It is a *monadic* connective. Each of the other connectives we shall study joins two statements; they are *dyadic* connectives.) S1 is symbolized:

(F1) –D

This formula is read "Not *D*" or "Dash *D*." As you will discover later in this section and in Section 7.2, the dash symbol does not "behave" like the minus sign of arithmetic, so it is *not* a good idea to read F1 "Minus D."

The following statements have the same content as S1:

(S2) *It is not true that* Al Gore is a dentist.
(S3) *It is false that* Al Gore is a dentist.
(S4) Al Gore is *not* a dentist.
(S5) Al Gore *isn't* a dentist.

Accordingly, they may be represented by F1. S2 and S3 are clearly compound statements. Each contains as a part the affirmative statement 'Al Gore is a dentist'. Are S4 and S5 also compound? As all four statements are symbolized by one formula, it is convenient to regard S4 and S5 as compound statements. However, this decision is somewhat arbitrary.

To avoid ambiguity when symbolizing negations, we adopt this principle concerning the use of parentheses:

> **Whenever the constituent of a negation is a conditional, conjunction, (looking ahead) biconditional, or disjunction, the constituent is enclosed in parentheses (or brackets, etc.). When the constituent of a negation is either a capital letter or a negation, it is not enclosed in parentheses.**

The following symbolizations illustrate this grouping principle:

(S6)   It is false that Tipper Gore is both a QUAKER and a LUTHERAN.
(F6)   –(Q & L)

(S7)   It is false that Tipper Gore is a Quaker and false that she is a Lutheran.
(F7)   –Q & –L

Note that S6 and S7 (F6 and F7) are *not* logically equivalent. S7 entails, but is not entailed by, S6. A third example is quoted from *The New Yorker*:

(S8)   "Henry Kissinger is no FOOL, but he is not infallible. . . . "

If we abbreviate 'Kissinger is fallible' with *A,* we can symbolize this statement with F8.

(F8)   –F & – –A

Consider these eight formulas:

(F9)   –A & B
(F10) A & –B
(F11) –A & –B
(F12) –(A & B)
(F13) –(–A & B)
(F14) –(A & –B)
(F15) –(–A & –B)
(F16) – –(A & B)

F9 through F11 are conjunctions. Each has at least one negative conjunct. F12 through F15 are negations of conjunctions. F16 is a negation of a negation (of a conjunction). It is important to know that there are no logically equivalent formulas in the set F9 through F16. This fact emphasizes the importance of correctly punctuating negations. It also establishes that the dash of logic does not have all the properties of the minus sign of arithmetic.

Capital letters abbreviate affirmative statements, not negative ones. This is a consequence of a convention adopted previously, as the following argument shows.

> Letters abbreviate only simple statements. Negative statements are not simple. So, letters do not abbreviate them.

(Can this argument be properly assessed by propositional logic? Exercise 8 in Chapter Six treats this question.)

Examine statements S17 through S19.

(S17) Some pilots are alcoholics.
(S18) Some pilots are not alcoholics.
(S19) It is not the case that some pilots are alcoholics.

The negation of S17 is not S18 but S19. S18 and S19 are not equivalent. One indication that S18 is not the negation of S17 is that both of these statements are true. A statement and its negation will never agree in truth (or falsity). If S17 is symbolized with F17, F19 will represent S19 but not S18.

(F17) P
(F19) −P

This illustrates once again the necessity of symbolizing *thoughtfully*.

Organic farmer J. I. Rodale (who crusaded against eating sugar) once claimed, "I'm going to LIVE to be 100 unless I'm RUN over by a sugar-crazed taxi driver."[1] This is a compound statement consisting of two simple statements joined by the connective 'unless'. This connective occurs frequently in our discourse. We can symbolize "unless" sentences by employing two of the connective symbols already introduced, the dash and the arrow. Rodale's statement is symbolized:

−R → L

We employ this principle in translating "unless" statements:

Negate the constituent that follows 'unless' and make the resulting negation the antecedent of a conditional; the other constituent of the original statement becomes the consequent of the conditional.

[1]He died at 72 while extolling his nutritional views during a taping of the Dick Cavett television show.

This principle applies both to statements where 'unless' occurs in the middle (like the Rodale claim) and to statements which begin with 'unless'. My summer-school contract provides an example of the latter case:

> *Unless signed copies are RETURNED by the specified date, this offer of employ-ment automatically EXPIRES.* $-R \to E$

In accordance with the principle stated, we arrive at:

$$-R \to E$$

Let's consider one more example. A newspaper space filler begins:

> *If the wedding is CANCELLED, wedding gifts must be RETURNED unless the bridegroom has DIED.*
>
> $C \to R(\dots D)$
> $C \to (-D \to R)$

It may help to symbolize this in two stages:

   (1) $C \to (R \text{ unless } D)$ OK
   (2) $C \to (-D \to R)$

     It might be suggested that a sentence containing 'unless' is equivalent to a *pair* of conditionals—not just one. Consider this newspaper headline: "DRIEST April ever for South Florida unless it RAINS." The translation principle given in the previous paragraph yields F20 as symbolization, while the suggestion in this paragraph is that F21 is the proper symbolization.

   (F20) $-R \to D$
   (F21) $(-R \to D) \& (R \to -D)$

Suppose that there is a small rain and still April retains the record for dryness. The headline would not be falsified, but F21 would (because its right conjunct would be falsified). So, F21 is not a satisfactory symbolization of the headline.

5.2 Dash In

One morning at the breakfast table my daughter Amy (then aged three) announced that she was now "big." My son Mike (five), who used a tableknife, rebuked her with these words:

> *If you were BIG you would have a KNIFE. But you don't have a knife. That tells me you aren't big.* $B \to K, -K, \therefore \vdash -B$

In symbols:

$$B \rightarrow K, -K \vdash -B$$

No one taught Mike to reason in this way. It is a basic pattern that each of us employs regularly. The pattern traditionally bears the label *modus tollens*,[2] meaning "in the mood of denying." An argument exhibiting this pattern has two premises. The first premise is a conditional, and the second is the negation of the consequent of that conditional. The conclusion is the negation of the antecedent of the first premise.

The "Knife" argument is clearly valid, but we are not yet able to establish this fact with our proof procedure. We can, however, provide an informal justification for the argument:

> *Assume* for a moment that Amy is big. From this assumption and the first premise it follows that she has a knife. But the second premise contradicts this. Therefore, the assumption that Amy is big was mistaken, and we conclude its negation.

We add to our stock of rules one that sanctions reasoning of this sort:

The Dash In Rule (–I): If from an assumed formula (and perhaps other assumptions) a standard contradiction can be derived, then derive the negation of the assumed formula.

The rule restated:

From the derivation of $\mathcal{B}$ & $-\mathcal{B}$ from assumption $\mathcal{A}$ (and perhaps other assumptions) derive $-\mathcal{A}$.

We define a *standard contradiction* as a conjunction whose right conjunct is the negation of the left conjunct; that is, the right conjunct consists of a dash followed by the left conjunct. Examples:

Standard Contradictions	Not Standard Contradictions
A & –A	–A & A
–B & – –B	(B & C) & (–B & –C)
(D → E) & –(D → E)	(D → E) & (D → –E)

Some of the formulas in the right column are contradictions and some are not–but none of them are *standard contradictions*. Note that a formula is a standard contradiction by virtue of its form–not its content. The Dash In Rule makes no reference to the content of the standard contradiction involved; any one will serve as well as any other. As we shall prove in Chapter Thirteen, all

---

[2]The second word is pronounced "TAH-lenz."

contradictions (and therefore all standard contradictions) are logically equivalent.

A proof for the "Knife" sequent:

1	(1)	B → K	A
2	(2)	–K	A
3	(3)	B	PA
1,3	(4)	K	1,3 →O
1,2,3	(5)	K & –K	4,2 &I
1,2	(6)	–B	3-5 –I

Lines 1 and 2 are original assumptions. Line 3 is a provisional assumption
made with the idea of the subsequent application of the Dash In Rule, a move
that is made on line 6. '3-5 –I' is short for 'Derived by the Dash In Rule from
the derivation of the standard contradiction on line 5 from the assumption on
line 3'. (The assumption line is always cited first.) Line 6 of the assumption-
dependence column was computed with the aid of this principle:

> **The formula derived by the Dash In Rule depends on all of the
> assumptions on which the standard contradiction depends–less
> the assumption whose negation is derived.**

Thus, line 6 depends on the assumptions of line 5 (1 through 3) less assumption 3; hence, it depends on 1 and 2. The Dash In step "wipes out" the provisional assumption.

Why is it legitimate to deduce '–B' on line 6 of the above proof? The
contradiction on line 5 follows from the assumptions on lines 1 through 3.
Only a contradictory set of assumptions will yield a contradiction and, thus,
lines 1 through 3 constitute a contradictory set. To avoid inconsistency, one of
the assumptions must be given up. The assumption-dependence entry on line
6 shows that we are retaining assumptions 1 and 2. We can retain 1 and 2 only
by rejecting the third assumption, *B,* which we do on line 6.

In the movie, *Oh God!,* when Jerry Landers (played by John Denver) tells
his wife, Bobbie (Teri Garr), that he has had an encounter with God, she tries
to persuade him that the experience was illusory.

> BOBBIE: *Did you see God or just hear him?*
> JERRY: *I only heard him.*
> BOBBIE: *Well, seeing is believing.*

Bobbie seems to be reasoning in this way:

> If you SAW God, then you should BELIEVE that he was there. You did
> not see God. So, you should not believe that he was there.

In symbols:

$$S \to B, -S \vdash -B$$

Does this argument have a valid form? Can you construct a Dash In proof of its validity?

The "God" argument superficially resembles a *modus tollens* inference but is in fact invalid. The first premise claims that S is a *sufficient* condition for B. That premise is quite compatible with there being other sufficient conditions for B (hearing God, for example). So, from S's denial nothing follows about B. The "God" argument has the same form as the "Cruise" argument (below), but the invalidity of the latter is more obvious (because we know the premises to be true and the conclusion to be false):

> If Tom Cruise plays professional football, then he is more than five feet tall. He does not play professional football. Therefore, he is not taller than five feet.

Both arguments display a pattern called the *fallacy of denying the antecedent*. Compare this pattern with that of *modus tollens*.

modus tollens: $\mathcal{P} \to \mathcal{Q}, -\mathcal{Q} \vdash -\mathcal{P}$ *(valid)*

denying the antecedent: $\mathcal{P} \to \mathcal{Q}, -\mathcal{P} \vdash -\mathcal{Q}$ *(invalid)*

Because the "God" argument is invalid, if you completed a "proof" for it you committed at least one error.

The Dash In Rule is employed in the proofs of many arguments that do not exhibit the *modus tollens* pattern. I shall further illustrate the application of the rule by constructing proofs for two such arguments. The first is advanced by philosopher Bernard Bolzano:

> *That no proposition has truth disproves itself because it is itself a proposition and we should have to call it false in order to call it true.*[3]

The argument restated:

> The proposition that no proposition has truth is not true because if it is true then it is false.

Letting T abbreviate 'The proposition that no proposition has truth is true', the argument is symbolized:

$$T \to -T \vdash -T$$

---

[3]Bernard Bolzano, *Theory of Science,* ed. and trans. by Rolf George (Berkeley and Los Angeles: University of California Press, 1972), p. 39.

A proof of validity:

1	(1)	T → −T	A
2	(2)	T	PA
1,2	(3)	−T	1,2 →O
1,2	(4)	T & −T	2,3 &I
1	(5)	−T	2-4 −I

In constructing this proof, I employed the *Dash In strategy:*

> **When you aim to derive a negation such as '−T' (and a more direct route is not apparent), make a provisional assumption of 'T' and try to derive a standard contradiction.**

When employing the Dash In strategy it would be a good idea to set down some specific standard contradiction as a subgoal, and then attempt to reach it. But how do you choose the standard contradiction? There are no hard and fast rules, but if one of the lines above is a negation, there is a good chance that that negation should be the right conjunct of your standard contradiction. If no line is a negation, you might concentrate on a negation that is a part of some line.

One feature of the proof of the "Truth" sequent deserves special comment. The conclusion of the sequent is reached twice, at lines 3 and 5. It might seem, therefore, that the proof could have been concluded on line 3. A glance at the assumption-dependence column shows why this is not so. Line 3 does not depend solely on the original assumption; it also depends on the provisional assumption on line 2. This assumption is removed by the Dash In step at line 5.

When Jerry Jones, owner of the Dallas Cowboys, fired Coach Jimmy Johnson, the sports editor of the *Miami Herald* wrote a column predicting that Johnson would not land a job with the Miami Dolphins. He wrote:

> *Johnson and Shula will never share authority within the Dolphins.*
>
> . . .
>
> *The Dolphins' long-term future probably will include Shula, which means it will not include Johnson. . . . No team is big enough for both these personalities.*[4]

---

[4]Edwin Pope, "J.J., Shula Won't Work Together," *Miami Herald* (March 31, 1994), pp. 1D, 9D.

The editor's argument formalized and symbolized:

> It is not the case that both JOHNSON and SHULA will be Dolphins. Shula will be a Dolphin; therefore, Johnson won't.[5]

$$-(J \ \& \ S), \ S \vdash -J$$

Let's call this argument "Dolphins I." This proof demonstrates its validity.

1	(1)	$-(J \ \& \ S)$	A
2	(2)	S	A
3	(3)	J	PA
2,3	(4)	J & S	2,3 &I
1,2,3	(5)	$(J \ \& \ S) \ \& \ -(J \ \& \ S)$	4,1 &I
1,2	(6)	$-J$	3-5 $-$I

The pattern exhibited by "Dolphins I" is called *conjunctive argument.* Any argument exhibiting this pattern has two premises. The first premise is a negated conjunction, and the second is one of the conjuncts of that negated conjunction. The conclusion is the negation of the other conjunct.

Does the following argument ("Dolphins II") exhibit the conjunctive-argument pattern?

> It is not the case that both JOHNSON and SHULA will be Dolphins. Shula will not be a Dolphin; therefore, Johnson will.

$$-(J \ \& \ S), \ -S \vdash J$$

"Dolphins II" exhibits a distinct pattern that we may call the *fallacy of denying a conjunct.* Compare the following patterns:

conjunctive argument:	$-(\mathcal{P} \ \& \ \mathcal{Q}), \ \mathcal{P} \vdash -\mathcal{Q}$ *(valid)*
denying a conjunct:	$-(\mathcal{P} \ \& \ \mathcal{Q}), \ -\mathcal{P} \vdash \mathcal{Q}$ *(invalid)*

It would be instructive to attempt a "proof" of "Dolphins II." If you try, you will discover that the "proof" can be completed only by misapplying one or more rules.

5.3 Dash Out

Consider this extremely simple argument:

> It is false that Johnson won't be a Dolphin. So he will be a Dolphin.

---

[5]This argument is valid, but has a false conclusion; within two years Johnson was coaching the Dolphins. How can this happen? The second premise of the argument is false.

In symbols:

$$--J \vdash J$$

Clearly, the conclusion of this argument follows from its premise. But we are not yet in a position to construct a proof of validity. We require a companion for the Dash In Rule.

> **The Dash Out Rule (–O): If from an assumed negation (and perhaps other assumptions) a standard contradiction can be derived, then derive the constituent of the negation.**

The rule restated:

> **From the derivation of $\mathcal{B}$ & $-\mathcal{B}$ from assumption $-\mathcal{A}$ (and perhaps other assumptions) derive $\mathcal{A}$.**

The assumption-dependence principle for this rule parallels the one for the Dash In Rule.

With the help of the Dash Out Rule we can construct a proof of validity for the above argument.

1	(1)	$--J$	A
2	(2)	$-J$	PA
1,2	(3)	$-J \& --J$	2,1 &I
1	(4)	J	2-3 –O

Not only does '$--J$' entail 'J' (as we have just established), but 'J' entails '$--J$'. Thus, the two statements are logically equivalent.

In his *Autobiography,* Bertrand Russell writes:

> *I had had from the first a dark suspicion that the invitation [to lecture in China] might be a practical joke, and in order to test its genuineness I had got the Chinese to pay my passage money before I started. I thought that few people would spend £125 on a joke. . . .*[6]

Russell employed this argument (whose pattern resembles *modus tollens*):

> If the invitation is not GENUINE, the persons who extended it will not SPEND 125 pounds for my passage. Since they are spending it, the invitation must be genuine.

In symbols:

$$-G \rightarrow -S, S \vdash G$$

---

[6](Boston: Little, Brown, 1968), II, p. 172.

Proof:

1	(1)	−G → −S	A
2	(2)	S	A
3	(3)	−G	PA
1,3	(4)	−S	1,3 →O
1,2,3	(5)	S & −S	2,4 &I
1,2	(6)	G	3-5 −O

The *Dash Out strategy* is simple:

When you are seeking to derive a capital letter (or other affirmative formula) and you do not see a more direct route, make a provisional assumption of its negation and try to derive a standard contradiction.

When is the Dash Out strategy likely to be useful? When the following three features are all present the chances are good that the strategy should be employed:

1. The goal (or subgoal) is a capital letter.
2. The premise lines contain one or more dashes.
3. No more direct path from premises to goal is obvious.

When to use

In the previous section I suggested that often you can decide on a standard contradiction by looking for a negative line in the proof and making it the right conjunct of the contradiction. Now we need a qualification: It is generally *not* a good idea to use the Dash Out provisional assumption (which, of course, is always a negation) for this purpose.

It may be helpful to view Dash Out (as well as Dash In) proofs as involving subproofs. The subproof begins with the provisional assumption and concludes with the standard contradiction. I illustrate by repeating the proof of the "Russell" argument:

1	(1)	−G → −S	A
2	(2)	S	A
3	(3)	−G	PA
1,3	(4)	−S	1,3 →O
1,2,3	(5)	S & −S	2,4 &I
1,2	(6)	G	3-5 −O

← subproof

The first and last lines of the subproof are identified by the numbers in the justification entry of the Dash Out step (line 6). The subproof shows that (with the help of assumptions 1 and 2) one can derive line 5 from the assumption on line 3. The completion of the subproof justifies the Dash Out step on line 6. If the assumption of '−G' leads us into a contradiction, then we are justified in concluding its opposite, G. Viewing Dash Out (and Dash In) steps in terms of subproofs may help make sense out of proofs containing more than one provisional assumption (such as the proof displayed in the next paragraph).

In the first argument displayed on page 40 it was claimed that S2 and S4 are logically equivalent statements.

(S2) If Colin Powell is PRESIDENT of the United States, then he is a U.S. CITIZEN.

(S4) If Powell is not a U.S. citizen, then he is not president.

These two statements are equivalent if and only if each entails the other. We prove now that S4 entails S2. (Exercise 13 at the end of the chapter concerns the other entailment.)

1	(1)	$-C \rightarrow -P$	A	[1]
2	(2)	P	PA	[3]
3	(3)	$-C$	PA	[5]
1,3	(4)	$-P$	1,3 →O	[6]
1,2,3	(5)	$P \& -P$	2,4 & I	[7]
1,2	(6)	C	3-5 −O	[4]
1	(7)	$P \rightarrow C$	2-6 →I	[2]

This proof involves both Arrow In and Dash Out strategies. Note the proof-discovery column.

The type of reasoning the two Dash Rules sanction has traditionally been known as the *Reductio ad Absurdum* method of proof. One reduces some assumption to absurdity (by deriving a contradiction from it) and then concludes its denial. A logical justification of this method is provided by the following argument:

> Argument X is VALID if and only if it is LOGICALLY impossible for its premises to be true and its conclusion false. It is logically impossible for X's premises to be true and its conclusion false if and only if it is logically impossible for its premises and the DENIAL of its conclusion all to be true. If a CONTRADICTION can be derived from the premises of X and the denial of its conclusion, then it is logically impossible for the premises and the denial of the conclusion all to be true. Therefore, the derivation of a contradiction from the premises of X and the denial of its conclusion is a sufficient condition for the validity of X.

I prove the validity of this argument in the next chapter.

If you derive a standard contradiction in the course of constructing a proof, are you warranted in concluding by Dash In the negation of *any* formula occurring earlier in the proof? (A parallel question regarding Dash Out can be raised.) No; an examination of the rule shows that two conditions must be met: (1) The earlier formula must be an assumption. (2) The standard contradiction must be derived from that assumption (and perhaps other assumptions).[7]

With the addition of the two Dash Rules we are now in a position to validate these sequents:

$$A \vdash --A$$
$$--A \vdash A$$
$$A \rightarrow B, -B \vdash -A$$
$$-(A \& B), A \vdash -B$$
$$A \rightarrow B \vdash -(A \& -B)$$
$$-(A \& -B) \vdash A \rightarrow B$$
$$A \rightarrow B \vdash -B \rightarrow -A$$
$$-B \rightarrow -A \vdash A \rightarrow B$$

EXERCISES

1. Symbolize each statement using the suggested notation.

   (a) *(presidential candidate George Bush)* "[Read my lips,] no new TAXES." (T = I will raise taxes)

   *(b) *(newspaper)* "Notre Dame is not unbeatable." (B = Notre Dame is beatable)

   (c) *(Johnnie Cochran)* "If it [the prosecution's case] doesn't FIT, you must ACQUIT."

   (d) *(presidential candidate Bill Clinton)* "I EXPERIMENTED with marijuana a time or two, [but] I didn't LIKE it, I didn't INHALE, and never TRIED it again."

   (e) *(New Jersey governor-elect Christine Todd Whitman)* "Unlike the president, I inhaled. [And then I threw up.]" (P = The president inhaled, W = I inhaled)

   *(f) "If you're not CONFUSED, you're not well INFORMED."

---

[7]These conditions are implied by the particular formulation of the Dash In and Dash Out Rules presented in this book. There are other logically sound formulations of these rules that do not imply these conditions.

the small society

IF YOU'RE NOT CONFUSED, YOU'RE NOT WELL INFORMED—

BRICKMAN

Reprinted with special permission of King Features Syndicate.

(g) *(Sartre's Nausea)* "The CASHIER was not there, nor the WAITER— nor M. FASQUELLE."

(h) *(Hans Christian Andersen)* "Now we shall have duck EGGS, unless it's a DRAKE."

(i) *(headline)* "Hamilton can't PRESIDE without MOVING to city."

*(j) *(conversation)* "The May Day program will be THURSDAY afternoon—unless it RAINS, in which case it will be FRIDAY morning."

(k) *(Dickens dialogue)* "Unless I SEE it with my own eyes, and HEAR it with my own ears, I never will BELIEVE it."

(l) *(Hitler)* "If I do not get the oil of MAIKOP and GROZNY, then I must END this war."

(m) *(Police Benevolent Association bulletin)* "If you don't TAKE your money now and you let it ACCRUE to retirement, then our attorney has not HELPED you and you will not be asked to PAY a legal fee."

2. Translate each formula into an English sentence using this dictionary:

    D = Justice O'Connor is a Democrat
    R = Justice O'Connor is a Republican

    (a) $--R$
    *(b) $-D \& R$
    (c) $-(D \& R)$
    (d) $-D \& -R$

3. Complete the following proofs. Every assumption has been identified.

    (a) 1   (1) $-A \to B$ A
         2   (2) $-A \to -B$ A
         3   (3) $-A$ PA
                (4) B

		(5)		2,3 →O
	1,2,3	(6)	B & −B	
	1,2	(7)	A	3-6 −O
*(b)	1	(1)	C & D	A
	1	(2)	C	
	1	(3)	D	
	4	(4)	−D	PA
	1,4	(5)	D & −D	
	1	(6)	− −D	
	1	(7)	C & − −D	
(c)		(1)	E → F	A
		(2)	−(E & F)	A
		(3)	E	PA
		(4)		
		(5)		
		(6)	(E & F) & −(E & F)	
	1,2	(7)		3-6 −I
(d)		(1)	−G → H	A
		(2)	−H	PA
		(3)	−G	PA
		(4)		
		(5)		
	1,2	(6)		3-5 −O
	1	(7)	−H → G	2-6 →I

Instructions for exercises 4 through 15: Symbolize and construct proofs.

4. Lucy's argument:

> Beethoven never played hockey. Proof: if he had PLAYED hockey, he would have written some hockey MUSIC. However, he wrote no hockey music.

*5. A historic grist mill operating outside Tallahassee, Florida, got caught in a bureaucratic Catch-22 summarized in the following argument.[8]

[8]Tom Fiedler, "It Took Grits to Ease up on the Rules," *Miami Herald* (February 26, 1995), pp. 1M, 4M.

> The mill will GRIND corn only if CHANGES [mandated by the state De-
> partment of Agriculture] are made. But the mill is on the National REG-
> ISTER of Historic Places. And if so, then no changes will be made to the
> mill. Therefore, the mill will not grind corn.

(Florida's Governor, Lawton Chiles, rode to the mill's rescue and cut
through the red tape.)

6. Ethicist Burton Leiser writes:

> *Liberty for the restaurant owners [to serve whom they chose] was incompat-*
> *ible with liberty for black travelers [to eat where they wished]. The latter*
> *could acquire the liberty to eat along the highway in Georgia only if Lester*
> *Maddox and other restaurant owners were deprived of their liberty to refuse*
> *to serve them.*[9]

(Fortunately, Congress decided that freedom from racial discrimination
in public accommodations is more important than the freedom of restau-
ranteurs to pick their clientele.) Prove that the first sentence in the quotation follows logically from the second. (T = Black travelers are free to eat
along the highway, R = Restaurant owners are free to refuse to serve
black travelers)

7. In the children's book *I Can't Have Bannock But the Beaver Has a Dam,*[10] a
Native Canadian child asks his mother why she is unable to prepare bannock (a native bread) for him. Her explanation (paraphrased):

> I can make BANNOCK for you only if the oven will get HOT. The oven
> will get hot only if the ELECTRICITY is on. The electricity is on only if
> the power LINES are up. But a tree [brought down by a beaver] FELL
> on the power lines. If a tree fell on the power lines, then they are not up.
> And that is why I can't make bannock for you.

This explanation takes the form of an argument; the conclusion is the last
sentence.

8. The medical examiner had another reason for rejecting the claim that
Blanche Block committed suicide (see page 1):

> Blanche was RIGHT-handed. Two wounds were on the LEFT side of
> her head. If Blanche committed SUICIDE and was right-handed, she
> would not have wounds on the left side of her head. Hence, she did not
> commit suicide.

*9. In the "Phaedo" Plato argues in the following way for the doctrine of im-
mortality:

> *Besides, Socrates, rejoined Cebes, there is that theory which you have often*
> *described to us—that what we call learning is really just recollection. If that*
> *is true, then surely what we recollect now we must have learned at some*

[9]Burton M. Leiser, ed., *Liberty, Justice, and Morals,* 2nd ed. (New York: Macmillan,
1979), p. 1.

[10]Bernelda Wheeler (Winnipeg, Canada: Pemmican Publications, 1984).

"Why is the electricity off?"

"Because the electricity is off. Without electricity, the oven won't get hot, so I can't make bannock."

Bernelda Wheeler, © 1984, 1993, Peguis Publishers, Winnipeg, Canada.

time before, which is impossible unless our souls existed somewhere before they entered this human shape. So in that way too it seems likely that the soul is immortal.[11]

The argument restated:

> Learning is actually RECOLLECTION. If that is true, then what we recollect now must have been learned before BIRTH. It is impossible that what we recollect was learned before birth unless the soul is immortal. So, the soul is immortal.

(M = The soul is mortal)

10. Joseph Heller's famous Catch-22:

> *There was only one catch and that was Catch-22, which specified that a concern for one's own safety in the face of dangers that were real and immediate was the process of a rational mind. Orr was crazy and could be grounded. All he had to do was ask; and as soon as he did, he would no longer be crazy and would have to fly more missions. Orr would be crazy to fly more missions and sane if he didn't, but if he was sane he had to fly them. If he flew them he was crazy and didn't have to; but if he didn't want to he was sane and had to. Yossarian was moved very deeply by the absolute simplicity of this clause of Catch-22 and let out a respectful whistle.*
>
> *"That's some catch, that Catch-22," he observed.*
>
> *"It's the best there is," Doc Daneeka agreed.*[12]

One analysis of the argument contained in this passage:

> Orr's ASKING to be grounded would be proof of his SANITY. Asking to be grounded is a necessary condition for being GROUNDED. If Orr is sane, then he cannot be grounded. All of which shows that Orr cannot be grounded.

11. Prove the validity of the second argument displayed on page 40. Use these abbreviations:

> B = S3 is equivalent to S5
> C = S1 is equivalent to S3
> D = S1 is equivalent to S5
> A = The word 'only' in S1 affects the meaning of S1

12. News story:

> *TALLAHASSEE—At least three votes cast during Thursday's debate in the House on the governor's environmental agency bill were illegal. . . .*
>
> *House rules provide that members must be present to vote on any motion, amendment or bill.*

---

[11]72e–73a. Hugh Tredennick, trans., "Phaedo," in *The Collected Dialogues of Plato,* ed. by Edith Hamilton and Huntington Cairns (Princeton, N.J.: Princeton University Press, 1961), p. 55.

[12]*Catch-22* (New York: Dell Pub. Co., 1961), p. 47.

Jacksonville Rep. Jon Forbes was recorded as voting for the bill creating the new Department of Environmental Affairs.
Forbes, however, was in Jacksonville when the vote was taken.[13]

The reporter reasoned:

> Rep. Forbes voted LEGALLY only if he was in TALLAHASSEE when the vote was taken. Therefore, since he was in JACKSONVILLE at the time, he did not vote legally. Obviously, he was not in both cities when the vote was taken.

*13. It was shown in Section 5.3 that S4 entails S2.

> (S2)   If Colin Powell is PRESIDENT of the United States, then he is a U.S. CITIZEN.
>
> (S4)   If Powell is not a U.S. citizen, then he is not president.

Now show that S2 entails S4 (thereby establishing logical equivalence).

14. The ontological argument for the existence of God was advanced by St. Anselm in the eleventh century.[14] He presented at least two versions of the argument, one of which may be paraphrased as follows:

> God exists in REALITY. The proof: God is a being a GREATER than which cannot be conceived. We understand the TERM 'God'. If we understand this term, then God exists in the UNDERSTANDING. If God exists in the understanding but not in reality, then [because we could conceive of a being who is like God except that he exists both in the understanding and in reality] God is *not* a being a greater than which cannot be conceived.

(G = God is a being a greater than which cannot be conceived) Don't symbolize the bracketed material in premise four.

15. The philosopher John Hick writes:

> *As a challenge to theism, the problem of evil has traditionally been posed in the form of a dilemma: if God is perfectly LOVING, he must WISH to abolish evil; and if he is all-POWERFUL, he must be ABLE to abolish evil. But evil EXISTS; therefore God cannot be both omnipotent and perfectly loving.*[15]

Add this obviously true suppressed premise:

> If God wishes to abolish evil and is able to do so, then evil does not exist.

---

[13]Rick Eyerdam, "3 Illegal Votes Cast during House Debate," *Miami News* (March 4, 1972), p. 1A.

[14]See his *Proslogion,* the relevant part of which is reprinted in John Hick, ed., *The Existence of God* (New York: Macmillan, 1964), pp. 25–27.

[15]*Philosophy of Religion* (Englewood Cliffs, N.J.: Prentice-Hall, 1963), p. 40. Hick examines this argument but does not subscribe to it.

16. Solve the puzzle.

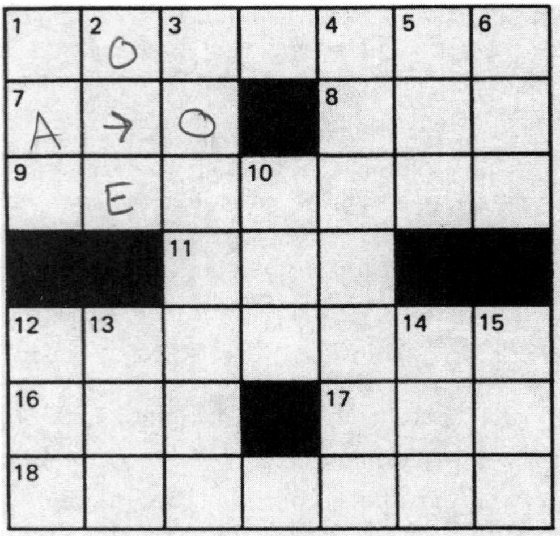

(crossword grid with handwritten entries: cell 2 contains "O"; row 7 reads "A → O"; cell 9 area contains "E")

Across

1. '– –N' _____ from 14d.
7. He is an OHIOAN since he lives in AKRON.
8. Follows from 'O → U' and 'O'.
9. Tacks on a dash.
11. Entailed by '–R → –I'.
12. Premise word.
16. Logically equivalent to '–(U & –A)'.
17. From 'T & L' in three steps.
18. In a mood.

Down

1. Rooter.
2. She's OLD, *ergo* ELIGIBLE.
3. Denying the antecedent is not _____ .
4. Rids a connective.
5. I'll WRITE while you E-MAIL.
6. Conclusion words.
10. If she's ABSENT, she's absent.
12. Conjunction word.
13. Only if he's OLD is he ELIGIBLE.
14. SUFFICIENT conditions are antecedents; NECESSARY conditions are consequents.
15. French conjunctions.

17. (CHALLENGE) Symbolize each statement using the suggested notation.

(a) *(comic strip dialogue)* "Not only did Mrs. Viking TREAT me with contempt–but you IGNORED me."

(b) *(Warren Christopher)* "I think it's so essential that both parties in this negotiation [the Israelis and the Palestinians] emerge as winners; otherwise both will be losers."

    A = The Israelis win
    B = The Palestinians win
    C = The Israelis lose
    D = The Palestinians lose

(c) *(Time)* "If both Mao and Chiang claimed to rule all of China, only one could be right."

    A = Mao claims to rule all of China
    B = Chiang claims to rule all of China
    C = Mao's claim to rule all of China is correct
    D = Chiang's claim to rule all of China is correct

(d) *(quarterback)* "I'll REPORT to camp, but I won't PLAY in an exhibition game without a signed CONTRACT." (Provide two symbolizations.)

(e) *(newspaper)* "The DONATION of the Virginia Key property, [Goode said,] should be made only if the university will USE the land only to expand the Marine and Atmospheric Sciences school and if the land will REVERT to Metro if CONSTRUCTION has not begun within three years from the date of transfer of title." (D = Metro should donate the Virginia Key property, U = The university uses the land only to expand the Marine and Atmospheric Sciences school)

18. (CHALLENGE) Symbolize each statement using only capitals, grouping symbols, dashes, and ampersands.

(a) It is not the case that either AL or BETH will quit.
(b) Al and/or Beth will quit.
(c) Either Al or Beth will quit, but not both.

Instructions for exercises 19 through 23: Symbolize and construct proofs.

19. (SEMICHALLENGE)

(a) $-(R \, \& \, T) \vdash T \to -R$

What can you infer from the fact that sequents 6 (page 74) and 19(a) are both valid?

(b) In what logical relation do these two formulas stand:

$-(R \, \& \, -T)$
$R \to T$

Demonstrate the correctness of your answer.

20. (CHALLENGE) In Rudyard Kipling's short story "Rikki-Tikki-Tavi," Nagaina, the recently widowed King Cobra, seeks vengeance:

> *"Son of the big man that killed Nag," she hissed, "stay still. I am not ready yet. Wait a little. Keep very still. . . . If you move I strike, and if you do not move I strike."* [16]

Demonstrate that her last statement entails 'I STRIKE'. (M = You move)

21. (CHALLENGE)

$A \, \& \, -A \vdash B$

---

[16] *The Jungle Book* (Garden City, N.Y.: Doubleday, 1964), p. 146.

This peculiar sequent is discussed in Section 13.1. A five-line proof is possible. Remember the second restriction on the Dash Rules.

22. (CHALLENGE)

    $-T \vdash T \to M$

An eight-line proof is possible.

This sequent is the mate of sequent 19 in Chapter Four. Sequent 22 is demonstrably valid, but some English arguments that seem to have this form are of questionable validity. An example:

> Tipper Gore does not have two husbands. Hence, if she has two husbands she is monogamous.

Sequents 19 (Chapter Four) and 22 are commonly referred to as the "paradoxes of material implication." These paradoxes are discussed in Appendix Two.

23. (CHALLENGE) A newspaper editorial advocating taxing land instead of buildings contains these sentences:

> *Taxing buildings discourages the construction of housing, which increases rents and unemployment. Not taxing land enough causes inflated land prices, one of the major causes of inflation.*[17]

The passage suggests this argument:

> Taxing BUILDINGS results in more UNEMPLOYMENT. Not taxing LAND leads to increased INFLATION. It follows that we can avoid both higher unemployment and greater inflation only if land is taxed but buildings are not.

---

[17]"The Tax Bite," *Springfield* [Ohio] *News & Sun* (January 16, 1979).

6

Iff

6.1 Symbolizing Biconditionals

A statement consisting of two constituent statements joined by the connective 'if and only if' is called a *biconditional.* An example:

>   (S1) Norma will do GRADUATE work if and only if she receives a FELLOWSHIP.

A biconditional is equivalent to the conjunction of a pair of conditionals. Thus, S1 is logically equivalent to S2.

>   (S2) Norma will do graduate work if she receives a fellowship, and she will do graduate work only if she receives a fellowship.

S2 is, of course, symbolized by F2:

>   (F2) $(F \rightarrow G)$ & $(G \rightarrow F)$

We could employ F2 as a symbolization of S1 and dispense with a special symbol for the locution 'if and only if'. However, because the locution is common in logical discourse, it will prove convenient to adopt the *double arrow* ($\leftrightarrow$) as an abbreviation of it. We symbolize S1 with F1:

>   (F1) $G \leftrightarrow F$

F1 is read "*G* if and only if *F*" or "*G* double arrow *F*." The expressions 'is a necessary and sufficient condition for' and 'just in case' (in one of its senses) are approximately synonymous with 'if and only if' and are also abbreviated by the double arrow.

The conventions for punctuating formulas containing arrows and ampersands also apply to formulas containing double arrows. For example, F3 represents a biconditional whose left constituent is a conjunction, and F4 symbolizes a conjunction whose right conjunct is a biconditional.

> (F3) (A & B) $\leftrightarrow$ C
> (F4) A & (B $\leftrightarrow$ C)

Although biconditionals occur regularly in logical and philosophical language, they occur only infrequently in many other areas of discourse. I suspect that (in the case of English) this infrequent usage is due in part to the cumbersomeness of the pentasyllabic expression 'if and only if'. Some logicians have coined the shorter term 'iff' to remedy this difficulty; I will use this expression for the remainder of the book. (A defect of this expression is that it is phonetically indistinguishable from 'if'. Perhaps in the future a short biconditional connective will evolve in English.) The logician Bas Van Fraassen saves one syllable with his expression 'exactly if'.

In the absence of such a convenient term, people will sometimes employ either 'if' or 'only if' when they mean 'if and only if'. Thus, someone may utter S5 or S6 intending to claim S7.

> (S5) I will make the flight if I rush.
> (S6) I will make the flight only if I rush.
> (S7) I will make the flight if and only if I rush.

However, we need to distinguish between what a *person* means to claim and what the uttered *sentence* means. Strictly speaking, S5 and S6 express only conditionals.

6.2   Double Arrow In and Out

Examine this simple argument:

> Norma MOVES to Chapel Hill iff she does GRADUATE work. So, she does graduate work iff she moves to Chapel Hill.

In symbols:

> M $\leftrightarrow$ G $\vdash$ G $\leftrightarrow$ M

This is a valid sequent. (The double arrow is commutative.) We can prove the validity of this sequent with the help of a pair of inference rules governing the double arrow.

The Double Arrow In Rule ($\leftrightarrow$**I**): From $A \rightarrow B$ and $B \rightarrow A$ **derive** $A \leftrightarrow B$.

The Double Arrow Out Rule ($\leftrightarrow$**O**): From $A \leftrightarrow B$ **derive either** $A \rightarrow B$ **or** $B \rightarrow A$.

Note that the Double Arrow In Rule sanctions a move from two premises, whereas the Double Arrow Out Rule sanctions a move from one premise. The standard assumption-dependence principle applies to both rules.

A proof for the "Chapel Hill" argument:

(1)   M $\leftrightarrow$ G   A
(2)   M $\rightarrow$ G   1 $\leftrightarrow$O
(3)   G $\rightarrow$ M   1 $\leftrightarrow$O
(4)   G $\leftrightarrow$ M   3,2 $\leftrightarrow$I

In the justification entry for a statement derived by the Double Arrow In Rule, I cite first the premise whose antecedent is identical with the biconditional's left constituent.

I illustrate the application of these two rules by constructing proofs for three other arguments. The first is suggested by an editorial in the *Huntington* [West Virginia] *Herald-Dispatch:*

> *Since the First Amendment to the Constitution forbids government from restraining the publication of news, it clearly follows that the government is equally powerless to compel the publication of news or opinion.*[1]

The argument formalized and symbolized:

> The government may RESTRAIN the publication of news iff it may COMPEL the publication of news. Since government may not restrain publication, it clearly follows that it also is not permitted to compel the publication of news.
>
> R $\leftrightarrow$ C, –R $\vdash$ –C

The proof:

1   (1)   R $\leftrightarrow$ C   A
2   (2)   –R   A
3   (3)   C   PA
1   (4)   C $\rightarrow$ R   1 $\leftrightarrow$O

[1]Reprinted in *Miami News* (September 3, 1973), p. 12A.

1,3	(5)	R	4,3 →O
1,2,3	(6)	R & −R	5,2 &I
1,2	(7)	−C	3-6 −I

At the end of Section 5.3 I provided a justification for the Dash In and Dash Out Rules. This justification was formulated as an argument that is symbolized:

$$V \leftrightarrow -L, -L \leftrightarrow -D, C \rightarrow -D \vdash C \rightarrow V$$

Proof:

1	(1)	V ↔ −L	A
2	(2)	−L ↔ −D	A
3	(3)	C → −D	A
4	(4)	C	PA
3,4	(5)	−D	3,4 →O
2	(6)	−D → −L	2 ↔O
2,3,4	(7)	−L	6,5 →O
1	(8)	−L → V	1 ↔O
1,2,3,4	(9)	V	8,7 →O
1,2,3	(10)	C → V	4-9 →I

The third illustrative proof concerns this argument:

> Norma MOVES to Chapel Hill iff she does GRADUATE work. She does graduate work iff she receives a FELLOWSHIP. Hence, Norma moves to Chapel Hill just in case she gets a fellowship.

This is the biconditional version of a chain argument. In symbols:

$$M \leftrightarrow G, G \leftrightarrow F \vdash M \leftrightarrow F$$

Proof:

1	(1)	M ↔ G	A	[1]
2	(2)	G ↔ F	A	[2]
3	(3)	M	PA	[6]
1	(4)	M → G	1 ↔O	[8]
1,3	(5)	G	4,3 →O	[9]
2	(6)	G → F	2 ↔O	[10]
1,2,3	(7)	F	6,5 →O	[7]
1,2	(8)	M → F	3-7 →I	[4]

9	(9)	F	PA	[11]
2	(10)	F → G	2 ↔O	[13]
2,9	(11)	G	10,9 →O	[14]
1	(12)	G → M	1 ↔O	[15]
1,2,9	(13)	M	12,11 →O	[12]
1,2	(14)	F → M	9-13 →I	[5]
1,2	(15)	M ↔ F	8,14 ↔I	[3]

Note the proof-discovery numbers.

Both Double Arrow rules are "choice" rules. This is obvious in the case of Double Arrow Out, but not so evident for Double Arrow In. When Double Arrow In is applied to a pair of conditionals, either of two biconditionals may be deduced. The following proof illustrates:

(1)	D → E	A
(2)	E → D	A
(3)	D ↔ E	1,2 ↔I
(4)	E ↔ D	2,1 ↔I
(5)	(D ↔ E) & (E ↔ D)	3,4 &I

Strategic suggestions for the Double Arrow rules:

> *Double Arrow In*: **If one of the goal lines is a biconditional, search the premise lines for the two associated conditionals (that is, the conditionals with the same constituents). If you find both conditionals, apply Double Arrow In. If you find only one of the associated conditionals, add the other as a goal line. If you find neither conditional among the premise lines, add both as goal lines.**

> *Double Arrow Out*: **If one of the premise lines is a biconditional, apply Double Arrow Out (once or twice).**

Consider these valid sequents involving the double arrow:

> A ↔ B, A ⊢ B
> A ↔ B, −A ⊢ −B
> A ↔ B ⊢ B ↔ A
> A ↔ (B ↔ C) ⊢ (A ↔ B) ↔ C
> A ↔ −B ⊢ −(A ↔ B)
> −(A ↔ B) ⊢ A ↔ −B
> A ↔ B ⊢ −A ↔ −B

Some of these sequents are easily proved; the proofs for others are very challenging.

EXERCISES

1. Symbolize each statement using the suggested notation.

   (a) *(newspaper column)* "Our JUSTICE system works if, and only if, witnesses are willing to come FORWARD."

   *(b) *(bulletin)* "If and only if it [a motion on racial research] is APPROVED by a majority of the AAA membership will it become an official POSITION of the American Anthropological Association."

   (c) I'll let you pay for the MEAL just in case you allow me to leave the TIP.

   (d) *(professor)* "I will READ Grimm's logic qualifier—but only if the first two readers disagree." (A = The first two readers agree)

   (e) *(Section 5.3)* "These two statements [S2 and S4] are EQUIVALENT if and only if each entails the other." (A = S2 entails S4, B = S4 entails S2)

   *(f) *(minutes)* "The assistantship will be offered to McGRAW if and only if he does not get a tuition WAIVER; and it will be offered to SPIEGELMAN if not offered to McGraw."

   (g) *(newspaper editorial)* "Greta's father will DONATE the kidney she needs—but not unless he's HERE [in the United States]."

   (h) *(insurance premium notice)* "No receipt will be FURNISHED except by WRITTEN request."

   (i) *(Kofi Annan)* "If all of us in this hall together . . . can make this organization [the UN] LEANER, more EFFICIENT, and MORE effective, more responsive to the WISHES and NEEDS of its members and more realistic in its GOALS and COMMITMENTS, then and only then will we serve both this organization's high PURPOSE and the planet's best INTERESTS."

2. Translate each formula into an English sentence using this dictionary:

   B = Smith wins the batting crown
   S = Smith makes an out
   H = Smith gets a hit
   J = Jones makes an out

   (a) $B \leftrightarrow -S$
   *(b) $B \leftrightarrow (H \,\&\, J)$
   (c) $(B \leftrightarrow H) \,\&\, J$
   (d) $H \rightarrow (B \leftrightarrow J)$

3. Complete the following proofs. Every assumption has been identified.

   (a)

(1)	$A \leftrightarrow B$		A
(2)	$C \leftrightarrow B$		A
(3)	A		PA
(4)			1 $\leftrightarrow$ O
(5)			
(6)			2 $\leftrightarrow$ O

1,2,3	(7)		
1,2	(8)	A → C	3-7 →I
*(b)	(1)	D ↔ E	A
	(2)	(E → D) → (G → F)	A
	(3)	(D → E) → (F → G)	A
	(4)	E → D	
	(5)	G → F	
	(6)		
	(7)		
	(8)	F ↔ G	
(c)	(1)	H ↔ (I & J)	A
	(2)	I → H	A
	(3)	H	PA
	(4)		1 ↔O
	(5)		
	(6)		
	(7)		3-6 →I
1,2	(8)	H ↔ I	7,2 ↔I

Instructions for exercises 4 through 15: Symbolize and construct proofs.

4. NBC News correspondent Pete Williams, reporting on doctor-assisted suicide:

   The doctors [interviewed] argue that it's already legal to help terminally ill patients on life support pull the plug when they want to die, so they say it's unfair to refuse help to terminally ill patients who also want to die but aren't on life support.[2]

   The doctors' argument can be expressed like this:

   Doctor-assisted suicide for patients NOT on life support should be legal if and only if doctor-assisted suicide for patients ON life support is legal. The latter is legal. Therefore, the former should be legal as well.

*5. Administrators at a junior high school in Ohio ordered some students to stop wearing to school T-shirts featuring satanic messages.[3] The satanists then argued that T-shirts with Christian themes should also be banned:

   T-shirts with CHRISTIAN messages should be permitted just in case T-shirts with SATANIC messages are allowed. Since the latter are not allowed, the former shouldn't be permitted either.

6. One formalization of Snoopy's (and Charlie Brown's) reasoning:

   The RED dish is the supper dish iff the YELLOW dish is the water dish. There is WATER in the yellow dish. If so, then the yellow dish is the water dish. Which means the red dish must be the supper dish.

---

[2] NBC Evening News, January 5, 1997.

[3] "T-Shirts with Spiritual Messages Stir School Debate," *Miami Herald* (November 4, 1996), p. 3A.

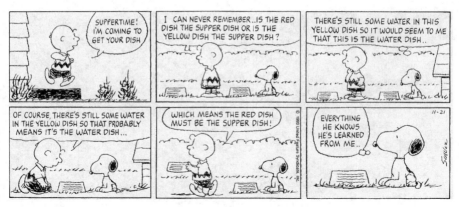

PEANUTS © United Feature Syndicate. Reprinted by permission.

7. The logicians Hughes and Cresswell write:

> *It should be noted that whenever we have a thesis of the form* Cab *we can always use TR3 to obtain* ⊢ LCab, *and hence, by Def F,* ⊢ Fab. *Moreover, whenever we have* ⊢ Fab *we can, by Def F, substitution of* Cab *for* p *in A5, and Modus Ponens, obtain* ⊢ Cab. *I.e. whenever* Cab *is a thesis, so is* Fab, *and vice versa.*[4]

Their reasoning may be paraphrased:

> If *Cab* is a theorem, then *LCab* is also, and if *LCab* is a theorem, then *Fab* is a theorem. Moreover, if *Fab* is a theorem, then *Cab* is too. This proves that *Cab* is a theorem iff *Fab* is a theorem.

(C = *Cab* is a theorem, L = *LCab* is a theorem, F = *Fab* is a theorem)

8. The argument about symbolizing negative statements displayed on page 61 may be symbolized in propositional logic as:

> L, –N ⊢ –A

The following argument establishes that that symbolization is inadequate:

> If propositional logic is **ADEQUATE** for evaluating the argument, the **ENGLISH** argument is valid just in case the **SYMBOLIZED** version is valid. The English argument is valid, but the symbolization isn't. It follows that propositional logic is inadequate for evaluating the argument.

*9. An opinion column appearing soon after the Oklahoma City bombing contained this passage:

> *But it's sadly clear that the kind of police-power restrictions stipulated by the founders and consistently enlarged by courts ever since are viable over the*

[4]G. E. Hughes and M. J. Cresswell, *An Introduction to Modal Logic* (London: Methuen, 1968), p. 31. I have replaced their notation by one that is more readily printed.

long haul if, and only if, civilization reigns. In other words, if no sanity prevails in office buildings and in the streets, then constitutional and other buffers cannot survive as we have come to know them over two centuries-plus.[5]

The quotation strongly suggests this argument:

Restrictions on police powers will be VIABLE iff society remains CIVILIZED. Hence, if society does not remain civilized, police-power restrictions will no longer be viable.

10. The philosopher Norman Malcolm[6] was critical of the view that brain phenomena and mental phenomena are identical. I paraphrase one of his arguments as follows:

If brain phenomena are IDENTICAL with mental phenomena, then the former's having spatial location constitutes a necessary and sufficient condition for the latter's having spatial location. BRAIN phenomena can be located spatially. Provided that MENTAL phenomena are spatially locatable, it will be meaningful to assign spatial location to a THOUGHT. It is not meaningful to do this. So, it is false that brain phenomena and mental phenomena are identical.

11. This argument provides the rationale for wiring backup lights through the transmission.

Backup lights are NEEDED only if the car is in REVERSE. [Because they are connected to the transmission] they are ON just in case the car is in reverse. If they are on only if the car is in reverse, then they use very LITTLE power. Therefore, the backup lights are on if needed, yet they use very little power.

12. A news story about a meeting of the Coral Gables City Commission contains this passage:

Politics has taken up residence in the old Biltmore Hotel. . . .

The issue is whether the city wants to try to obtain the 19.8-acres from the federal government. . . .

After a series of confusing votes Friday, the commission's answer depends on your political viewpoint.

"Yes," commissioners said, "the city wants the property if voters agree." On the other hand commissioners said "no, the city doesn't want it, unless voters say they do." [7]

There is the implication in this story that the two views expressed in the final paragraph are unclear or perhaps inconsistent. Yet, the two views taken together (see S1) are logically equivalent to S2, a perfectly straightforward biconditional.

[5]Mitchell B. Pearlstein, "Fear Itself; No Choice But to Look Hard at Those Who Look Different," *Star Tribune* (Minneapolis, April 23, 1995), p. 21A.

[6]See "[Abstract of] Scientific Materialism and the Identity Theory," *Journal of Philosophy,* LX (October 24, 1963), 662–663.

[7]Louis Salome, "Biltmore: Yes, the City Wants It; No, It Doesn't . . . Unless the Voters Do," *Miami News* (March 16, 1971), p. 5A.

(S1) The CITY wants the property if the VOTERS want it, and the city doesn't want it unless the voters want it.

(S2) The city wants the property iff the voters want it.

Prove that S1 entails S2.

*13. Prove that S2 in the preceding exercise entails S1. These two proofs establish the logical equivalence of S1 and S2.

14. In a *Star Trek* episode, the crew of the starship *Enterprise* is held captive by a powerful computer. The crew escapes after one of them says to the computer, "I am lying to you." This inference blew the computer's fuses:

> He SAYS that he is lying. If he says that he is lying and he *is* LYING, then he isn't lying. But also, if he says that he is lying and he *isn't* lying, then he is lying. This proves that he is lying exactly if he isn't lying.

15. There are people who believe that at some time after their death God will re-create their bodies. Would the re-creation of, say, Elvis Presley be Elvis or merely a *replica* of Elvis? The realization that it is logically possible that God produce two re-creations of Elvis (label them *A* and *B*) may count against the view that either re-creation would be Elvis. Argument 15 pursues this point.

> A is Elvis just in case B is Elvis. It is not true that both A and B are Elvis. Therefore, A is not Elvis and neither is B.

(A = A is Elvis, B = B is Elvis)

16. (CHALLENGE) (a) Prof. M.G. Yoes, Jr. has symbolized the following sentence with a formula consisting of 16 symbols (connectives, letters, and grouping symbols). Can you provide an equally short (or shorter) symbolization?

> Exactly one of these three people will be hired: BURTT, DAVIS, and MASON.

(b) Symbolize Catbert's dress code using this dictionary:

O = It is OK for me to wear casual clothes to work today
F = Today is Friday
S = Someone sees me at work today

DILBERT © United Feature Syndicate. Reprinted by permission.

Instructions for exercises 17 through 20: Symbolize and construct proofs.

17. (CHALLENGE)

> Norma's receiving a FELLOWSHIP is a necessary and sufficient condition for her doing GRADUATE work. Consequently, her not receiving a fellowship is a necessary and sufficient condition for her not doing graduate work.

18. (CHALLENGE)

$$-D \leftrightarrow E \vdash -(D \leftrightarrow E)$$

19. (CHALLENGE) If you invent an expression, you are entitled to assign a meaning to it. Suppose someone coined the sentence 'Blubs grub' and assigned it this meaning: "If the statement 'Blubs grub' is true, then God exists." The person would then be in a position to advance the following argument for the existence of God:

> [By definition] BLUBS grub iff, if the statement 'Blubs grub' is TRUE then GOD exists. The statement 'Blubs grub' is true iff blubs do grub. It follows that God exists.

Prove that this argument has a valid logical form. Of course, there is something wrong with the argument's content. What is it?

20. (CHALLENGE) In the *Ethics*,[8] Spinoza examines (and rejects) an argument that corporeal substance is finite. The argument assumes that corporeal substance could be divided into equal parts we can call *A* and *B*.

> If corporeal substance is infinite and parts A and B are both finite, then the infinite is made up of TWO finite parts. But this is absurd. If corporeal substance is infinite and parts A and B are both infinite, then one infinite is twice as GREAT as another. This is also absurd. Part A is infinite iff part B is infinite. Therefore, corporeal substance is FINITE.

(A = Part A is finite, B = Part B is finite) This is the toughest proof problem so far; my proof has 24 lines.

---

[8]Scholium to Book I, Proposition 15 (Indianapolis: Hackett Publishing, 1982), pp. 40–41.

7

Or

7.1 Symbolizing Disjunctions

A statement consisting of two constituent statements joined by the connective 'or' is called a disjunction; the component statements are called *disjuncts*. Often, the first disjunct is preceded by the word 'either'. A sample disjunction:

> Either one of the CHILDREN is up or there is an INTRUDER in the house.

We introduce the *wedge* (v) as an abbreviation for the connective 'or'. Accordingly, the above disjunction is symbolized:

> C v I

This formula is read *"C or I"* or *"C wedge I."* We adopt the conventions concerning the use of parentheses that we developed for the other dyadic connectives.

Very often, when we assert a disjunction we intend to admit the possibility that both disjuncts are true. For example, the disjunction above would not be proved false by the discovery that one of the children was up *and* there was an intruder in the house. In such a case 'or' is said to be used in the *inclusive* sense. When we wish to make it quite clear that we are including the possibility that both disjuncts are true, we may use one of these locutions:

> A *or* B *or both.*
> A *and/or* B.

Sometimes when we utter an "or" sentence for the purpose of telling people what they *should* do or what they are *permitted* to do, we intend to rule out the case where both disjuncts are true. A mother who says "You may have an ice-cream sandwich or a Popsicle" is very likely excluding the case where the child gets both. In such a sentence 'or' is said to be used in the *exclusive* sense. When we wish to be explicit about excluding the case where both disjuncts are true, we employ this expression:

A *or* B *but not both.*

To sum up, when S1 means the same as S2, the 'or' in S1 has the inclusive sense; when S1 means the same as S3, the 'or' in S1 has the exclusive sense.

(S1) A or B.
(S2) A or B or both.
(S3) A or B but not both.

What shall we say about this disjunction?

Erma is in Seattle or Dallas.

Is the 'or' being used in the inclusive or the exclusive sense? The answer is that there is no satisfactory way to tell in which sense it is being used. The two disjuncts, because of their content, cannot both be true. Inasmuch as (independently of the way in which 'or' is being used here) they rule each other out, it is impossible to determine that, in addition, the 'or' is being used in a "strong" sense that excludes their both being true.

Logic cannot tolerate ambiguity. We must decide whether the wedge abbreviates the inclusive 'or' or the exclusive 'or'. The decision is easily reached. Most (all?) clear-cut cases of an exclusive 'or' involve regulative language (that is, command-giving language) and not descriptive language. The logic we are piecing together is a logic of descriptive language, in which 'or' is generally used in the inclusive sense. Hence, we ascribe that sense to the wedge and adopt the following convention:

Disjunctions shall be treated as exclusive iff they contain the expression 'but not both' (or a similar locution).

How shall we symbolize exclusive disjunctions (for example, the following sentence)?

Either the CASHIER or the MANAGER will be fired, but not both.

F4 is the literal translation, but let's accept F5 and F6 also.

(F4) (C ∨ M) & –(C & M)
(F5) C ↔ –M
(F6) –C ↔ M

F5 and F6 don't track the English well, but their admirable succinctness offsets that shortcoming. (I shall prove the logical equivalence of F4 and F5 in Section 13.2.)

How shall we symbolize this sentence?

Either the SUSPECT or the WITNESS or the DETECTIVE lied.

Three possibilities:

(F7X) S ∨ W ∨ D
 (F8) S ∨ (W ∨ D)
 (F9) (S ∨ W) ∨ D

We exclude F7X because accepting it would complicate the statement of the wedge inference rules (and techniques developed later in the book). F8 and F9 track the sentence adequately and are logically equivalent (the wedge is associative), and, hence, both are satisfactory symbolizations. Exercise 17 involves half the task of showing that the wedge is associative.

7.2   Wedge In

Consider this argument:

> If Norma is offered either a FELLOWSHIP or a teaching ASSISTANT-SHIP, she will do GRADUATE work. Therefore, she will do graduate work if she is offered a fellowship.

In symbols:

$$(F \vee A) \rightarrow G \vdash F \rightarrow G$$

The validity of this argument is quite obvious. To construct a proof for the argument, we need to adopt a rule for deriving disjunctions.

***The Wedge In Rule* (vI): From a formula derive a disjunction which has that formula as one disjunct and any formula as the other disjunct.**

The rule restated:

From $\mathcal{A}$ derive either $\mathcal{A}$ ∨ $\mathcal{B}$ or $\mathcal{B}$ ∨ $\mathcal{A}$.

This is a *choice* rule with a vengeance; it offers the proof constructor *two* choices: (1) The premise of a Wedge In step must reappear as one of the disjuncts of the formula derived, but it may be either the left or the right disjunct. (2) The other disjunct of the formula derived may be any formula whatever. We use the standard assumption-dependence principle with this rule.

Now we can construct a proof for the "Fellowship" sequent:

1	(1)	$(F \lor A) \to G$	A
2	(2)	F	PA
2	(3)	$F \lor A$	2 $\lor$I
1,2	(4)	G	1,3 $\to$O
1	(5)	$F \to G$	2-4 $\to$I

The *Wedge In proof strategy* is obvious:

If one of the goal lines is a disjunction, search the premise lines for one of the disjuncts. If you find such a premise, apply Wedge In.

When people first study the Wedge In Rule, they often regard it as being excessively liberal. "You mean you can introduce *any* formula—even one that does not appear elsewhere in the proof—as the other disjunct?" I will attempt to justify the rule with an argument:

> An inclusive disjunction is TRUE whenever even one of its disjuncts is true. If so, then WHENEVER the premise of a Wedge In inference is true the conclusion is also. The Wedge In Rule is "SAFE" if whenever the premise of an inference made according to it is true the conclusion is also true. Hence, Wedge In is a "safe" rule.

Is this argument valid?

One explanation of the skeptical attitude people often exhibit when first exposed to the Wedge In Rule is that it sanctions an inference pattern that we are not accustomed to employing. We rarely reason in this way because having learned the truth of a certain statement, we are not concerned with demonstrating that the disjunction of that statement and some other statement is also a truth. The disjunctive statement is less specific and, therefore, less informative than the statement already established. Nevertheless, we do occasionally reason in this way. My 14-year-old brother-in-law was bugging his father for a lightweight Honda motorcycle. My father-in-law told him, "I will either buy you the most powerful Honda made or no Honda at all." Had my father-in-law been asked to justify his statement, I'm confident he would have replied, "I'm not buying him a Honda." The argument 'I'm not buying him a Honda; therefore, I'll either buy him the most powerful Honda or no Honda' is, of course, an inference sanctioned by the Wedge In Rule.

A logic text that I have used contains this sequent:

$$P \& Q \vdash P \lor Q$$

Many of my students constructed the following "proof" for the sequent:

(1)   P & Q   A
(2)   P   1 &O
(3)   Q   1 &O
(4)   P v Q   2,3 vI (ERROR!)

The error lies in treating Wedge In as a two-premised inference. These two proofs of the sequent are correct:

(1)   P & Q   A
(2)   P   1 &O
(3)   P v Q   2 vI

(1)   P & Q   A
(2)   Q   1 &O
(3)   P v Q   2 vI

How should we symbolize S1 (quoted from a newspaper article)?

(S1) The Orange Bowl is neither ORANGE nor a BOWL.

As 'neither O nor B' is a contraction of 'not either O or B', the literal symbolization is F1:

(F1) –(O v B)

F1 is logically equivalent to F2, another acceptable symbolization.

(F2) –O & –B

F3 and F4 are not equivalent to F1 and F2 and are not acceptable symbolizations of S1.

(F3) –(O & B)
(F4) –O v –B

Can you explain why F3 and F4 do not correctly symbolize S1?

We can show that F1 and F2 are logically equivalent by demonstrating that each entails the other. I prove now that F1 entails F2; in Chapter Ten I will prove that F2 entails F1.

1	(1)	–(O v B)	A	[1]
2	(2)	O	PA	[5]
2	(3)	O v B	2 vI	[6]
1,2	(4)	(O v B) & –(O v B)	3,1 &I	[7]
1	(5)	–O	2-4 –I	[3]
6	(6)	B	PA	[8]
6	(7)	O v B	6 vI	[9]
1,6	(8)	(O v B) & –(O v B)	7,1 &I	[10]
1	(9)	–B	6-8 –I	[4]
1	(10)	–O & –B	5,9 &I	[2]

Note the proof-discovery numbers.

7.3 Wedge Out

In his speech to the Athenian jury that sentenced him to death (as recounted in Plato's "Apology"), Socrates argues that death is not something to be feared, but rather is a benefit:

> ... *Death is one of two things. Either it is annihilation, and the dead have no consciousness of anything, or, as we are told, it is really a change—a migration of the soul from this place to another. Now if there is no consciousness but only a dreamless sleep, death must be a marvelous gain. ... If death is like this, then, I call it a gain, because the whole of time, if you look at it in this way, can be regarded as no more than one single night. If on the other hand death is a removal from here to some other place, and if what we are told is true, that all the dead are there, what greater blessing could there be than this, gentlemen? ... Put it in this way. How much would one of you give to meet Orpheus and Musaeus, Hesiod and Homer?*[1]

Socrates' argument expressed simply:

> Death is either ANNIHILATION or MIGRATION. If death is annihilation it is a BENEFIT. If, on the other hand, it is migration it is still a benefit. So, death is a benefit.

In symbols:

A v M, A → B, M → B ⊢ B

The pattern of inference exhibited by this argument is one form of the *dilemma*. Two characteristics shared by all dilemmas are (1) a disjunctive

[1]40c–41a. Hugh Tredennick, trans., "Apology," in *The Collected Dialogues of Plato*, ed. by Edith Hamilton and Huntington Cairns (Princeton, N.J.: Princeton University Press, 1961), p. 25.

premise and (2) two conditional premises. Logicians recognize several species of dilemma; the two most common forms:

$$\text{simple constructive:} \quad \mathcal{P} \vee \mathcal{Q}, \mathcal{P} \to \mathcal{R}, \mathcal{Q} \to \mathcal{R} \vdash \mathcal{R}$$
$$\text{complex constructive:} \quad \mathcal{P} \vee \mathcal{Q}, \mathcal{P} \to \mathcal{R}, \mathcal{Q} \to \mathcal{S} \vdash \mathcal{R} \vee \mathcal{S}$$

Socrates advanced a simple constructive dilemma. Examples of each type will be found in the exercises at the end of this chapter.

We can base our Wedge Out Rule on the obviously sound simple constructive dilemma.

***The Wedge Out Rule* (vO): From $\mathcal{A} \vee \mathcal{B}$, $\mathcal{A} \to \mathcal{C}$, and $\mathcal{B} \to \mathcal{C}$ derive $\mathcal{C}$.**

I will illustrate the employment of the rule by constructing four proofs, beginning with a proof of Socrates' argument:

(1)   A ∨ M   A
(2)   A → B   A
(3)   M → B   A
(4)   B   1,2,3 vO

The Wedge Out Rule is applicable because the formula on line 4 matches the consequent of both conditionals and the antecedents of those conditionals match the disjuncts in line 1. The justification entry for any Wedge Out step will include three line numbers. I cite first the disjunctive premise, and second the conditional whose antecedent matches the left disjunct of the disjunctive premise.

The second proof concerns this simple argument:

> Death is either ANNIHILATION or MIGRATION. Thus, it is either migration or annihilation.

In symbols:

A ∨ M ⊢ M ∨ A

The sequent is valid; the wedge is commutative. The proof for this sequent is going to involve both the Wedge Out Rule (because of the disjunctive premise) and the Wedge In Rule (because of the disjunctive conclusion). The dominant pattern in the proof is Wedge Out. To apply the Wedge Out Rule at the conclusion of the proof, we will need (in addition to the disjunctive premise) two conditional formulas. We can tell exactly what those conditionals will be:

A → (M ∨ A)
M → (M ∨ A)

The antecedent of the first conditional will match the left disjunct of the disjunctive premise and the antecedent of the second will match the right disjunct. Both conditionals will have a consequent that matches the conclusion to be reached by Wedge Out. The two conditionals will be derived by means of the Arrow In Rule. The proof goes as follows:

1	(1)	A ∨ M	A
2	(2)	A	PA
2	(3)	M ∨ A	2 ∨I
	(4)	A → (M ∨ A)	2-3 →I
5	(5)	M	PA
5	(6)	M ∨ A	5 ∨I
	(7)	M → (M ∨ A)	5-6 →I
1	(8)	M ∨ A	1,4,7 ∨O

Note that lines 4 and 7 depend on *no* assumptions. Line 4, for example, depends upon whatever line 3 depends on (namely, 2) less line 2; that is, nothing. This phenomenon is discussed in Section 12.1 below. The standard assumption-dependence principle applies to the Wedge Out Rule. Line 8 depends on all of the assumptions on which lines 1, 4, and 7 depend.

A peculiar feature of the proof above (and of many Wedge Out proofs) is that the same formula occurs on three lines (3, 6, and 8). However, the lines differ in assumption dependence, and only line 8 is free of dependence on a provisional assumption. Putting the same point differently, when you reach line 3 you have validated the sequent 'A ⊢ M ∨ A', and when you get to line 6 you have validated 'M ⊢ M ∨ A', but you haven't validated the sequent to be proven, 'A ∨ M ⊢ M ∨ A', until you reach line 8.

The *Wedge Out strategy* may be summarized as follows:

If one of the premise lines is a disjunction, search the other premise lines for two conditionals whose antecedents match the disjuncts and whose consequents (both) match some goal line. If you find both conditionals, apply Wedge Out. If you find only one of the two conditionals, add the other as a goal line. If you find neither conditional among the premise lines, add both as goal lines.

The Wedge Out strategy will be further illustrated in a third proof that establishes the validity of a complex constructive dilemma. In a letter to James C. Conkling, Abraham Lincoln writes about the Emancipation Proclamation:

> *But the proclamation, as law, either is valid, or not valid. If it is not valid, it needs no retraction. If it is valid, it cannot be retracted, any more than the dead can be brought to life.*[2]

---

[2]Quoted in Irving M. Copi, *Introduction to Logic,* 7th ed. (New York: Macmillan, 1986), p. 259.

By transposing the last two premises and adding the unstated conclusion, we reach a dilemma in standard form:

> The proclamation is either VALID or not valid. If it is valid, it cannot BE retracted. If it is not valid, it does not NEED to be retracted. Therefore, either the proclamation cannot be retracted or it does not need to be retracted.

$$V \vee -V,\ V \rightarrow -B,\ -V \rightarrow -N \vdash -B \vee -N$$

This argument is a *complex*, rather than a *simple*, dilemma. Note that the consequents of the conditionals do not match; instead, each consequent matches one of the disjuncts of the conclusion. To complete a Wedge Out proof for this sequent it will be necessary to deduce two conditionals (lines 7 and 11 in the proof below) whose consequents match the sequent's conclusion.

1	(1)	$V \vee -V$	A
2	(2)	$V \rightarrow -B$	A
3	(3)	$-V \rightarrow -N$	A
4	(4)	V	PA
2,4	(5)	$-B$	2,4 $\rightarrow$O
2,4	(6)	$-B \vee -N$	5 vI
2	(7)	$V \rightarrow (-B \vee -N)$	4-6 $\rightarrow$I
8	(8)	$-V$	PA
3,8	(9)	$-N$	3,8 $\rightarrow$O
3,8	(10)	$-B \vee -N$	9 vI
3	(11)	$-V \rightarrow (-B \vee -N)$	8-10 $\rightarrow$I
1,2,3	(12)	$-B \vee -N$	1,7,11 vO

The fourth proof shows that formula F1 entails F2.

(F1) A & (B v C)
(F2) (A & B) v (A & C)

F2 also entails F1 (exercise 13 at the end of the chapter), and, so, the two formulas are logically equivalent. Their equivalence constitutes one of the two main cases of a principle known as *distribution*. The other main case of distribution involves formulas like F3 and F4.

(F3) D v (E & F)
(F4) (D v E) & (D v F)

The proof that F1 entails F2:

1	(1)	A & (B ∨ C)	A	[1]
1	(2)	A	1 &O	[3]
1	(3)	B ∨ C	1 &O	[4]
4	(4)	B	PA	[7]
1,4	(5)	A & B	2,4 &I	[9]
1,4	(6)	(A & B) ∨ (A & C)	5 ∨I	[8]
1	(7)	B → [(A & B) ∨ (A & C)]	4-6 →I	[5]
8	(8)	C	PA	[10]
1,8	(9)	A & C	2,8 &I	[12]
1,8	(10)	(A & B) ∨ (A & C)	9 ∨I	[11]
1	(11)	C → [(A & B) ∨ (A & C)]	8-10 →I	[6]
1	(12)	(A & B) ∨ (A & C)	3,7,11 ∨O	[2]

Note the proof-discovery numbers.

Many Wedge Out proofs will incorporate two Arrow In subproofs; the last three proofs have been of this sort. In constructing the second subproof, one must avoid incurring dependence on the provisional assumption that begins the first subproof. If this does occur, then the formula derived by Wedge Out will depend on the first provisional assumption and the proof will not be complete.

Consider these valid sequents involving the wedge:

A ∨ B ⊢ B ∨ A
A ∨ (B ∨ C) ⊢ (A ∨ B) ∨ C
(A ∨ B) → C ⊢ A → C
A → B, C → B ⊢ (A ∨ C) → B
A ∨ B, A → C, B → D ⊢ C ∨ D
A ∨ (B & C) ⊢ A ∨ B
A ∨ B, −A ⊢ B
−(A ∨ B) ⊢ −A & −B
−(A & B) ⊢ −A ∨ −B

Proofs for some of these sequents are simple; proofs for others are complex.

EXERCISES

1. Symbolize each statement using the suggested notation.
   (a) *(Plautus dialogue)* "This woman must be either MAD or DRUNK."
   *(b) *(forensic pathologist)* "Either the eyewitnesses are mistaken or this is not the body of Nathaniel Cater." (E = The eyewitnesses are correct, N = This is the body of Nathaniel Cater)
   (c) *(dust jacket ad)* "Webster's New Collegiate does not begin with 'A' or end with 'Z'." (A = *Webster's New Collegiate* begins with 'A', Z = *Webster's New Collegiate* ends with 'Z')

(d) *(newspaper, lottery winner discussing her grandchildren)* "They'd better lose the ATTITUDE and listen to their DAD, or they won't get diddly CRAP."

(e) *(ad)* "If our TV repairman SAYS he'll be there Thursday he'll BE there Thursday or the cost of the LABOR is on us."

*(f) *(college newspaper)* "Nottage will DIE if he does not CONTINUE the dialysis treatment or UNDERGO the kidney transplant."

(g) *(newspaper)* "Either AMBASSADOR Aoki had to take responsibility, or FOREIGN Minister Ikeda had to take responsibility, or the PRIME minister had to take responsibility."

(h) *(newspaper)* "If Rutgers doesn't PROTECT its quarterbacks any better than Pitt did, LUCAS and/or FORTAY will be bludgeoned."

(i) *(Supreme Court Justice John Harlan)* "Our Constitution is color BLIND and neither KNOWS nor TOLERATES classes among citizens."

*(j) *(Everglades sign)* "It is illegal to FEED or HARASS alligators." (F = It is legal to feed alligators, H = It is legal to harass alligators)

(k) *(Section 10.1)* "If either S2 or S3 or both are false, then S1 is false." (A = S2 is true, B = S3 is true, C = S1 is true)

(l) We will hire RACHELS or ALLISON but not both.

(m) *(newspaper)* "The FIESTA [Bowl] is guaranteed a 1–2 matchup unless the Big Ten or Pac-10 champion is No. 1 or No. 2."

> A = The Big Ten champion is No. 1
> B = The Big Ten champion is No. 2
> C = The Pac-10 champion is No. 1
> D = The Pac-10 champion is No. 2

*(n) *(Rasputin to Empress Alexandra)* "If I DIE or YOU desert me, you will lose your SON and your CROWN within six months." (S = You lose your son within six months, C = You lose your crown within six months)

(o) *(biologist)* Humans are more closely related to orangutans than they are to either CHIMPANZEES or GORILLAS. (C = Humans are more closely related to orangutans than they are to chimpanzees, G = Humans are more closely related to orangutans than they are to gorillas)

(p) *(newspaper)* "If the BRAVES and GIANTS both win or both lose today, they will play a one-game PLAYOFF Monday night in San Francisco."

(q) *(attorney)* "Neither Amy nor Brian intended to cause nor in fact did cause any harm to the deceased."

> D = Amy intended to cause harm to the deceased
> E = Brian intended to cause harm to the deceased
> F = Amy caused harm to the deceased
> G = Brian caused harm to the deceased

*(r)   *(Arabian Nights)* "Your head shall answer for my son's life, unless he returns safe, or unless I hear that he is alive." (H = I shall cut your head off, R = My son returns safely, A = I hear that my son is alive)

(s)   *(newspaper)* "If it becomes necessary to PULL equipment off the line for repairs or if an ACCIDENT saps generating capacity, the company could be forced to REDUCE power to all areas or BLACK out some sections of the Gold Coast."

(t)   *(Plato)* "Unless either PHILOSOPHERS become kings or KINGS philosophers, there can be no rest from troubles for STATES, nor yet for all MANKIND."

2. Translate each formula into an English sentence using this dictionary:

E = Zero is even
O = Zero is odd
P = Zero is positive
N = Zero is negative
C = Zero is a cardinal number

(a)   −E v −O
*(b)   −(P v N)
(c)   C → (E v O)
(d)   E v −(E v O)

3. Complete the following proofs. Every assumption has been identified.

(a)
	(1)	−(A v B)	A
	(2)	A & B	PA
	(3)	A	
	(4)	A v B	
	(5)	(A v B) & −(A v B)	
1	(6)	−(A & B)	

*(b)
	(1)	(C → D) & (E → D)	A
	(2)	C → D	
	(3)		1 &O
	(4)		PA
	(5)		4,2,3 vO
1	(6)	(C v E) → D	4-5 →I

(c)
	(1)	(C v E) → D	A
	(2)	C	PA
	(3)	C v E	
	(4)	D	
	(5)	C → D	
	(6)		PA
	(7)	C v E	
	(8)	D	
	(9)	E → D	
1	(10)	(C → D) & (E → D)	

(d)
	(1)	F v (G & H)	A
	(2)	F	PA
	(3)		2 vI

	(4)		2-3 →I
	(5)		PA
	(6)		5 &O
	(7)		6 vI
	(8)		5-7 →I
1	(9)	F v G	1,4,8 vO

4. The sequent 'A ⊢ B' is clearly not valid. Therefore, the "proof" below must contain some error. Find it.

1	(1)	A	A
1	(2)	B v A	1 vI
3	(3)	B	PA
1,3	(4)	A & B	1,3 &I
1,3	(5)	B	4 &O
1	(6)	B → B	3-5 →I
7	(7)	A	PA
1,3,7	(8)	A & B	7,5 &I
1,3,7	(9)	B	8 &O
1,3	(10)	A → B	7-9 →I
1	(11)	B	2,6,10 vO

Instructions for exercises 5 through 14: Symbolize and construct proofs.

5. A news story begins:

> Democrat Helen Boosalis will face Republican state Treasurer Kay Orr in the nation's first woman-against-woman campaign for governor, after yesterday's primaries guaranteed that Nebraska will have its first female chief executive.[3]

The quotation involves this simple dilemma:

> Either BOOSALIS or ORR will win the election for governor of Nebraska. If Boosalis wins, Nebraska will have its first FEMALE governor. If Orr wins, Nebraska will have its first female governor. So, Nebraska will have its first female governor.

*6. A & B ⊢ (C v A) v D

7. −(E v −F) ⊢ −E & F

If you find this proof difficult, study the proof on page 97.

8. A news story concerns one Willie Dennis who, in exchange for a reduction of charges against him from murder to manslaughter, agreed to testify in the trial of a second man. However, the testimony Dennis gave in the trial of the other man differed from what he had previously told the state attorney; whereupon the judge ordered Dennis's manslaughter conviction vacated and directed the state to indict him for murder. The newspaper account quotes the judge as giving the following justification of his action:

> *"His [Dennis's] in-court statement was a confession to first-degree murder and contradicted his story to the state attorney," Sepe said. "He reneged and lied—either to the state attorney or to the jury."*

[3]"Women Vie for Top Nebraska Post," *Miami News* (May 14, 1986), p. 2A.

"He did not cooperate with the state, an essential condition to his plea to the lesser charge of manslaughter." [4]

Judge Sepe's reasoning may be paraphrased with this argument:

> Dennis's in-court statement CONTRADICTED the story he told the state attorney. If this is so, then he lied either to the JURY or to the state ATTORNEY or perhaps both. Provided that he lied to the jury, he did not cooperate with the STATE. And if he lied to the state attorney, he also did not cooperate with the state. Since Dennis's cooperating with the state was a necessary condition for dropping the charge of MURDER, the state will charge him with murder.

9. Horace Kephart, chronicler of life in the southern Appalachians a century ago, writes about the angry reception the author John Fox received when he read to an audience from his book of short stories:

> *They had no comprehension of the nature of fiction. Mr. Fox's stories were either true or false. If they were true, then he was "no gentleman" for telling all the family affairs of people who had entertained him with their best. If they were not true, then, of course, they were libellous upon the mountain people.*[5]

Supply the unstated conclusion of the audience's reasoning. Use this dictionary:

T = The stories are true
F = The stories are false
G = Fox is a gentleman
L = Fox is a libeler

Symbolize the last premise as 'F → L' (rather than as '−T → L') in order to avoid a more difficult proof.

*10. Add to the report the suppressed premise and conclusion:

> We either FIGHT or RETREAT, or SURRENDER or stay HERE. So, we'll be KILLED.

Reprinted with special permission of King Features Syndicate.

[4] "Murder Suspect-Witness Stripped of Lesser Plea," *Miami News* (October 7, 1971), p. 5A.

[5] *Our Southern Highlanders* (New York: Macmillan, 1913), p. 282.

11. Because the author of *Alice in Wonderland*, Lewis Carroll, was a logician, it is not surprising to find Alice employing deductive arguments:

> *Soon her eye fell on a little glass box that was lying under the table: she opened it, and found in it a very small cake, on which the words "EAT ME" were beautifully marked in currants. "Well, I'll eat it," said Alice, "and if it makes me larger, I can reach the key; and if it makes me smaller, I can creep under the door; so either way I'll get into the garden, and I don't care which happens!"*[6]

Alice's argument:

> The cake will make me either LARGER or SMALLER. If it makes me larger, I can reach the KEY; and if it makes me smaller, I can CREEP under the door. If I reach the key, I'll get into the GARDEN; and if I creep under the door, I'll get into the garden. So [either way] I'll get into the garden.

12. Flo's problem:

> If I talk about OTHERS Andy thinks I'm a GOSSIP, and if I talk about MYSELF he thinks I'm a BORE. If I talk to ANDY I talk either about others or about myself. Hence, if I talk to Andy he thinks I'm a gossip or a bore.

Reprinted with special permission of North America Syndicate.

13. Prove that F2 entails F1.

(F1) $A \;\&\; (B \lor C)$
(F2) $(A \;\&\; B) \lor (A \;\&\; C)$

*14. From *The Death of King Arthur*:

> " ... *When Sir Gawain knoweth thereof that Sir Gareth is slain, I shall never have rest of him till I have destroyed Sir Lancelot's kin and himself both, other else he to destroy me. And therefore," said the king, "wit you well, my heart was never so heavy as it is now.... Such a fellowship of good knights shall never be together in no company."* [7]

---

[6]Lewis Carroll, *Alice in Wonderland* (London: Dent, 1961), pp. 8–9.

[7]Sir Thomas Malory, *King Arthur and His Knights* (Oxford: Oxford University Press, 1975), pp. 173–174.

This argument is suggested:

> The FELLOWSHIP of knights continues only if both LANCELOT and I live. But at least one of us will die. Therefore, the fellowship will not continue.

(A = Arthur lives)

15. (CHALLENGE) Symbolize each statement using the suggested notation.

(a) Exactly one of these two women will be hired: Jackson and Steele. (J = Jackson is hired, S = Steele is hired)

(b) More than one of these three men will be hired: BURTT, DAVIS, and MASON.

(c) *(parental lecture)* "A 'no' from one of us means a 'no' from both of us." (M = Mother says "no," F = Father says "no")

(d) *(Around the World in Eighty Days)* "If then—for there were 'ifs' still—the SEA did not become too boisterous, if the wind did not VEER round to the east, if no accident happened to the BOAT or its MACHINERY, the *Henrietta* might CROSS the three thousand miles from New York to Liverpool in the nine days, between the 12th and the 21st of December."

(e) *(umpire to Cleveland and Detroit managers)* "If either pitcher throws at any-one again, both the pitcher and the manager will be out of the game."

> A = The Cleveland pitcher throws at someone again
> B = The Cleveland pitcher is out of the game
> C = The Cleveland manager is out of the game
> D = The Detroit pitcher throws at someone again
> E = The Detroit pitcher is out of the game
> F = The Detroit manager is out of the game

(f) *(newspaper)* "If the [LSU] Tigers lose (or tie) either the Tulane game or the Mississippi game, the Orange Bowl will try to shift to the Texas-Arkansas loser, providing it is Arkansas."

> C = LSU loses the Tulane game
> D = LSU ties the Tulane game
> E = LSU loses the Mississippi game
> F = LSU ties the Mississippi game
> O = The Orange Bowl tries to shift to the Texas-Arkansas loser
> A = Arkansas loses to Texas

(g) *(newspaper)* "[There will be] a No. 1 vs. No. 2 matchup in the FI-ESTA Bowl if the Big East Conference champion, Atlantic Coast Conference champion, or Notre Dame occupy the top two spots in the coalition poll at the end of the regular season."

> G = The Big East Conference champion is ranked first in the coalition poll at the end of the regular season
> H = The Big East Conference champion is ranked second . . .
> I = The Atlantic Coast Conference champion is ranked first . . .

J = The Atlantic Coast Conference champion is ranked second . . .
K = Notre Dame is ranked first . . .
L = Notre Dame is ranked second . . .

(h) (*Senator Robert Dole*) "We can't DEPLOY American forces to Haiti without Congressional AUTHORIZATION, unless there's some emergency need to EVACUATE American people or unless there's some NATIONAL interest and you don't have TIME to go to Congress or unless the President CERTIFIES that the safety [of the military is] involved."

(i) (*newspaper*) "The Dolphins are in the PLAYOFFS if they beat St. LOUIS, and either INDIANAPOLIS loses, or two of the three AFC West teams (OAKLAND, San DIEGO and SEATTLE) lose." (I = Indianapolis loses, etc.)

16. (CHALLENGE) Construct two four-line proofs for exercise 20 in Chapter Four. In one proof use a Wedge Rule; in the other employ a Dash Rule.

Instructions for exercises 17 through 20: Symbolize and construct proofs.

17. (CHALLENGE)

S v (W v D) ⊢ (S v W) v D

Proving the validity of this sequent constitutes half the demonstration that the wedge is associative.

18. (CHALLENGE) A newspaper article begins, "Saudi Arabia is threatening to raise its oil prices if Congress does not approve a windfall profits tax." Later in the story Treasury Secretary G. William Miller states the Saudi position as, "Either you put in a windfall profits tax or we're going to be raising prices."[8] Prove the logical equivalence of these two statements by showing that each entails the other. (R = Saudi Arabia raises its oil prices, A = Congress approves a windfall profits tax)

19. (CHALLENGE)

(a) A *simple destructive dilemma*:

F → G, F → H, –G v –H ⊢ –F

(b) A *complex destructive dilemma*:

I → J, K → L, –J v –L ⊢ –I v –K

20. (CHALLENGE) I received a birthday card with the following message:

Some Philosophy for Your Birthday: WHY WORRY??? There are only two things to worry about, either you're healthy or you're sick. If you're healthy, there's nothing to worry about and if you're sick . . . there are two things to worry about . . . either you'll get well or you won't. If you get well there is nothing to worry about, but if you don't, you'll have two things to

---

[8]Saudis Put Pressure upon U.S. to Enact Windfall Profits Tax," *Miami Herald* (November 25, 1979), p. 1A.

worry about . . . either you'll go to heaven or to hell. If you go to heaven you
have nothing to worry about and if you go to hell you'll be so busy shaking
hands with all of us that you'll have no time to worry.

This is an argument whose unstated conclusion is 'Either you have nothing
to worry about or you'll have no time to worry'. Use these abbreviations:

H = You are healthy
S = You are sick
W = You have something to worry about
A = You will get well
B = You will go to heaven
C = You will go to hell
T = You will have time to worry

8

Résumé

8.1 Summary

In this section we list in one place many of the symbolization principles presented above along with one or two new tips, and we set down together all of the inference rules that we have learned so far.

Symbolization Guide

P although Q P but Q P even though Q P however Q P moreover Q P yet Q	P & Q
P only if Q P is a sufficient condition for Q	P → Q
P if Q P provided that Q P is a necessary condition for Q	Q → P
P exactly if Q P just in case Q P is a necessary and sufficient condition for Q P, but only if Q	P ↔ Q
P or Q or both P and/or Q	P v Q

Symbolization Guide

P or Q but not both	(P v Q) & –(P & Q) *or* P ↔ –Q
Neither P nor Q	–(P v Q) *or* –P & –Q
P unless Q Unless Q, P	–Q → P *or* P v Q
Not P without Q	–(P & –Q) *or* –Q → –P

In the preceding six chapters eleven proof rules have been introduced. Ten of these rules sanction deductions and may be called *inference rules*. (The Rule of Assumptions will be considered a proof rule but not an inference rule.) For each of the five statement connectives there is an inference rule that sanctions a move *to* a formula containing that connective; these are the five "In" rules. And for each of the connectives there is a rule that sanctions a move *from* a formula that contains the connective; these, of course, are the five "Out" rules.[1] The ten inference rules are summarized in the following table. We call the rules "primitive" (original, primary) so as to distinguish them from additional rules introduced in the next chapter.

Primitive Inference Rules

	In	Out
→	From the derivation of B from assumption A (and perhaps other assumptions) derive $A → B$.	From $A → B$ and A derive B.
&	From A and B derive $A \& B$.	From $A \& B$ derive either A or B.
v	From A derive either A v B or B v A.	From A v B, $A → C$, and $B → C$ derive C.
↔	From $A → B$ and $B → A$ derive $A ↔ B$.	From $A ↔ B$ derive either $A → B$ or $B → A$.
–	From the derivation of $B \& –B$ from assumption A (and perhaps other assumptions) derive $–A$.	From the derivation of $B \& –B$ from assumption $–A$ (and perhaps other assumptions) derive A.

[1]This type of proof system (employing "In" and "Out" rules for each connective) was developed by Gerhard Gentzen and published in a German mathematics journal in 1934. Logicians call the approach "natural deduction" because the rules correspond to intuitive patterns of reasoning.

Recall that each of these inference rules applies to *whole* lines but not to *parts* of lines. This sequent is invalid:

$$A \to B \vdash (A \lor C) \to B$$

Can you show it to be invalid?[2] By applying one of the inference rules to a part of a line, we can construct a "proof" for the sequent.

(1) $A \to B$ A
(2) $(A \lor C) \to B$ 1 $\lor$I (ERROR!)

For each of the ten inference rules and the Assumption Rule a principle has been provided for determining the assumption dependence of any formula introduced into a proof by that rule. These principles are listed in the following table.

Assumption-Dependence Principles for the
Primitive Proof Rules

A, PA	An assumption depends on itself.
$\to$I	$\mathcal{A} \to \mathcal{B}$ depends on whatever assumptions $\mathcal{B}$ depends on (less the assumption $\mathcal{A}$).
$-$I	$-\mathcal{A}$ depends on whatever assumptions $\mathcal{B}$ & $-\mathcal{B}$ depends on (less the assumption $\mathcal{A}$).
$-$O	$\mathcal{A}$ depends on whatever assumptions $\mathcal{B}$ & $-\mathcal{B}$ depends on (less the assumption $-\mathcal{A}$).
other rules	The formula derived depends on all of the assumptions on which the premise(s) of the step depend(s).

In working the exercises for the preceding chapters, you have constructed proofs for a large number of valid sequents. The following question may have occurred to you:

Just how powerful *is the proof procedure (the set of eleven proof rules) we have developed? What proportion of the total collection of valid propositional sequents can be demonstrated by this procedure? Thirty percent? Perhaps sixty percent?*

The answer, surprisingly, is that our set of eleven rules has maximum power; it is sufficient to demonstrate the validity of *every* valid propositional sequent.[3] In

---

[2]Try devising an argument exhibiting this form that has a true premise and a false conclusion.

[3]Of course, this does not mean that a given individual will be able to complete a proof for any valid propositional sequent. It means that for each such sequent a proof is in principle possible.

logicians' terminology, our set of rules is *complete*. This answer seems more surprising when you realize that the number of possible distinct valid propositional sequents is infinite. A second question:

> *How* safe *is our set of proof rules? Can we by correctly applying these rules construct "proofs" for some invalid propositional sequents?*

The answer is that our rule set is completely safe. In logicians' terms our set of rules is *sound* or *consistent*. If the set were unsound, it would not provide a means of establishing the validity of arguments and, hence, would be of no value to us. The issues raised by these two questions are discussed in detail in Appendix One.

A third question:

> *Is the set of proof rules presented here the only one that is both complete and sound?*

The answer is that there are a great many such rule sets. The set given here, however, is an especially attractive one. It is more compact than most rule sets; it is especially suited to exercising a proof-builder's ingenuity and developing ability to plot strategy; and it is highly symmetrical (with one "In" rule and one "Out" rule for each connective).

8.2   Proof Strategy

As you have discovered, devising proofs requires insight and ingenuity; it is not a mechanical enterprise. Herein lies the challenge of constructing proofs. Proofs exercise our creative abilities. Because proof construction is essentially creative, I cannot provide a set of directions that when mechanically applied will enable you to devise an elegant proof for any valid propositional sequent. I can, however, offer some suggestions that should help you plot proof strategy. I begin by displaying in one place (on page 115) the suggestions made in earlier chapters—one suggestion for each rule of inference. I don't recommend committing this table to memory; I do recommend studying the suggestions until you fully understand them, and also referring back to the table when a proof has you stumped.

Some of the strategies suggested in this table should be given precedence over others because employing them usually gives an overall structure to the proof. I have in mind the strategies for Arrow In, Dash In, and Wedge Out. The Dash Out strategy also gives an overall structure to a proof, but it is often used as a last resort when other approaches fail.

Proof Strategies

When a Goal Line Is a:	Consider this Strategy:
conditional	Make a provisional assumption of the antecedent and add the consequent as a goal line. ($\rightarrow$I strategy)
conjunction	Search the premise lines for the two conjuncts. If you find both conjuncts, apply &I. If you find only one conjunct, add the other as a goal line. If you find neither conjunct among the premise lines, add both as goal lines. (&I strategy)
disjunction	Search the premise lines for one of the disjuncts. If you find such a premise, apply vI. (vI strategy) The –O strategy may be tried as well.
biconditional	Search the premise lines for the two associated conditionals (that is, the conditionals with the same constituents). If you find both conditionals, apply $\leftrightarrow$I. If you find only one of the associated conditionals, add the other as a goal line. If you find neither conditional among the premise lines, add both as goal lines. ($\leftrightarrow$I strategy)
negation	(If a more direct way of reaching the goal line is not apparent) make a provisional assumption of the formula less its initial dash and try to derive a standard contradiction. (–I strategy)
capital letter (or other affirmative formula)	(If a more direct way of reaching the goal line is not apparent) make a provisional assumption of the negation of the formula and try to derive a standard contradiction. (–O strategy)

When a Premise Line Is a:	Consider this Strategy:
conditional	Search the other premise lines for the antecedent. If you find it, apply $\rightarrow$O. If you do not find the antecedent among the premise lines, add it as a goal line. ($\rightarrow$O strategy)
conjunction	Apply &O (once or twice). (&O strategy)
disjunction	Search the other premise lines for two conditionals whose antecedents match the disjuncts and whose consequents (both) match some goal line. If you find both conditionals, apply vO. If you find only one of the two conditionals, add the other as a goal line. If you find neither conditional among the premise lines, add both as goal lines. (vO strategy)
biconditional	Apply $\leftrightarrow$O (once or twice). ($\leftrightarrow$O strategy)

I will illustrate how some of these strategies can be applied by constructing a proof for an argument advanced by Bertrand Russell during the height of the Cold War:

> *There can be no permanent peace unless there is only one Air Force in the world,—with the degree of international government that that implies.*[4]

Supplying the unstated conclusion, this argument emerges:

> There can be no permanent PEACE unless there is only one AIR force in the world. There will be one air force only if there is an INTERNATIONAL government. Therefore, the existence of an international government is a necessary condition for permanent peace.
>
> $-A \rightarrow -P, A \rightarrow I \vdash P \rightarrow I$

Simple proofs can be constructed "top-to-bottom." The premises of the sequent are recorded at the top of the proof; then formulas are derived from others higher in the list until the conclusion of the sequent is reached. Some proofs are best done "backwards." First, you put the conclusion at the bottom of a sheet. Then, on the next line up, you put the formula that enables you to deduce the conclusion. You repeat this procedure until you reach the premises at the top of the proof. Of course, when you employ this method you are not making deductions but setting subgoals; and after reaching the top of the proof you have to turn around and descend, filling in the justification column indicating how the formulas are to be deduced.

Many proofs are best done by combining the forward and backward approaches. The premises of the sequent are recorded at the top and the conclusion at the bottom; then the gap in the middle is reduced by alternately making deductions and provisional assumptions (above the gap) and setting subgoals (below the gap). The aim in this approach is to eliminate the gap in the middle. The proof of Russell's argument is best done in this fashion. To understand my strategy, read the bracketed comments in the right-hand column in numerical order.

(1)	$-A \rightarrow -P$	A	
(2)	$A \rightarrow I$	A	
(3)	P	PA	[1. In accordance with the Arrow In strategy, I provisionally assume *P* on line 3 and set down *I* as the first subgoal.]

---

[4] *The Autobiography of Bertrand Russell* (Boston: Little, Brown, 1968), II, p. 365.

(4)   −A   PA   [3. Seeing no more direct route for the proof, I fall back on the Dash Out strategy and provisionally assume the negation of my highest subgoal, *A*. I keep in mind the need to reach a standard contradiction.]

(5)   −P   1,4 →O   [4. The Arrow Out strategy dictates this deduction.]

(6)   P & −P   3,5 &I   [5. My subgoal of deducing a standard contradiction, combined with the Ampersand In strategy, leads to the deduction of line 6. Now the gap in the middle of the proof has been eliminated, since I can reach *A* by Dash Out.]

     A   [2. Normally, the Arrow In provisional assumption makes some deduction immediately possible, but that is not true in this proof. I notice that the subgoal *I* matches the consequent of line 2, which leads me to apply the Arrow Out strategy to line 2 and set down *A* as another subgoal.]

  I

  P → I

Having successfully closed the gap between premise lines and goal lines, all that I have to do now is add the remaining line numbers and justification entries and fill in the assumption-dependence column:

1	(1)	−A → −P	A
2	(2)	A → I	A
3	(3)	P	PA
4	(4)	−A	PA
1,4	(5)	−P	1,4 →O
1,3,4	(6)	P & −P	3,5 &I
1,3	(7)	A	4-6 −O
1,2,3	(8)	I	2,7 →O
1,2	(9)	P → I	3-8 →I

Now let's consider a more complex proof problem. The "Sally Forth" comic strip presents this argument:

> Sally can't both have the report READY first thing tomorrow and be home by 8:00 TONIGHT. If the report isn't ready, her BOSS will be disappointed. And if she isn't home by 8:00, her HUSBAND will be disappointed. So, at least one of them will be disappointed.
>
> $-(R \& T)$, $-R \to B$, $-T \to H \vdash B \lor H$

Reprinted with special permission of King Features Syndicate

There is no obvious direct path to the conclusion, so we should try the Dash Out strategy and provisionally assume the negation of the conclusion:

$-(B \lor H)$

It is clear that the next-to-last line in the proof will be a standard contradiction, but which one? Very likely the first premise will supply the right conjunct, so the contradiction will be:

$(R \& T) \& -(R \& T)$

Now how will we get the left conjunct of this contradiction? Presumably by Ampersand In from R and T, so we set them down as subgoals. And how will we reach these subgoals? Try Dash Out subproofs. What is the clue that we should do that? One indication is that if we assume '$-R$' and (later) '$-T$' we will be able to make further moves immediately. And what will the standard contradiction be for these two Dash Out subproofs? The right conjunct will probably be the first provisional assumption ('$-(B \lor H)$'), which would otherwise not figure into the proof. I encourage you to stop reading and attempt this proof now. Your proof will probably contain 17 lines.

8.3   Definitions

Since Chapter Two we have been operating with the concept of "formula," but I have nowhere provided a definition of it. I now turn to this task. To make the definition brief, I will first define the terms 'capital', 'connective', 'grouper', and 'symbol'. In stating these definitions, I abbreviate 'equals by definition' as '$=_{df}$'.

capital	$=_{df}$	an upper-case letter of the English alphabet with or without prime symbols[5]
connective	$=_{df}$	an arrow, ampersand, double arrow, wedge, or dash
grouper	$=_{df}$	a parenthesis, bracket, or brace
symbol	$=_{df}$	a capital, connective, or grouper

Now I am able to define 'formula'.

formula	$=_{df}$	a symbol or a horizontal string of symbols

According to this definition, F1 through F3 are formulas.

(F1) $I \rightarrow (J \rightarrow K)$
(F2) $I \rightarrow J \rightarrow K$
(F3) $I \rightarrow \rightarrow JK)($

In our past usage of the term 'formula' we would be inclined to say that F1 is a "proper" formula, F2 an incorrectly punctuated formula, and F3 no formula at all but, rather, a jumble of symbols. It will prove convenient to use the term 'formula' with the broader meaning assigned above and to introduce a second term, 'well-formed formula', to distinguish F1 from F2 and F3. The expression 'well-formed formula' (abbreviated 'wff'[6]) will correspond closely to the term 'formula' as we used it in earlier chapters. To facilitate defining 'wff', I define the expressions 'left-hand grouper', 'matching right-hand grouper', and 'dyadic connective'.

left-hand grouper	$=_{df}$	either the mark '(' or '[' or '{'
matching right-hand grouper	$=_{df}$	the mirror image of a left-hand grouper
dyadic connective	$=_{df}$	connective other than the dash

The term 'wff' is defined by the following set of statements:

1. **Any capital is a wff.**
2. **A dash followed by a wff is a wff.**

---

[5]We add prime symbols if we need more than 26 capital letters. In practice, 26 letters will always suffice.

[6]'Wff' rhymes with 'hoof'.

3. **A left-hand grouper followed by a wff followed by a dyadic connective followed by another wff followed by a matching right-hand grouper is a wff.**

4. **No formula is a wff unless its being so follows from clauses one through three.**

This definition belongs to a special type called *recursive definitions,* found mainly in logic and mathematics. The principal feature of a recursive definition is that one must often apply the various clauses in the definition again and again in order to discover whether some object falls within the scope of the term defined. Let's illustrate this, using the definition of 'wff' just given. Is F4 a wff by that definition?

(F4) $-(L \rightarrow -M)$
(F5) L
(F6) M
(F7) $-M$
(F8) $(L \rightarrow -M)$

By clause one of the definition, F5 and F6 are wffs. Because F6 is a wff, by clause two F7 is also a wff. As F5 and F7 are wffs, by clause three F8 is a wff. And since F8 is a wff, by clause two F4 is one too. Is F9 a wff by our recursive definition?

(F9) $(N-\rightarrow O)$
(F10) $N-$

F10 is not a wff by any of the first three clauses of the definition; hence, by virtue of clause four it is not a wff. Neither of the first two clauses applies to F9; therefore, it is a wff (by the third clause) iff F10 is a wff. But we already established that F10 is not a wff; it follows that F9 is not a wff. In a similar manner you can decide whether any formula—no matter how long—is a wff or not.

You may have noticed that according to the definition proposed, F11 is a wff, whereas F12 is not.

(F11) $(P \rightarrow Q)$
(F12) $P \rightarrow Q$

This does not agree with our practice in earlier chapters, according to which we would say that F12 is a proper formula but that F11 contains a superfluous pair of parentheses. The justification for making this change is that by doing so we greatly simplified the definition of 'wff'. If you doubt that this is so, try to formulate an alternative definition. As a test of correctness for your definition, be sure that it includes F1 and excludes F2 (see above). It must be admitted that the parentheses in F11 do no work (preclude no ambiguity), so in practice we will omit any pair of groupers that begin and end a wff.

There is one other unusual result stemming from our definition. In addition to F13, F14 and F15 count as wffs.

(F13) –[(R & S) → T]
(F14) –([R & S] → T)
(F15) –[[R & S] → T]

There is no harm in this; none of the formulas are ambiguous. The justification for this change is the same as the one given in the previous paragraph; it simplified the definition of 'wff'. Experimenting with the definition will convince you that this is so. Again, in practice we will conform to our old ways, which in this case means preferring F13 over the other two formulas.

With the exception of the two matters just discussed, the definition of 'wff' agrees completely with the punctuation principles adopted in Chapters Two through Seven. For example, it excludes F16 and F17.

(F16) (U & V → W)
(F17) (X & Y & Z)

F16 is viciously, and F17 benignly, ambiguous. You should study the definition until you see how they are excluded.

An examination of the definitions of 'formula' and 'wff' will reveal that wffs are a species of formula. Specifically, wffs are formulas that are structured in accordance with the formation rules of our logic. The formation rules are contained in the definition of 'wff'. The notion of a "wff" in logic is analogous to the concept of a "grammatical sentence" in a natural language.

With 'wff' defined, I am now able to define 'sequent'.

sequent $=_{df}$ a wff, or a string of wffs separated by commas, followed by a turnstile followed by a wff

The following obvious definitions will prove useful in a moment:

premise of sequent S $=_{df}$ a wff of S that precedes the turnstile
conclusion of sequent S $=_{df}$ the wff of S that follows the turnstile

In Section 2.3, I provided a rough account of the concept of "formal proof." Now I can give a precise definition.

formal proof of sequent S = $_{df}$ a list of wffs such that:

> (i) each wff either is an assumption or is deduced from wffs (or derivations of wffs) above it in the list by one of the stated rules of inference,
>
> (ii) the last wff is the conclusion of S, and
>
> (iii) every assumption on which the last wff depends is a premise of S

EXERCISES

1. On the basis of the definition of 'wff' provided in Section 8.3, determine for each of the following formulas whether it is a wff. (This is the only exercise in the book in which the outermost groupers are included.)

   (a) $(-A \rightarrow B)$

   *(b) $-(C \rightarrow - - -D)$

   (c) $(E–F)$

   (d) $(G \rightarrow H \& I)$

   (e) $\{J \vee -[(K \vee -L) \leftrightarrow M]\}$

   *(f) N O

   (g) $\leftrightarrow P$

2. Complete the following proofs. Every assumption has been identified.

   (a)

1	(1)	D v (E & F)	A
2	(2)	D	PA
2	(3)		2 vI
2	(4)		2 vI
2	(5)		3,4 &I
	(6)		2-5 →I
7	(7)	E & F	PA
7	(8)		7 &O
7	(9)		8 vI
7	(10)		7 &O
7	(11)		10 vI
7	(12)		9,11 &I
	(13)		7-12 →I
1	(14)	(D v E) & (D v F)	1,6,13 vO

   *(b)

	(1)	T v P	A
	(2)	–P	A
	(3)	T	PA
	(4)	T & –P	
	(5)	T	
	(6)	T → T	
	(7)	P	PA
	(8)	–T	PA
	(9)	P & –P	

$$(10) \quad (P \,\&\, {-}P) \,\&\, {-}T$$
$$(11) \quad P \,\&\, {-}P$$
$$(12) \quad T$$
$$(13) \quad P \rightarrow T$$
$$1,2 \quad (14) \quad T$$

Instructions for exercises 3 through 18: Symbolize and construct proofs.

3. Calvin's argument:

   If Einstein's theory is CORRECT, then if we ACCELERATE, time will SLOW. We accelerated, but time didn't slow. So, Einstein is wrong.

CALVIN AND HOBBES © Watterson. Dist. by UNIVERSAL PRESS SYNDICATE.

*4. A newspaper editorial includes this passage:

> There is a lot of evidence that Judge Person suffered a serious lapse of judgment, but no evidence has been presented that he is corrupt. If there was, the FBI would have pulled him in already, since the investigation has been going on for over a year. There is no ground, therefore, for any criminal prosecution.[7]

The argument:

> If there is evidence that Judge Person is CORRUPT, the FBI would have ARRESTED him. They have not done so. If there is no evidence that the judge is corrupt, then there is no ground for a criminal PROSECUTION. Therefore, there is no ground for prosecution.

5. *Newsweek*'s Jerry Adler interviews Elizabeth Thomas, author of *The Hidden Life of Dogs*:

> THOMAS: *. . . If we [humans] go to heaven, so do they [dogs].*
> ADLER: *How do you know?*
> THOMAS: *Because if dogs are not there, it is not heaven.*[8]

This argument is suggested:

> If HUMANS are in heaven, so are DOGS, because if humans are in heaven but dogs are not, then humans are not in heaven.

6. The political cartoon on page 125, published at the start of World War I, suggests this argument:

> If AUSTRIA attacks Serbia, RUSSIA will attack Austria. Provided that Russia attacks Austria, GERMANY will attack Russia. And if Germany attacks Russia, both FRANCE and ENGLAND will attack Germany. Therefore, "if Austria attacks Serbia, Russia will fall upon Austria, Germany upon Russia, and France and England upon Germany."

7. One version of the "pragmatic" justification of induction.[9]

> If INDUCTION does not work, then no METHOD of inference about the future will work; for these reasons: If there are UNIFORMITIES in nature, induction will work. And if there is a method of inference about the future which works, then there are uniformities in nature.

*8. A newspaper sports story:

> BALTIMORE, July 20–Earl Weaver, the Baltimore Oriole manager, thinks he has finally found a foolproof protest.

---

[7] *Miami Times* (January 20, 1994), reprinted in the *Miami Herald* (January 21, 1994), p. 17A.

[8] "The (Secret) World of Dogs," *Newsweek* (November 1, 1993), p. 61.

[9] Wesley C. Salmon discusses this argument in *The Foundations of Scientific Inference* (Pittsburgh: University of Pittsburgh Press, 1967), pp. 52–54.

"A Chain of Friendship"—"If Austria attacks Serbia, Russia will fall upon Austria, Germany upon Russia, and France and England upon Germany." (*The Brooklyn Eagle*, 1914. Professor Oron J. Hale provided the cartoon.)

Last week in Oakland, Weaver was arguing about a hit-batsman call and the umpires refused to allow his pitcher, Sam Stewart, to warm up during the argument. He protested the game, contending there was no such rule in the book. That protest is pending.

Last night, when Manager Jim Fregosi of California was arguing in the same situation, the umpires allowed Dave LaRoche, the Angel pitcher, to continue warming up. Weaver again protested the game.

"I want to see how he gets out of this one," said Weaver, referring to Lee MacPhail, the American League president. "There is no chance of losing both protests. If they don't allow at least one of them, we'll have a rule-book-burning promotion night."[10]

Weaver's argument may be phrased as follows:

We will win the FIRST protest exactly if we do not win the SECOND. So, we will not lose both protests.

[10]"Weaver Sets up an Umpire Trap," *New York Times* (July 21, 1979), p. 15.

9. In a letter to the editor of the *Proceedings and Addresses of the American Philosophical Association,* Professor Philip Devine protests the association's passing resolutions on matters of public policy:

> *The argument takes the form of a dilemma. Either the issue in question is amenable to philosophical argument, and the passing of resolutions prejudices philosophical discussion. Or it is not, and philosophers as such have no competence to decide it.*[11]

Devine's argument (applied to a specific issue of public policy):

> Either the issue is AMENABLE to philosophical argument and passing a resolution PREJUDICES philosophical discussion, or it is not amenable and philosophers have no special COMPETENCE to decide it. It follows that either passing a resolution prejudices philosophical discussion of the issue or philosophers have no special competence to decide the issue.

10. In William Harvey's day it was generally accepted that blood is created in the heart and flows from that organ only in an outward direction. Harvey's main attack on that theory is summarized by this argument.[12]

> In an hour, a human heart THROWS out more blood than the human's own weight. If this is so and if blood flows only OUTWARD from the heart, then the heart creates MORE blood in an hour than the weight of a human. But the heart cannot do this. If the blood does not flow only out of the heart, then it must CIRCULATE through the body and REENTER the heart. Thus, the view that blood flows only out of the heart is false, and the view that blood circulates through the body and reenters the heart is true.

11. In the "Peanuts" strip, Shermy reasons:

> If there is a SANTA Claus, then it does not MATTER how I act. And if there isn't any Santa Claus, then it still doesn't matter how I act. So, it does not matter how I act.

PEANUTS © United Feature Syndicate.

---

[11]LIII (1980), 501.

[12]See Herbert Butterfield, *The Origins of Modern Science* (New York: Free Press, 1957), pp. 64–65.

*12. A newspaper article[13] appearing after the O.J. Simpson civil trial contained this argument (paraphrased):

> If Simpson APPEALS, he can POSTPONE payment only if he posts a BOND of $12.75 million. He cannot post such a bond. If he doesn't appeal, he cannot postpone payment. It follows that he cannot postpone payment.

13. A paraphrase of St. Thomas Aquinas's third cosmological argument for the existence of God.[14]

> There is a NECESSARY being who has created some contingent beings. Proof: There have been contingent beings for either a FINITE or an INFINITE period of time. If the former, then provided that no contingent beings have created themselves, there must be a necessary being which has created some contingent beings. No contingent beings have created themselves. On the other hand, if there have been contingent beings for an infinite period of time, then all the POSSIBLE combinations of the existence and nonexistence of contingent beings have been realized. If all the possible combinations have been realized, then there was a TIME in the past when no contingent being existed. If there was such a time in the past and if no contingent beings have created themselves, then there are contingent BEINGS today only if there is a necessary being who has created some contingent beings. Of course, there are contingent beings today.

Use these symbols:

N = There is a necessary being who has created some contingent beings
F = There have been contingent beings for a finite period of time
I = There have been contingent beings for an infinite period of time
D = Some contingent beings have created themselves
P = All the possible combinations of the existence and nonexistence of contingent beings have been realized
T = There was a time in the past when no contingent being existed
B = There are contingent beings today

This exercise exemplifies the utility and power of the logical system we have presented. The argument is so complex that, for most of us, it falls outside the range of logical intuition. Although symbolizing and proving the sequent involve some time, neither procedure is particularly difficult. And in symbolizing and constructing a proof, one gains an insight into the structure of the English argument.

---

[13]"O.J. Hit for 25 Million More," *Miami Herald* (February 11, 1997), pp. 1A, 6A.

[14]See the selection from *Summa Theologica* in John Hick, ed., *The Existence of God* (New York: Macmillan, 1964), p. 84.

14. A realtor gave my son, Mark, this explanation for why he couldn't accept Mark's application to rent an apartment:

    I can't accept an application for the apartment without a deposit, and I can't take a deposit without showing the apartment, and I can't show the apartment while it is still occupied.

    Add this unexpressed premise:

    The apartment is currently OCCUPIED.

    The conclusion is the matter to be explained:

    I will not accept your APPLICATION for this apartment.

    You can simplify the proof by treating the argument as having four premises (rather than two). The first three premises are best symbolized as negated conjunctions. (D = I accept a deposit for the apartment, S = I show you the apartment)

15. (CHALLENGE) A variation on exercise 8:

    We will win the FIRST protest exactly if we do not win the SECOND. So, we will win at least one of them.

16. (CHALLENGE) (a) A newspaper story includes this passage:

    The Federal Communications Commission turned down a request by [The] Tribune [Company] for a permanent waiver of federal ownership rules so that it may continue to own the Sun-Sentinel *and WDZL-Channel 39. . . .*

    Tribune will have 12 months to divest one of the media properties. . . .[15]

    This argument is suggested:

    The Tribune Company will not own both the *SUN-SENTINEL* and CHANNEL 39. Thus, either it will not own the *Sun-Sentinel* or it will not own Channel 39.

    (b) Show that the conclusion entails the premise (thereby demonstrating logical equivalence).

17. (CHALLENGE) Symbolize and construct proofs for the arguments in these exercises following Chapter Nine:

    (a) Exercise 3
    (b) Exercise 15
    (c) Exercise 11
    (d) Exercise 16
    (e) Exercise 17

18. (SUPERCHALLENGE) Construct a proof for this sequent:

    $-(D \leftrightarrow E) \vdash -D \leftrightarrow E$

    My proof has 28 lines. Compare exercise 18 with exercise 18 in Chapter Six.

---

[15]"FCC Tells Tribune: Make a Choice," *Miami Herald* (March 22, 1997), p. 1C.

9

Derived Rules

9.1 Derived Rules 1

A newspaper story describes the difficulties of a married couple:

> *About a year ago, their troubles began. Mrs. Mathias was having medical prob-*
> *lems and went to a doctor who told her "she either had a tumor or was pregnant,"*
> *Mathias said.*
> *"We were scared because she couldn't be pregnant and we thought it had to*
> *be a tumor," he said.*[1]

The couple believed that the wife could not be pregnant since she had under-
gone a sterilization operation. They employed this simple argument to reach a
frightening conclusion:

> Mrs. Mathias either has a TUMOR or she is PREGNANT. But she can't
> be pregnant. Thus, she has a tumor.

In symbols:

> T ∨ P, −P ⊢ T

The inference pattern exhibited here is known as *disjunctive argument.* Any argument embodying this pattern has two premises. The first is a disjunction,
and the second is the negation of one of the disjuncts of the first premise; the
conclusion is the other disjunct. This argument pattern is obviously valid, yet

---

[1]Bill Gjebre, "Unplanned Birth Nearly Cost Marriage," *Miami News* (February 2, 1976),
p. 1A.

the conclusion of the argument was false–Mrs. Mathias did not have a tumor. The second premise was false; the sterilization had failed and the woman was pregnant.

Compare this argument with a superficially similar but invalid inference:

> Mrs. Mathias either has a tumor or she is pregnant. She is pregnant. Thus, she does not have a tumor.

$$T \vee P, P \vdash -T$$

This argument is invalid because it is possible for both its premises to be true although its conclusion is false–she could have a tumor *and* be pregnant. Look again at the first argument and note that it could *not* have two true premises and a false conclusion. We term the pattern exhibited by the second argument the *fallacy of affirming a disjunct.* Compare these patterns:

> disjunctive argument: $P \vee Q, -Q \vdash P$ *(valid)*
> affirming a disjunct: $P \vee Q, Q \vdash -P$ *(invalid)*

Despite the simplicity of the valid "Tumor" argument, it is quite difficult to prove using only primitive proof rules. The following proof is the simplest proof we can construct. (You have already encountered this proof as exercise 2(b) in the last chapter.)

1	(1)	T ∨ P	A
2	(2)	–P	A
3	(3)	T	PA
2,3	(4)	T & –P	3,2 &I
2,3	(5)	T	4 &O
2	(6)	T → T	3-5 →I
7	(7)	P	PA
8	(8)	–T	PA
2,7	(9)	P & –P	7,2 &I
2,7,8	(10)	(P & –P) & –T	9,8 &I
2,7,8	(11)	P & –P	10 &O
2,7	(12)	T	8-11 –O
2	(13)	P → T	7-12 →I
1,2	(14)	T	1,6,13 ∨O

The odd maneuver on lines 4 and 5 is done to satisfy the second restriction on the Arrow In Rule when it is applied on line 6. A friend of mine calls such moves "unnatural acts." Another unnatural act is performed on lines 10 and 11; what is the point of that maneuver?

It is of interest to show that a proof employing just primitive rules can be constructed for the "Tumor" sequent. But you would not want to travel that tortuous path whenever you encountered a sequent that exhibits this pattern. For this reason I propose that we add to our stock of rules one that will sanction a direct move from lines 1 and 2 to line 14, in the above proof.

> ***The Disjunctive Argument Rule*: From a disjunction and the negation of one of the disjuncts derive the other disjunct.**

The rule restated:

> **From $\mathcal{A} \vee \mathcal{B}$ and $-\mathcal{A}$ derive $\mathcal{B}$. From $\mathcal{A} \vee \mathcal{B}$ and $-\mathcal{B}$ derive $\mathcal{A}$.**

With the help of this rule (which we abbreviate 'DA'), the proof of the "Tumor" sequent becomes suitably simple:

(1)	T ∨ P	A
(2)	–P	A
(3)	T	1,2 DA

We may speak of Disjunctive Argument as a *derived* inference rule, in contrast with the *primitive* inference rules summarized in Chapter Eight. It is a derived rule in the sense that it sanctions deductions that could be made without its help by employing only primitive rules. In any proof that involves a Disjunctive Argument step, that step could be omitted at the cost of increasing the length of the proof by eleven lines. The first proof of the "Tumor" sequent provides us with a "recipe" for constructing the lengthened proof. It follows that if the eleven primitive proof rules are "safe," then the Rule of Disjunctive Argument must also be "safe."

Having added one derived rule to our stockpile, we must decide whether to add others. The reason for adding more rules, of course, is to make proofs generally simpler or shorter or both. In principle, we could add an infinite number of derived rules because there is an infinite number of distinct argument patterns whose validity can be established with the primitive rules. In practice, however, it is desirable to keep the set of rules compact. With this in mind, I propose to add a set of eight derived rules, half of them in this section and half in the next. The first four rules are displayed below.

Modus Tollens (MT)	From $\mathcal{A} \rightarrow \mathcal{B}$ and $-\mathcal{B}$ derive $-\mathcal{A}$.
Disjunctive Argument (DA)	From $\mathcal{A} \vee \mathcal{B}$ and $-\mathcal{A}$ derive $\mathcal{B}$. From $\mathcal{A} \vee \mathcal{B}$ and $-\mathcal{B}$ derive $\mathcal{A}$.
Conjunctive Argument (CA)	From $-(\mathcal{A} \ \& \ \mathcal{B})$ and $\mathcal{A}$ derive $-\mathcal{B}$. From $-(\mathcal{A} \ \& \ \mathcal{B})$ and $\mathcal{B}$ derive $-\mathcal{A}$.
Chain Argument (CH)	From $\mathcal{A} \rightarrow \mathcal{B}$ and $\mathcal{B} \rightarrow \mathcal{C}$ derive $\mathcal{A} \rightarrow \mathcal{C}$.

The standard assumption-dependence principle applies to these rules.

Each rule corresponds to an argument pattern that we have met before. I will illustrate the use of these rules by constructing two proofs. In *The Long Winter*, Laura Ingalls Wilder writes:

> *Laura looked at the four pounds of beef. She thought of the few potatoes left and she saw the partly filled sack of wheat standing in the corner. . . .*
> *Laura could not help asking, "Pa, you couldn't shoot a rabbit?"*
> *Pa . . . did not answer Laura's question. She knew what the answer was. There was not a rabbit left in all that country. They must have gone south when the birds went. Pa never took his gun with him when he was hauling hay, and he would have taken it if he had ever seen so much as one rabbit's track.*[2]

Laura inferred the answer to her question with this reasoning:

> Pa did not take his GUN with him. Pa would have taken it if he had seen rabbit TRACKS. Had there been RABBITS in the area, he would have seen their tracks. Hence, there was not a rabbit left in all that country.
>
> $-G, T \rightarrow G, R \rightarrow T \vdash -R$

The addition of derived rules increases our options in proof construction; for example, we can construct two proofs for the "Rabbit" argument:

(1)	$-G$	A		(1)	$-G$	A
(2)	$T \rightarrow G$	A		(2)	$T \rightarrow G$	A
(3)	$R \rightarrow T$	A		(3)	$R \rightarrow T$	A
(4)	$R \rightarrow G$	3,2 CH		(4)	$-T$	2,1 MT
(5)	$-R$	4,1 MT		(5)	$-R$	3,4 MT

Four months after the crash of TWA Flight 800 off the coast of New York, the top FBI official investigating the tragedy announced that mechanical failure was the likely cause.[3] He reasoned by elimination:

> The crash was caused by a mechanical PROBLEM, a BOMB or a MISSILE. It wasn't caused by a bomb and it wasn't caused by a missile. So, the cause was a mechanical problem.
>
> $P \lor (B \lor M), -B \& -M \vdash P$

---

[2](New York: Harper & Row, Pub., 1953), pp. 214–215.

[3]"Mechanical Failure Likely Caused TWA Crash, FBI Investigator Says," *Miami Herald* (November 21, 1996), p. 15A.

1	(1)	P v (B v M)	A
2	(2)	−B & −M	A
3	(3)	−P	PA
1,3	(4)	B v M	1,3 DA
2	(5)	−B	2 &O
1,2,3	(6)	M	4,5 DA
2	(7)	−M	2 &O
1,2,3	(8)	M & −M	6,7 &I
1,2	(9)	P	3-8 −O

Here are strategic suggestions for these four rules:

MT	If a premise line is a conditional and the negation of its antecedent is a goal line, search the other premise lines for the negation of the consequent. If you find it, apply Modus Tollens. If you do not find the negation of the consequent among the premise lines, add it as a goal line.
DA	If a premise line is a disjunction and one of its disjuncts is a goal line, search the other premise lines for the negation of the other disjunct. If you find it, apply Disjunctive Argument. If you do not find the negation of the other disjunct among the premise lines, add it as a goal line.
CA	If a premise line is the negation of a conjunction and the negation of one of the conjuncts is a goal line, search the other premise lines for the other conjunct. If you find it, apply Conjunctive Argument. If you do not find the other conjunct among the premise lines, add it as a goal line.
CH	If the consequent of one conditional premise line matches the antecedent of another, apply Chain Argument.

EXERCISES

1. Complete the justification column for each proof. Each line requiring justification is a derived line (not an assumption).

(a)
(1)	−B → C	A
(2)	A → −B	A
(3)	C → −D	A
(4)	− −D	A
(5)	A → C	
(6)	A → −D	
(7)	−A	

*(b)

1	(1)	$E \rightarrow (F \vee G)$	A
2	(2)	$-(F \& -H)$	A
3	(3)	$-H$	A
4	(4)	E	PA
1,4	(5)	$F \vee G$	
2,3	(6)	$-F$	
1,2,3,4	(7)	G	
1,2,3	(8)	$E \rightarrow G$	

Instructions for exercises 2 through 7: Symbolize and construct proofs. In each proof employ at least one derived rule.

2. Part of the parental reasoning recounted by the student in panels three and four of the "Hi and Lois" comic strip is the chain whose conclusion is 'If I don't get good MARKS, I won't have a good LIFE.' (C = I get into a good college, J = I get a good job)

Reprinted with special permission of King Features Syndicate.

*3. A news report includes these paragraphs:

> *Beach police theorized the trio of robbers who invaded the Tepper residence at 4830 Pine Tree Dr. about 9:15 a.m. yesterday arrived by boat. They got away with $5,000 in jewelry and currency.*
>
> *A crew of linemen in the street outside the home saw no cars arrive or leave during the robbery. But the rear of the house has a dock on Indian Creek.*[4]

The police theory and the data supporting it are contained in this argument:

> The robbers entered the house either from the FRONT or from the REAR. Had they entered from the front, the line crew would have SEEN their car. But the linemen did not see their car. If the robbers entered the house from the rear, they must have arrived by BOAT. This proves that the robbers came by boat.

4. When I asked Mike and Amy to pick up Sea Grape leaves in the yard, I received this reply from Amy (then aged four):

> *We are not going to pick them up, because I won't do it without Mike and he won't do it.*

This is an explanation cast as an argument. 'Amy won't pick up without Mike' amounts to 'It is false that AMY does pick up while MIKE does not'.

5. Construct proofs for the arguments in these exercises from earlier chapters.

   (a) Exercise 9(a) in Chapter Four
   (b) Exercise 12 in Chapter Five
*(c) Exercise 10 in Chapter Eight
   (d) Exercise 14 in Chapter Eight
   (e) Exercise 7 in Chapter Eight

6. From Justice Hugo Black's opinion for the Supreme Court in the famous case of *Youngstown Sheet & Tube Co.* v. *Sawyer* (343 U.S. 579 (1952)):

> *The President's power, if any, to issue the order [to seize the steel mills]*[5] *must stem either from an act of Congress or from the Constitution itself. There is no statute that expressly authorizes the President to take possession of property as he did here. Nor is there any act of Congress . . . from which such a power can fairly be implied.*
>
>   . . .
>
> *It is clear that, if the President had authority to issue the order he did, it must be found in some provision of the Constitution.*

Summarize the second and third sentences as 'The President's power to issue the order does not stem from an ACT of Congress'. (C = The Presi-

---

[4]Milt Sosin, "Doctor Gets Call from Thief: 'You'd Better Go Home,'" *Miami News* (April 25, 1972), p. 5A.

[5]To avert a nationwide strike of steel workers in April 1952, which he believed would jeopardize national defense, President Truman issued an Executive Order directing the Secretary of Commerce to seize and operate most of the steel mills. The steel companies then sued the Secretary.

dent's power to issue the order stems from the Constitution, O = The President has the authority to issue the order)

*7. Dialogue from George Orwell's classic novel *Nineteen Eighty-Four:*

> "*. . . When once they get hold of us there will be nothing, literally nothing, that either of us can do for the other. If I confess, they'll shoot you, and if I refuse to confess they'll shoot you just the same. Nothing that I can do or say, or stop myself from saying, will put off your death for as much as five minutes. . . .*"[6]

Show that the second sentence entails 'They'll SHOOT you." (C = I confess)

9.2   Derived Rules 2

"THE CHILD-LABOR LAWS HAVE NO TEETH IN THEM.
I STILL HAVE TO CLEAN MY ROOM."

© 1979 McCall's Magazine. Reprinted by permission of Orlando Busino.

The youngster's argument:

> The child-labor laws have no TEETH. Proof: If they had teeth I wouldn't have to clean my ROOM. However, I do have to clean it.
>
> $T \rightarrow -R, R \vdash -T$

Consider this putative proof for the sequent:

(1) $T \rightarrow -R$ A
(2) R A
(3) $-T$ 1,2 MT (ERROR!)

The inference from lines 1 and 2 to line 3 may appear to be sanctioned by the Rule of Modus Tollens, but in fact it is not. The second premise of a deduction

[6](New York: Harcourt, Brace & Co., 1949), p. 167.

sanctioned by that rule consists of a dash followed by the consequent of the first (conditional) premise. Clearly, line 2 of the above "proof" does not fit this description because it contains no dash at all. Let's generalize the point into a rule:

> **You haven't applied an inference rule correctly unless every connective in the rule pattern appears (in the appropriate location) on the proof lines involved.**

Here are two more examples of violations of this principle:

(1)	–C v D	A
(2)	C	A
(3)	D	1,2 DA (ERROR!)

(1)	–(E & –F)	A
(2)	E	A
(3)	F	1,2 CA (ERROR!)

Look at the rules involved and satisfy yourself that line 3 in each proof violates the principle displayed above. Notice, on the other hand, that the following proof does *not* violate the principle.

(1)	–C v –D	A
(2)	– –C	A
(3)	–D	1,2 DA

Compound wffs (such as '–C' and '–D') may always be substituted for the script '$\mathcal{A}$'s and '$\mathcal{B}$'s in the rules.

Someone might respond as follows to the claim that the putative proof on page 136 is not acceptable:

> *You are being too picky here. Anyone can* see *that the move made on line 3 amounts to the same thing as Modus Tollens.*

Here is our reply:

> *We do not accept appeals to logical intuition ("I see that this amounts to that") as justifications for proof moves, for two reasons: (1) Logical intuition is usually reliable, but not always reliable. (2) Proofs should be an* objective *instrument. A completed proof should convince not only the deviser of the proof, but any knowledgeable inspector of the proof. Inasmuch as I may not share all of your logical intuitions, a proof of yours containing justifications that refer to your intuitions may not convince me.*

To complete the proof for "Child-Labor" we are going to need another derived rule, a rule we call "Double Negation." Let's adopt that rule and three more; these four rules will complete our "stable" of inference rules. Note that all of the inference rules are collected in one place at the back of the book.

Double Negation (DN)	From A derive $--A$ and vice versa.
De Morgan's Law (DM)	From $-(A \,\&\, B)$ derive $-A \vee -B$ and vice versa. From $-(A \vee B)$ derive $-A \,\&\, -B$ and vice versa. From $-(-A \,\&\, -B)$ derive $A \vee B$ and vice versa. From $-(-A \vee -B)$ derive $A \,\&\, B$ and vice versa.
Arrow (AR)	From $A \rightarrow B$ derive $-A \vee B$ and vice versa. From $-A \rightarrow B$ derive $A \vee B$ and vice versa. From $A \rightarrow B$ derive $-(A \,\&\, -B)$ and vice versa. From $-(A \rightarrow B)$ derive $A \,\&\, -B$ and vice versa.
Contraposition (CN)	From $A \rightarrow B$ derive $-B \rightarrow -A$ and vice versa. From $A \rightarrow -B$ derive $B \rightarrow -A$. From $-A \rightarrow B$ derive $-B \rightarrow A$.

The De Morgan's Law Rule (named after the nineteenth-century mathematician-logician who promulgated it) shows how to replace ampersands with wedges (and vice versa) at the cost of adding or deleting dashes. The Arrow Rule provides equivalent formulations for conditionals (and negated conditionals). The Contraposition Rule indicates how to validly reverse the elements in a conditional.

These four rules differ in an important respect from all the rules presented above; namely, they can be used "in two directions," from left to right and from right to left. Double Negation, for example, can be used to add two dashes to a wff or to delete them, as this proof shows:

(1)   G   A
(2) $--$G   1 DN
(3)   G   2 DN

The standard assumption-dependence principle works for these rules. We will apply these four rules, like all the other rules we have adopted, to entire lines but not to line parts.[7]

I will illustrate the use of these rules by constructing proofs for four arguments, beginning with "Child Labor." Both of these proofs work:

---

[7]It is logically sound to apply these four rules (but none of the other rules) to line parts, but in the interest of uniformity of treatment I have decided to use them only with whole lines. Your instructor may prefer the other stance and direct you to apply these rules to parts of lines.

(1)	T → −R	A	(1)	T → −R	A
(2)	R	A	(2)	R	A
(3)	− −R	2 DN	(3)	R → −T	1 CN
(4)	−T	1,3 MT	(4)	−T	3,2 →O

In Section 7.3 I discussed an argument contained in Plato's "Apology"; here is another passage from that source:

> *If it is a fact that I [Socrates] am in process of corrupting some of the young, and have succeeded already in corrupting others, and if it were a fact that some of the latter, being now grown up, had discovered that I had ever given them bad advice when they were young, surely they ought now to be coming forward to denounce and punish me. And if they did not like to do it themselves, you would expect some of their families—their fathers and brothers and other near relations—to remember it now, if their own flesh and blood have suffered any harm from me.*[8]

Socrates' defense:

> If I have CORRUPTED the young, then either they or their RELATIVES will accuse me. But my young FOLLOWERS do not accuse me, and neither do their relatives. It follows that I have not corrupted the young.
>
> C → (F v R), −F & −R ⊢ −C

A proof of validity for this sequent that employs just primitive rules of inference is 19 lines in length. The use of derived rules shortens the proof by 15 lines:

(1)	C → (F v R)	A
(2)	−F & −R	A
(3)	−(F v R)	2 DM
(4)	−C	1,3 MT

A second advantage of this proof over the primitive-rules proof is that the assumption-dependence column is eliminated. The De Morgan's Law Rule comprises eight subrules; the subrule used in deducing line 3 is the "right-to-left" half of the second line of the rule.

Strategic suggestions for these four rules:

[8]33c–33d. Hugh Tredennick, trans., "Apology," in *The Collected Dialogues of Plato*, ed. by Edith Hamilton and Huntington Cairns (Princeton, N.J.: Princeton University Press, 1961), p. 19.

DN	If a premise or goal line is a double negation, consider using Double Negation.
DM	If a premise or goal line is a negated conjunction or a negated disjunction, consider using De Morgan's Law.
AR	If a conditional premise line and a disjunctive goal line (or vice versa) have identical components except for an initial dash, apply Arrow to the premise line. If a premise or goal line is a negated conditional, consider using Arrow.
CN	If a conditional premise or goal line has (one or two) negated constituents, consider using Contraposition.

I'm going to explain and then illustrate a trick that can help you construct difficult proofs (whether they involve derived rules or not). The trick relies on the fact that typically a proof line (other than the conclusion line) is used once and only once as a premise line in a deduction. (Conjunctions and biconditionals are the most obvious exceptions; often they are used twice as premise lines.) So, when you are in the midst of devising a proof it makes sense to concentrate your attention on *all* of the lines that have *not yet* been used as premises in deductions. We can keep track of matters by placing a check mark by the lines that have already been used.

I'll illustrate the technique by constructing a proof for an argument given by the philosopher Ludwig Wittgenstein.[9] Wittgenstein attacked the view that the meaning of a proper name is the individual who bears the name; let's call this view the "Bearer Theory." His refutation of the Bearer Theory:

> If the BEARER Theory is correct and John Jones is DEAD, then the NAME 'John Jones' has no meaning. But if that name has no meaning, then the SENTENCE 'John Jones is dead' also has no meaning. Obviously, the sentence 'John Jones is dead' is meaningful although John Jones is dead. Therefore, the Bearer Theory is mistaken.

$$(B \& D) \rightarrow -N, -N \rightarrow -S, S \& D \vdash -B$$

I shall interject comments as I build the proof for this sequent. I use the strategy suggestion for Chain Argument to deduce line 4 and then I place check marks before lines 1 and 2. I apply Ampersand Out (twice) to line 3, and check it.

✓ (1) $(B \& D) \rightarrow -N$ A
✓ (2) $-N \rightarrow -S$ A

[9] See *Philosophical Investigations,* 3rd ed. (New York: Macmillan, 1958), p. 20.

✓	(3)	S & D	A
	(4)	(B & D) → –S	1,2 CH
	(5)	S	3 &O
	(6)	D	3 &O

Now I focus on the unchecked lines, 4 through 6, looking for some connection between two of them. The most promising connection involves lines 4 and 5 and the letter *S*. I see two routes to take: (1) double negating line 5 and then applying Modus Tollens, and (2) contraposing line 4 and then applying Arrow Out. One route is as good as the other; let's take the second:

✓	(4)	(B & D) → –S	1,2 CH
✓	(5)	S	3 &O
	(6)	D	3 &O
✓	(7)	S → –(B & D)	4 CN
	(8)	–(B & D)	7,5 →O

Examining the two remaining unchecked lines I realize that a step of Conjunctive Argument will complete the proof:

	(9)	–B	8,6 CA

In *Around the World in Eighty Days,* Jules Verne writes:

> *The situation, in any event, was a terrible one, and might be thus stated: if Phileas Fogg was honest he was ruined; and if he was a knave, he was caught.*[10]

Verne presents an argument with this unstated conclusion: Phileas Fogg was either RUINED or CAUGHT.

$$(H \rightarrow R) \,\&\, (–H \rightarrow C) \vdash R \vee C$$

(H = Phileas Fogg was honest) This is a simple sequent whose validity is obvious. The proofs for it, however, are not simple–not even when derived rules are available. As a general rule, proofs for sequents with disjunctive conclusions tend to be tough. For this reason it will be useful to have a plan for devising such proofs. I will suggest two strategies.

One of these may be called the *De Morgan's Law strategy.* It consists of making a provisional assumption of the negation of the conclusion (anticipating a later Dash Out move) and transforming this assumption into a conjunction by De Morgan's Law. The conjunction, of course, yields its ingredients

---

[10] *The Jules Verne Omnibus* (Philadelphia: Lippincott, n.d.), p. 472.

through applications of Ampersand Out. I illustrate with this proof for the "Fogg" sequent:

1	(1)	$(H \to R)$ & $(-H \to C)$	A
1	(2)	$H \to R$	1 &O
1	(3)	$-H \to C$	1 &O
4	(4)	$-(R \lor C)$	PA
4	(5)	$-R$ & $-C$	4 DM
4	(6)	$-R$	5 &O
1,4	(7)	$-H$	2,6 MT
1,4	(8)	C	3,7 $\to$O
4	(9)	$-C$	5 &O
1,4	(10)	C & $-C$	8,9 &I
1	(11)	$R \lor C$	4-10 $-$O

The other plan for proving sequents with disjunctive conclusions may be labeled the *Arrow strategy*. The idea here is to set as a subgoal a conditional wff that can be converted by the Arrow Rule into the disjunctive conclusion. Notice that the antecedent of the conditional will contain one more or one less dash than the left disjunct of the disjunction. The rationale of the Arrow strategy is that it is usually easier to derive a conditional than a disjunction. Conditionals can be derived by applying Arrow In or Chain Argument (among other rules). The following proof for the "Fogg" sequent employs the Arrow strategy:

(1)	$(H \to R)$ & $(-H \to C)$	A
(2)	$H \to R$	1 &O
(3)	$-H \to C$	1 &O
(4)	$-R \to -H$	2 CN
(5)	$-R \to C$	4,3 CH
(6)	$R \lor C$	5 AR

The De Morgan's Law strategy is probably easier for beginners to employ; however, I prefer the Arrow strategy because it usually leads to shorter proofs. Also, the former strategy always requires a provisional assumption (and therefore an assumption-dependence column), but with the Arrow strategy you can often avoid making provisional assumptions.

The eight derived rules presented in this chapter comprise 28 subrules. Each of the 28 can be shown sound by constructing a proof that utilizes only primitive rules. Five of these subrules have been validated above. The student who has worked all of the exercises so far (including the challenges) has constructed proofs that validate 10 more subrules. Exercise 21 at the end of the chapter is concerned with validating the remaining subrules.

EXERCISES

8. Complete the justification column for each proof. Each line requiring justification is a derived line (not an assumption).

    (a)   (1)   A ∨ –B   A
               (2)   B   A
               (3)   – –B
               (4)   A

   *(b)   (1)   C → D   A
               (2)   –D   A
               (3)   –C
               (4)   – – –C

    (c)   (1)   E → –F   A
               (2)   G → F   A
               (3)   F → –E
               (4)   G → –E
               (5)   –(G & – –E)

    (d)   (1)   –[(H & –I) & J]   A
               (2)   J   A
               (3)   –(H & –I)
               (4)   –H ∨ – –I
               (5)   H → – –I

9. Identify and explain the errors committed in the following putative proofs:

    (a)   (1)   –(A & –B)   A
               (2)   A   A
               (3)   B   1,2 CA

   *(b)   (1)   –(C & D)   A
               (2)   –C   A
               (3)   D   1,2 CA

    (c)   (1)   E → F   A
               (2)   F → G   A
               (3)   G → –H   A
               (4)   E → –H   1-3 CH
               (5)   –(E & H)   4 AR

    (d)   (1)   –I → –J   A
               (2)   –K → I   A
               (3)   –J → –I   1 CN
               (4)   I → –K   2 CN
               (5)   –J → –K   3,4 CH

    (e)   (1)   –(–L & M)   A

	(2)	M	A
	(3)	L v –M	1 DM
	(4)	L	3,2 DA
*(f)	(1)	–(–N & O)	A
	(2)	N & O	1 DN
(g)	(1)	P → Q	A
	(2)	P & R	A
	(3)	–P & –R	2 DN
	(4)	–P	3 &O
	(5)	–Q	1,4 MT

Instructions for exercises 10 through 18: Symbolize and construct proofs. In each proof employ at least one derived rule.

10.　(a)　Exercise 8 in Chapter Five

　　*(b)　Exercise 9 in Chapter Five

　　(c)　Exercise 14 in Chapter Five

　　(d)　Exercise 14 in Chapter Seven

11.　The philosopher G. E. Moore writes:

> *I* do *know that this pencil exists; but I could not know this, if Hume's principles were true; therefore, Hume's principles, one or both of them, are false.*[11]

(K = I know that this pencil exists, A = Hume's first principle is true, B = Hume's second principle is true)

*12.　Newspapers employed deductive reasoning to predict the resignation of Israel's prime minister:

> *TEL AVIV–Prime Minister Menachem Begin ... will resign next week, setting up elections as soon as this summer, Israeli newspapers predicted today.*
>
> 　　*Begin will quit unless a compromise is reached on salary demands by the nation's 58,000 teachers, and both Finance Minister Yigael Hurvitz and Education Minister Zevulun Hammer decide to stay in office, the papers said.*
>
> 　　*Hurvitz, seeking to cap an inflationary spiral that left Israel with the world's highest inflation rate–131 percent–last year, has threatened to quit if the Begin government gives in to the teachers' demands for higher pay. Hammer says he will resign if the teachers don't get salary hikes.*[12]

The argument formalized:

> If the teachers get RAISES, the FINANCE Minister will resign. And the EDUCATION Minister will resign *unless* they get raises. Since the PRIME Minister will resign if either of these ministers resigns, it follows that he will resign.

[11] *Some Main Problems of Philosophy* (London: Allen & Unwin, 1953), pp. 119–120.

[12] "Begin Will Quit Next Week, Israeli Newspapers Predict," *Miami News* (January 8, 1981), p. 4A.

13. A newspaper sports story begins:

> *Last week Roy Wilfork insisted that Jackson High's track team would have to win all three relay events to win the Class AAAA state meet in Winter Park over the weekend.*
>   *The Jackson coach was wrong. But he was not disappointed.*
>   *The Generals won two of the relays Saturday night—the sprint medley and the 880—and won the state championship.*[13]

The reporter's argument:

> The Generals did not win all the RELAY events but they won the state CHAMPIONSHIP anyway. Hence, it is false that their winning all the relays was a necessary condition for taking the state championship.

14. (a) Exercise 12 in Chapter Six

  *(b) Exercise 3 in Chapter Eight

  (c) Exercise 17 in Chapter Six

  (d) Exercise 9 in Chapter Seven

15. Huckleberry Finn reports a conversation with his raft companion Jim:

> *He said that when I went in the texas[14] and he crawled back to get on the raft and found her gone he nearly died, because he judged it was all up with him anyway it could be fixed; for if he didn't get saved he would get drowned; and if he did get saved, whoever saved him would send him back home so as to get the reward, and then Miss Watson would sell him South, sure.*[15]

Jim reasoned:

> If I'm not SAVED I'll DROWN, and if I am saved I'll be sent HOME. If I'm sent home, then I'll BE sold South. So, I'll either drown or be sold South.

*16. Here is my solution to the puzzle presented in exercise 3 following Chapter One. Eight triplets have 36 as a product. I list them (along with their sums):

triplet			sum
36,	1,	1	38
18,	2,	1	21
12,	3,	1	16
9,	4,	1	14
9,	2,	2	13
6,	6,	1	13
6,	3,	2	11
4,	3,	3	10

---

[13]"Coach Wrong; but Jackson's Still a Runaway," *Miami News* (May 15, 1972), p. 2B.

[14]The "texas" was a structure on nineteenth-century Mississippi riverboats that contained the pilothouse and the officers' quarters.

[15]Mark Twain, *The Adventures of Huckleberry Finn* (New York: Collier Books, 1962), p. 87.

The solution expressed as an argument:

> If the answer has a UNIQUE sum, then Man 2 would not need another clue [beyond the clue about the building number]. But he did need another CLUE. If the answer does not have a unique sum, then it is either 9-2-2 or 6-6-1. If the answer is 6-6-1, then there is no oldest son. But there is an OLDEST son. Hence, the answer is 9-2-2.

(A = The answer is 9-2-2, B = The answer is 6-6-1)

17. In the ABC television mini-series *Masada*, Eleazar ben Yair tells his followers that the Roman soldiers will soon enter their mountaintop fortress, and recommends mass suicide:

    > *You can choose to fight them in the morning—they'll kill you or enslave you. You can choose to hide from them—they'll find you. Or you can take their victory from them. They will remember you.*

    One analysis of ben Yair's reasoning:

    > If we FIGHT, they will KILL or ENSLAVE us. If we HIDE they WILL find us, and if they find us they will kill us or enslave us. We either fight, hide, or commit SUICIDE. Thus, committing suicide is the only way we can avoid being killed or enslaved by the Romans.

18. In *A Problem of Evidence: How the Prosecution Freed O.J. Simpson* Joseph Bosco advances several arguments critical of the prosecution's case. I paraphrase one of them as follows:[16]

    > If the PROSECUTION is correct, then Ronald Goldman dropped his keys IMMEDIATELY after he was attacked. If he dropped them immediately, then the blood on the keys could be his only if the blood from his wounds went instantly to his FINGERS. But the blood did not do this. If the prosecution is correct, the blood on Ron's keys is his or NICOLE'S, or O.J.'s. It is not Nicole's blood. And if the blood belonged to O.J., the prosecution would have used the keys as EVIDENCE; they did not do this. It follows that the prosecution is not correct.

    (R = The blood on the keys is Ron's, O = The blood on the keys is O.J.'s) The second and fifth premises appear weak.

19. Solve the puzzle.

---

[16](New York: William Morrow, 1996), p. 71.

¹	²	³	▪	⁴	⁵	⁶
⁷			▪	⁸		
⁹			▪	¹⁰		
▪	▪	¹¹	¹²		▪	▪
¹³	¹⁴			▪	¹⁵	
▪	¹⁶					▪
¹⁷		▪		▪	¹⁸	
▪	▪	¹⁹		²⁰	▪	▪
²¹	²²		▪	²³	²⁴	²⁵
²⁶			▪	²⁷		
²⁸			▪	²⁹		

Across

1. To '–I → W' by derived rule.
4. Logically equivalent to 'B & T'.
7. From '−−(F & F)' by derived rule.
8. Entailed by 'U'.
9. From 'F → F' and 'F → F' by ↔I.
10. Not a wff.
11. Try this when all strategies fail.
13. Double choice.
15. Derived rule involving only '→' and '–'.
16. A valid argument may have all _____ premises.
17. Letter addition.
18. Derived rule.
19. NYC zone.
21. 'v' homophone.
23. Diamond stat.
26. From 'U → A' and 'A → R' by derived rule.
27. She's from URUGUAY but he's NICARAGUAN.
28. Poetic contraction.
29. Measures.

Down

1. If and only if.
2. The commutative connectives.
3. 'P' and '–P' are, but '↔P' and 'P & Q v R' aren't.
4. Conclusion word.
5. The key connectives in the variations of DM.
6. Conjunction word.
12. Troublesome terms.
14. Antecedent introducers.
15. Winged pest.
19. Makes a mistake.
20. A valid argument may have a _____ conclusion.
21. Word with black and cook.
22. From '–I → –A' by derived rule.
24. From '−(–B v –N)' by derived rule.
25. Election winners.

20. (SEMICHALLENGE) Symbolize (where necessary) and construct proofs.

    (a) Exercise 20 in Chapter Five
    (b) Exercise 22 in Chapter Five
    (c) Exercise 19 in Chapter Four
    (d) Exercise 8 in Chapter Eight
    (e) Exercise 21 in Chapter Five

In each proof employ at least one derived rule. The length of my proofs: (a) seven lines, (b) three, (c) three, (d) four, and (e) five.

21. (CHALLENGE) Fifteen of the 28 derived subrules are justified either by proofs in the book or by proofs you have constructed for exercises. Now complete the job of justification by constructing proofs for sequents corresponding to the remaining 13 subrules. Employ only primitive rules, of course.

    (a) $A \vdash - -A$
    (b) $-(A \,\&\, B),\ A \vdash -B$
    (c) $A \,\&\, -B \vdash -(A \rightarrow B)$
    (d) $A \rightarrow -B \vdash B \rightarrow -A$
    (e) $A \rightarrow B \vdash -A \vee B$
    (f) $-(-A \vee -B) \vdash A \,\&\, B$
    (g) $-(-A \,\&\, -B) \vdash A \vee B$
    (h) $A \vee B \vdash -(-A \,\&\, -B)$
    (i) $-(A \rightarrow B) \vdash A \,\&\, -B$
    (j) $A \vee B,\ -A \vdash B$
    (k) $-A \vee B \vdash A \rightarrow B$
    (l) $A \,\&\, B \vdash -(-A \vee -B)$
    (m) $-A \,\&\, -B \vdash -(A \vee B)$

Instructions for exercises 22 and 23: Symbolize and construct proofs. You may use derived rules.

22. (SUPERCHALLENGE)

       $C \leftrightarrow (D \leftrightarrow E) \vdash (C \leftrightarrow D) \leftrightarrow E$

Proving the validity of sequent 22 constitutes half the demonstration that the double arrow is associative. This is the second most difficult exercise in the book. Prof. Robert E. Rodes, Jr. devised a 38-line proof for this exercise.

23. (GONZO CHALLENGE) This situation arises as you play the computer game Minesweeper™:

A	B	C	D	E
	2	1	2	

(The labels *A* through *E* are not part of the game; they are added to simplify reference. Cells A through E have not yet been uncovered. The first and last cells in the bottom row are empty. The bottom row of the diagram is the bottom row of the puzzle.) Knowing the rules of the game, you deduce the following:

> Exactly two of the cells A, B, and C are mines. Exactly one of the cells B, C, and D is a mine. And exactly two of the cells C, D, and E are mines.

Show that this information entails:

> A, C, and E are—and B and D are not—mines.

(A = A is a mine, etc.) My proof exceeds 100 lines.

10

Truth Tables

10.1 Full Truth Tables

In the preceding chapters we have developed an efficient and powerful instrument for demonstrating the validity of propositional arguments. However, this device has one major limitation: It does not demonstrate *in*validity. For example, consider the "Brooks" argument, discussed in Section 1.2:

> Gwendolyn Brooks is an AMERICAN. Therefore, she is an American and she is also a POET.

Symbolized:

> A ⊢ A & P

Intuitively, we know this argument to be invalid. We may also be certain that we cannot construct a formal proof for it. However, an individual's failure to construct a proof for an argument *does not* demonstrate the invalidity of the argument. For there is always at least a theoretical possibility that the failure to complete the proof results from the thickheadedness of the proof constructor rather than from the invalidity of the argument under evaluation.

A system of logic that has no method of demonstrating the invalidity of arguments is an inadequate tool for individuals who want to *apply* logic to the arguments they encounter. Some of the arguments that confront us in daily life are invalid, and we want to be able to establish their invalidity. For this reason, in the present chapter and the next we present logical methods that will demonstrate invalidity as well as validity. We begin with the full-truth-table method.[1]

---

[1]Gottlob Frege introduced an early version of this technique in his 1879 monograph, *Begriffsschrift*.

Every statement—simple or compound—has a *truth-value*; that is, every statement is either true or false. The truth-value of a conjunction (S1, for example) is determined by the truth-values of its conjuncts (S2 and S3).

(S1) Brooks is an American and she is a poet.
(S2) Brooks is an American.
(S3) Brooks is a poet.

If both S2 and S3 are true, then S1 is true. If either S2 or S3 or both are false, then S1 is false. The same can be said of F1 through F3, the symbolizations of these statements. The truth-value of F1 is entirely determined by the truth-values of F2 and F3.

(F1) A & P
(F2) A
(F3) P

We will regard each of the five connective symbols as having this characteristic: The truth-value of a wff in which that symbol is the major connective is determined by the truth-values of the wff or wffs it connects. In logicians' jargon, the five connectives are *truth-functional*.[2] The specific ways in which the truth-values of wffs are determined by the truth-values of constituent wffs are shown in the following *basic truth table*:[3]

	Guide Columns		(1)	(2)	(3)	(4)	(5)
	P	Q	$-P$	$P \& Q$	$P \lor Q$	$P \to Q$	$P \leftrightarrow Q$
(a)	T	T	F	T	T	T	T
(b)	F	T	T	F	T	T	F
(c)	T	F		F	T	F	F
(d)	F	F		F	F	T	T

Column 3 (to take an example) shows that a disjunctive wff is true when both disjuncts are true (row a), is also true when one disjunct is true (rows b and c), but is false when both disjuncts are false (row d). Column 1 (to take another example) indicates that a negative wff is false when the fragment following the dash is true (row a) and is true when the negated constituent is false (row b).

[2]Because the connectives studied in propositional logic are truth-functional, this branch of logic is often called *truth-functional logic*.

[3]One may wonder whether the five connective symbols as interpreted by this basic truth table are faithful translations of English connective expressions. This interesting and important question is discussed in Appendix Two.

One cannot employ the truth-table method without learning the information contained in the basic truth table. But, fortunately, this information can be presented in a way that is easier to retain. The entire content of the basic truth table is captured in these five principles:

(P1) **A wff and its *negation* have opposite truth-values.**

(P2) **A *conjunction* is true iff both conjuncts are true.**

(P3) **A *disjunction* is false iff both disjuncts are false.**[4]

(P4) **A *conditional* is false iff its antecedent is true and its consequent is false.**

(P5) **A *biconditional* is true iff its two components have the same truth-value.**

Satisfy yourself that these five principles accurately summarize the basic truth table. These principles should be memorized because you will employ them repeatedly in working exercises.

With the aid of these five principles we can determine the truth-value of *any* compound wff (belonging to propositional logic), provided that we know the truth-values of the simple wffs (capitals) it contains. I will illustrate with wff F4:

(F4)

Suppose in this case that the capitals abbreviate true statements. We indicate this by placing *T*'s beneath the capitals. By applying principle P1, we determine that the fragment '−B' is false. Then, by applying P4, we learn that the entire wff is false. For a second example consider F5:

(F5) −[(C & D) ↔ E]
       T F   T
        F
          F
       T

We begin with the information that *C* and *E* are true and *D* is false. By applying P2, P5, and P1 (in that order), we establish that F5 is true. Notice that we began with the truth-values of the smallest fragments of F5 (namely, the capi-

---

[4]P3 may also be stated: A *disjunction* is true iff at least one disjunct is true.

tals) and then considered in turn larger and larger fragments until we reached the complete wff. It will soon prove important to economize on vertical space. We can do this by writing all the T's and F's on one row, as in the following:

(F5) $\underline{-[(C \& D) \leftrightarrow E]}$
  T T F F F T]

I have employed this convention: each T (F) is located under the major symbol in the fragment to which it applies. For example, the major symbol in 'C & D' is the ampersand; hence, the F located under the ampersand indicates that the conjunction is false.

We have seen how to determine the truth-value of a wff, given the actual truth-values of its simple constituents. We can also determine the truth-values that a wff *would* have for each of the *possible* assignments of truth-values to its simple constituents. The chart in which these possibilities are worked out is called a *truth table*. We return to wff F4 for an illustration. There are four possible assignments of truth-values to its simple constituents:

A	B
T	T
F	T
T	F
F	F

A convenient way of listing these combinations is to alternate T's and F's, singly in the first column and in pairs in the second column. These *guide columns* form the starting point for the truth table for F4. They are separated from the rest of the table by a pair of vertical lines.

A	B		A	$\rightarrow$	$-$	B
T	T		T	F	F	T
F	T		F	T	F	T
T	F		T	T	T	F
F	F		F	T	T	F
				*		
[1]	[2]		[3]	[6]	[5]	[4]

The bracketed numbers at the bottoms of the columns are not part of the truth table. They are included to simplify making references and to indicate the order in which I filled in the columns.

The 16 entries to the right of the double vertical line can be computed on a row-by-row basis by working from the top of the table to the bottom or by proceeding from one column to another. I will adopt the latter procedure because it is faster. Column 3 provides possible truth-values for the fragment A

and is copied from guide column 1. Column 4 is copied from column 2 in the same way. As column 3 is identical with column 1, 3 could be omitted from the table; column 4 could also be dropped. In the future I shall employ this shortcut. Column 5 gives possible truth-values for the fragment '−B'. It is computed by applying principle P1 to column 4. Column 6, which covers the entire wff, is constructed by applying P4 to columns 3 and 5. (Column 3 gives values for the antecedent of F4, and column 5 gives values for the consequent.) Column 6 informs us that wff F4 is false iff both its simple constituents are true. The column that gives values for the whole wff is marked with an asterisk. (The asterisk is omitted when there is only one column.)

If a wff contains three simple constituents, there will be eight possible assignments to consider. This truth table for F5 illustrates:

C	D	E		−[(C & D) ↔ E]		
T	T	T		F	T	T
F	T	T		T	F	F
T	F	T		T	F	F
F	F	T		T	F	F
T	T	F		T	T	F
F	T	F		F	F	T
T	F	F		F	F	T
F	F	F		F	F	T
				*		
[1]	[2]	[3]		[6]	[4]	[5]

(I insert a horizontal line between the fourth and fifth rows of an eight-row truth table to help align the entries in the various columns. This practice is not essential.) The third guide column is constructed by alternating T's and F's in quartets. How many rows of truth-values would a truth table with four guide columns have? How would the fourth column be constructed (assuming we continue with the scheme I have been using)? How many rows are there in a truth table with one guide column? What is the formula for computing the number of rows?[5]

You should realize that the pattern of truth-value assignments in the guide columns of the above table is only one of many feasible patterns. All that is essential is that each of the eight possible assignments to C, D, and E be included. You should also realize that it is immaterial whether the first column is headed with C, D, or E.

Column 4 of the truth table for F5 is computed by applying P2 to columns 1 and 2. Column 5 is constructed by using P5 on columns 4 and 3. Finally, column 6 is produced by applying P1 to column 5. Column 6 can be

---

[5] $r = 2^c$ (where r is the number of rows and c the number of guide columns)

constructed only after column 5 has been completed, and the completion of 5 must await the construction of 4. Do you see why?

So far we have learned how to construct truth tables for wffs. It is a simple matter to extend the technique to sequents. A truth table for the "Brooks" sequent looks like this:

	A	P	A	⊢ A & P
	T	T	T	T
	F	T	F	F
✓	T	F	T	F
	F	F	F	F

The wffs composing the sequent are separated from one another by single vertical lines. A turnstile marks the conclusion. By examining the truth table, we can determine whether the sequent is valid or invalid. We employ this principle:

A sequent is invalid iff there is one or more rows on its truth table where all the premises are true and the conclusion is false.

On the third row of the above truth table the premise is true and the conclusion is false; this establishes the invalidity of the "Brooks" sequent. We "check" the row exhibiting the crucial pattern. The third row of the table indicates that (whatever the actual truth-values of the premise and conclusion of the "Brooks" sequent) it is *possible* that the premise is true and the conclusion is false. By definition, it is impossible for a (one-premised) valid sequent to have a true premise and a false conclusion. Hence, the "Brooks" sequent is not valid.

In Section 2.3, I promised to provide a justification of the inference pattern *modus ponens*; the time to fulfill that promise has arrived. A truth table for a *modus ponens* sequent:

F	G	F → G	F	⊢ G
T	T	T	T	T
F	T	T	F	T
T	F	F	T	F
F	F	T	F	F

We search the table unsuccessfully for a row in which both premises are true and the conclusion is false. From the absence of such a row we conclude that this sequent (and, by extension, any *modus ponens* argument) is valid. Why is it sound to conclude this? The table sets forth all the possible combinations of the truth-values of the premises and conclusion. These do not include an instance where there are true premises and a false conclusion. The table reveals that, due to the form of the sequent alone, it is impossible that its premises are true and its conclusion is false. This is the defining characteristic of a valid sequent.

I also promised in Section 2.3 to demonstrate formally the invalidity of the "Revelation" argument, an instance of the fallacy of affirming the consequent.

	R	W		R → W	W	⊢ R
	T	T		T	T	T
✓	F	T		T	T	F
	T	F		F	F	T
	F	F		T	F	F

The critical pattern that establishes invalidity occurs on row 2.

In Section 7.2 a formal proof was constructed to demonstrate that F1 entails F2.

    (F1) –(O v B)
    (F2) –O & –B

I now establish by truth table that F2 also entails F1.

O	B		–O	&	–B	⊢ –(O v B)
T	T		F	F	F	F T
F	T		T	F	F	F T
T	F		F	F	T	F T
F	F		T	T	T	T F
				*		*
[1]	[2]		[3]	[5]	[4]	[7] [6]

The asterisks identify the principal columns. The critical pattern of a *T* in column 5 and an *F* in column 7 appears on no row; hence, F2 entails F1.

Notice how the truth-values in column 7 were calculated on the basis of a column (6) of values for the fragment 'O v B'. I have encountered the following faulty table devised by students.

O	B		–(O	v	B)
T	T		F	F	F
F	T		T	T	F
T	F		F	T	T
F	F		T	T	T
				*	
[1]	[2]		[3]	[5]	[4]

Column 3 was constructed by applying P1 to column 1, and column 4 was built by applying the same principle to column 2. Then 5 was computed by using P3 with columns 3 and 4. A comparison of column 5 from this table with column 7 of the preceding table indicates that something has gone wrong. The mistaken truth table above rests on the false supposition that F1 is equivalent to F4.

(F1) −(O v B)
(F4) −O v −B

The following table establishes the invalidity of the "Prime" argument, discussed in Sections 3.3 and 4.2:

	L	E	P	(L & E) → P		⊢ L → P
	T	T	T	T	T	T
	F	T	T	F	T	T
	T	F	T	F	T	T
	F	F	T	F	T	T
	T	T	F	T	F	F
	F	T	F	F	T	T
✓	T	F	F	F	T	F
	F	F	F	F	T	T
					*	

For the sake of simplicity I have written in this section as though a demonstration of the invalidity of a sequent constitutes a demonstration of the invalidity of the argument it symbolizes. However, the matter is not quite so simple. While every English argument symbolized by a *valid* sequent is *valid,* not every English argument symbolized by an *invalid* sequent is *invalid.* Consider an example:

> Some BUDDHISTS are musicians. Therefore, some Buddhists are musicians, and some MUSICIANS are Buddhists.

B ⊢ B & M

The English argument is valid (because it is impossible for its premise to be true and its conclusion false), but its propositional symbolization is invalid. The explanation for this anomaly is that the logical structure of the English argument goes beyond the resources of propositional logic. While we can reason directly from the validity of a sequent to the validity of the English argument it symbolizes, when invalidity is at issue we must qualify the principle:

An English argument that is symbolized by an invalid propositional sequent is itself invalid *unless it has some valid-making logical feature that escapes detection in propositional logic.*

All of the English arguments occurring in exercises in this book are suitable for treatment in propositional logic. So, this qualification is of only theoretical interest to us.

The full-truth-table and formal-proof techniques differ in several respects. The most obvious difference is that while truth tables demonstrate both validity and invalidity, formal proofs show only validity. Truth tables are an *effective* procedure—that is, a truth table will lead to a definite result in a finite number of steps. Formal proofs are not "effective." Also, truth tables are a *mechanical* procedure—that is, the method can be described by a completely explicit set of instructions that tell what step to take at every point in the procedure. The technique makes no demands on ingenuity or creativity. Formal proofs, of course, are not "mechanical."

Do the two methods yield consistent results? Yes. Every sequent for which a formal proof can be constructed will be assessed as valid by the full-truth-table test, and for every sequent judged valid by this method a formal proof is possible. For proofs that back up the assertions in this paragraph, see Appendix One.

EXERCISES

1. Complete each of the following truth tables. Remember to place a check mark by each critical row. Indicate for each sequent whether it is valid or invalid.

(a)

A	A	⊢ – –A
T		
F	F	F T
		*

   [1]   [2]   [4] [3]

*(b)

B	C	B → C	⊢ B v –C
T	T	T	T F
F	T		
T	F		
F	F	T	T T
			*

   [1] [2]   [3]   [5][4]

(c)

D	E	F	D → E	E v F	⊢ (D v F) → (E & F)
T	T	T	T	T	T T T
F	T	T			
T	F	T			
F	F	T			
T	T	F			
F	T	F			
T	F	F			
F	F	F	T	F	F T F
					*

(d)

G	H	I	(G & H) ↔ I	H	⊢ −(G & −I)
T	T	T	T T	T	T F F
F	T	T			
T	F	T			
F	F	T			
T	T	F			
F	T	F			
T	F	F			
F	F	F	F T	F	T F T

                                                      *   *

Instructions for exercises 2 through 12: Symbolize and test by the full-truth-table method. Indicate whether the sequent is valid or invalid.

2. This argument was discussed in Section 9.1:

   > Mrs. Mathias either has a TUMOR or she is PREGNANT. She is pregnant. Thus, she does not have a tumor.

*3. Evaluate the argument advanced in the middle panels of the "Sylvia" comic strip. (S = Women played team sports as children, C = Women fit smoothly into the corporate world)

© 1980 by Nicole Hollander.

4. From a philosophy midterm examination:

   > *The determinist says that if all actions are caused then no actions are free and no actions are free, therefore everything is caused.*

   (C = All actions are caused, F = Some actions are free)

5. Philosopher Carl Hempel examines—but does not endorse—this argument concerning the existence of theoretical entities:

   > *. . . When two alternative theories—such as the particle and wave theories of light before the "crucial experiments" of the nineteenth century—equally account for a given set of empirical phenomena, then, if "real existence" is granted to the theoretical entities assumed by one of them, it must be granted*

to the quite different entities assumed by the other; hence, the entities posited by none of the alternative theories can be held actually to exist.[6]

The argument reformulated:

> The theoretical entities postulated by the PARTICLE theory of light exist iff those postulated by the WAVE theory exist. It is not the case that the theoretical entities postulated by both theories exist. Hence, it is not true that the entities posited by either theory exist.

6. One of my students in Introduction to Philosophy advanced this argument:

> If God EXISTS, then he is all-POWERFUL. If he exists and is all-powerful, then the world hangs TOGETHER. This shows that God exists because the world does hang together.

This may be the first three-premised argument for which you have constructed a truth table. The critical pattern is $TTTF$.

*7. An article in a religious tract claims that among the world's religions, Christianity (and only Christianity) incorporates significant or meaningful statements. The author writes:

> *Jesus Christ made statements significant only if He was something more than a man, and He proved He was by dying and rising again—a physical transmigration. . . .*
> *He died and rose again to make His "game" meaningful and factually significant.*[7]

He is advancing the following argument:

> Jesus made SIGNIFICANT statements only if he was MORE than a man. If he ROSE from the dead, then he was more than a man. And he did rise from the dead. This proves that Jesus' statements are significant.

8. The television drama *Anne of Cleves* contains these words addressed to Anne by Thomas Cromwell.

> *If you fall I fall; if I fall you fall. And if both of us fall, the Church of England falls.*

Does it follow from Cromwell's remarks that the Church of ENGLAND falls if either ANNE or CROMWELL falls?

9. Business administration educator Eugene F. Brigham writes:

> *If stocks were negatively correlated, or if there were zero correlation, then a properly constructed portfolio would have very little risk. However, stocks tend to be positively (but less than perfectly) correlated with one another, so all stock portfolios tend to be somewhat risky.*[8]

---

[6]*Philosophy of Natural Science* (Englewood Cliffs, N.J.: Prentice Hall, 1966), p. 80.

[7]Bill Luck, "The Games People Play," *The Logos* (Miami, Fla.), September 1970, p. 3.

[8]*Fundamentals of Financial Management* (Hinsdale, Ill.: Dryden Press, 1978), p. 107.

'Stocks have zero correlation' is equivalent to 'Stocks are neither positively nor negatively correlated'. (N = Stocks are negatively correlated, P = Stocks are positively correlated, R = Stock portfolios involve significant risk)

10. After the California Angels suspended outfielder Alex Johnson without pay for "not showing the proper mental attitude" and fined him $3,750 for misconduct, an arbitration board ruled that his behavior was caused by emotional disturbance and ordered the club to pay Johnson $29,970 in back pay. However, the board upheld the disciplinary fines. A newspaper story gives this account of the reaction of an Angels official to the board's decision:

> *General Manager Dick Walsh called the ruling inconsistent and asked: If Johnson was not responsible for his actions, why allow the fines to stand? If he was, why not uphold the suspension?*
>
> *"Either Johnson was or was not responsible for his actions," Walsh said. "If he was responsible, then the suspension and fines were justified."* [9]

We can formalize Walsh's criticism as follows:

> The view [of the arbitration board] that the FINE was justified but the SUSPENSION was not is mistaken, for the following reasons: Either Johnson was or was not RESPONSIBLE for his actions. If he was, then the fine and the suspension were both justified. But if he wasn't responsible, then neither the fine nor the suspension was justified.

11. (CHALLENGE)

> Providing any one of my three children [Mike, Amy, and Mark] is telling the truth, then the other two are not. It follows that one of them is telling the truth and the other two are not.

(B = Mike is telling the truth, A = Amy is telling the truth, C = Mark is telling the truth)

12. (CHALLENGE) The following puzzle appears in *101 Puzzles in Thought and Logic,* by C. R. Wylie, Jr.:

> *The personnel director of a firm in speaking of three men the company was thinking of hiring once said,*
>
> *"We need Brown and if we need Jones then we need Smith, if and only if we need either Brown or Jones and don't need Smith."*
>
> *If the company actually needed more than one of the men, which ones were they?* [10]

Assume that the main connective in the personnel director's statement is 'if and only if'. Read no further if you want to solve the puzzle on your own. One proposed solution to the puzzle: 'The company needs Jones

---

[9]"Alex Wins, but . . . ; Bunning Retires," *Miami News* (September 29, 1971), p. 4B.

[10](New York: Dover, 1957), puzzle 42. Reprinted through permission of the publisher.

and Smith, but not Brown'. Discover whether this solution is correct by evaluating the argument that has it as conclusion and that has as premises the personnel director's statement and the claim that the company needs more than one of the men. (B = The company needs Brown, J = The company needs Jones, S = The company needs Smith)

13. (CHALLENGE) The following connectives are common in computer programming:

    (1) XOR (exclusive disjunction)
    (2) IF-THEN-ELSE

For a discussion of exclusive disjunction, see Section 7.1. Let's symbolize 'P XOR Q' as 'P X Q' and 'IF R THEN S ELSE T' as '*R,S,T'. (The 'ELSE' in 'IF R THEN S ELSE T' is short for 'AND IF NOT R THEN'.)

    1. Define both connectives with the help of other propositional-logic connectives.
    2. Construct basic truth tables for both connectives.
    3. Formulate an "In" rule and an "Out" rule for each connective. Aim for soundness and completeness (as explained in Section 8.1).

10.2   Brief Truth Tables

The truth-table method developed in the preceding section is an attractive test procedure. In the first place, it can establish invalidity as well as validity. Second, being a mechanical method that does not rely on the ingenuity of the tester, it does not fail when the tester's inventive powers fail. Finally, the method, when carried through, yields an evaluation of *any* argument within the province of propositional logic.[11]

The main defect in the method is a practical one. For arguments involving four or more simple statements the procedure consumes too much space and time. A full truth table has 2^n rows, where n is the number of guide columns in the table. A truth table with four guide columns is 2^4, or 16 rows long; one with five guide columns has 32 rows, and so on. A truth table for exercise 13 in Chapter Eight, with its seven simple statements, would contain 128 rows. Constructing a 128-row table is a snap for a computer, but it is unreasonable to ask a human to perform this task. For practical reasons, then, the full-truth-table procedure should be supplemented by other methods. The present section is devoted to explaining two techniques that are abridgments of the

---

[11]In view of these attractive features of the truth-table method, you may wonder why I bothered to develop the method of formal proofs in Chapters Two through Nine. Here are two reasons: (1) Learning to construct formal proofs strengthens a person's logical powers to a greater extent than does learning to employ the truth-table test. (2) Truth tables have only limited use beyond propositional logic, whereas formal-proof procedures are important in every branch of deductive logic. Thus, learning to construct proofs in propositional logic prepares you for study in other areas of logic.

truth-table test introduced in the last section; we call them *brief truth tables*. I explain first the brief-truth-table method of demonstrating invalidity, and then the brief-table method of establishing validity.

In a full truth table for a sequent, the existence of one row where the premises are assigned the value *T* and the conclusion is marked *F* establishes the invalidity of the sequent. The other rows on the table may be ignored; in fact, they need never have been constructed. This is the idea behind the brief-table method of establishing invalidity. The table contains only one row, which is *the* row (or one of the rows) exhibiting the crucial pattern of true premises and false conclusion.

I'll illustrate this brief-table method by establishing the invalidity of the "Oh God!" argument discussed in Section 5.2. In symbols:

$$S \rightarrow B, -S \vdash -B$$

The brief truth table:

	S	B		S → B	−S	⊢ −B
✓	F	T		T	T	F
	[4]	[5]		[1]	[2]	[3]

(The numbers enclosed by brackets indicate the order in which I inserted *T*'s and *F*'s; the numbers are not part of the truth table.) The portion of this table that lies above the horizontal line is completed as it would be for a full truth table. The crucial pattern (*T*'s under the premises and an *F* under the conclusion) is written in columns 1 through 3. Next I attempt to complete the row of truth values consistent with this critical pattern. The *T* in column 2 requires an *F* in guide column 4, and the *F* in column 3 requires a *T* in guide column 5. I omit placing *F*'s under the occurrences of *S* in the premises (and also omit placing *T*'s under the occurrences of *B* in the first premise and conclusion) as a shortcut; they may, of course, be included. The guide-column entries were selected so that they would support the entries in columns 2 and 3—but what of the entry in column 1? An application of principle P4 confirms the correctness of the entry in column 1. Thus, I have successfully extracted from a full truth table the row that shows that it is possible for the premises of the sequent to be true while the conclusion is false. I have produced the row that establishes invalidity without computing the insignificant rows. I add a check mark to the left of the truth-values to signal the successful completion of the demonstration of invalidity.

We may summarize the brief-truth-table procedure for demonstrating invalidity as follows:

Make a goal assignment of *T* to each premise and *F* to the conclusion. If the remaining assignments are completed consistently, the sequent is invalid.

The "Dolphins II" argument from Section 5.2 provides a second example. Symbolized:

$$-(J \ \& \ S), \ -J \vdash S$$

The brief truth table:

	J	S		$-(J \ \& \ S)$		$-J$	$\vdash S$
✓	F	F		T	F	T	F
				*			
	[5]	[4]		[1]	[6]	[2]	[3]

The crucial pattern is entered in columns 1 through 3. The *F* entry in column 3 requires a similar entry in guide column 4, and the *T* in column 2 forces an *F* into guide column 5. Having completed the guide columns in a way that conforms to columns 2 and 3, we check to see whether the guide columns are also consistent with the entry of *T* in column 1. The guide-column entries require the placement of *F* in column 6, and that entry supports the *T* in column 1. So the invalidity of the sequent is established. Where more than one truth-value is entered under a wff, we mark the principal value with an asterisk (just as we did with columns of values for full truth tables).

Why did I attend to the second premise and the conclusion before considering the first premise? Because they "force" additional truth-value assignments, whereas the first premise does not. The assignment of *T* to the first premise is compatible with several assignments in the guide columns. We adopt this procedural principle for the brief-truth-table technique:

Concentrate first on those wffs in the sequent whose truth-value assignments force additional assignments.

This sequent provides a final example:

$$A, (B \rightarrow A) \ \& \ (-C \ v \ B) \vdash C$$

The brief truth table:

	A	B	C		A		$(B \rightarrow A) \ \& \ (-C \ v \ B)$			$\vdash C$
✓	T	T	F		T		T	T	T	F
								*		
	[4]	[9]	[5]		[1]		[6]	[2] [7] [8]		[3]

The goal entries in columns 1 and 3 force entries in guide columns 4 and 5. The *T* in 4 leads to a *T* in 6 (because conditionals with true consequents are true). The *F* in 5 results in a *T* in 7, which in turn forces a *T* into column 8. The *T*'s in 6 and 8 support the goal entry of *T* in column 2. This shows that regardless of what letter is inserted in guide column 9, it is possible for the premises to be true and the conclusion false. The invalidity of the sequent is, therefore, established. To complete the table, I "flip a truth-value coin" and enter a *T* in column 9. This example shows that for some invalid sequents (a minority of those we are likely to encounter) more than one brief truth table is possible.

The brief-truth-table method of establishing validity is nearly identical to the technique explained above. I'll illustrate it by evaluating the "Brown v. Board of Education" argument from Section 2.3. That argument is symbolizd:

$$U \rightarrow V, U \vdash V$$

We draw up a brief truth table and make goal assignments to the premises and conclusion.

U	V	U → V	U	⊢ V
		T	T	F

When we make the additional truth-value assignments that are forced by these initial assignments we land in a contradiction!

U	V	U → V	U	⊢ V
T	F	T	T	F
		F		
[4]	[5]	[1]	[2]	[3]

The *T* in column 2 is copied over in column 4 and the *F* in column 3 is recorded in 5. When we check the first premise against the guide columns, "trouble" emerges. The antecedent of the first premise has been assigned *T* and the consequent *F*; but in this case the premise itself must be false—which conflicts with the initial assignment of *T* to that premise. Note that each truth-value entered after the initial assignments was forced by prior assigments. Therefore, ending with a contradiction (both *T* and *F* assigned to the first premise) shows that the initial goal assignment was impossible. But if it is impossible for the premises to be true and the conclusion false, then the sequent is valid.

Note that the contradiction could have "popped up" at other locations, for example:

U	V	U → V	U	⊢ V
T	T	T	T	F
				T
[4]	[5]	[1]	[2]	[3]

The *T* in column 2 is transferred to 4. Given that a true conditional with a true antecedent must have a true consequent, the *T*'s in columns 1 and 4 dictate that the consequent of the first premise also be true, and that information is recorded in column 5. When the *T* in 5 is transferred to the conclusion a contradiction erupts in column 3. Wherever the contradiction emerges, it is proof of validity–providing only that each assignment made was required by earlier assignments (going all the way back to the initial goal assignments).

We have developed a brief-truth-table test of validity, which may be summarized:

> **Make a goal assignment of T to each premise and F to the conclusion. If this assignment forces a contradictory assignment, the sequent is valid.**

For a second illustration of the method, I assess an argument of Albert Einstein's. Einstein said:

> *I am convinced that there is absolute truth. If there isn't an absolute truth, there cannot be a relative truth.*[12]

Einstein makes the (plausible) assumption that there is some sort of truth. His argument may be expressed as follows:

> There is ABSOLUTE truth. Proof: There is either absolute or RELATIVE truth. And if there isn't an absolute truth, there cannot be a relative truth.

Symbolized:

$$A \vee R, \; -A \to -R \vdash A$$

The brief truth table:

A	R	A ∨ R	−A → −R	⊢ A
F	T	T	T T F	F
			F	
			*	
[4]	[6]	[1]	[5] [2][7]	[3]

The goal entry in column 3 is transferred to guide column 4 and also entails the T in column 5. Because a true disjunction must have at least one true disjunct, the entries in columns 1 and 4 show that 'R' will receive the value T (recorded in 6), and this in turn places an F in column 7. But now the second premise has a true antecedent and a false consequent; so it is given an F–which contradicts its initial assignment.

For a third example I assess exercise 12 in Chapter Seven:

O	G	M	B	A	(O → G) & (M → B)	A → (O ∨ M)	⊢ A → (G ∨ B)
F	F	F	F	T	T T T	T T	F F
					*	* F	*
[11]	[9]	[12]	[10]	[6]	[4] [1] [5]	[2] [8]	[3] [7]

[12]Roger A. MacGowan and F. I. Ordway, *Intelligence in the Universe* (Englewood Cliffs, N.J.: Prentice Hall, 1966), p. 289.

Study this table (following the truth-value entries in the order indicated) until you understand how the initial goal assignments lead to the contradiction in column 8. If you need help, read the footnote.[13]

Occasionally you will encounter a valid sequent where the initial goal assignment does not force all the remaining truth-value assignments. When that occurs the method becomes more complex. When you reach an unforced assignment you will need to construct two rows of assignments: one where the unforced assignment is assigned T and a second where it is assigned F. If on each row all the remaining assignments are forced and lead to some contradiction, then the sequent has been shown valid. This sequent from Section 6.2 provides an example:

M	G	M $\leftrightarrow$ G	$\vdash$ G $\leftrightarrow$ M
T	T	T	F
			T
F	F	T	F
			T
[3]		[1]	[2]

The initial assignments in columns 1 and 2 forced no further assignments, so I assigned a T in column 3 and then later an F. Both assignments resulted in contradiction, so the sequent is valid.

This requirement that each step be forced (or else worked out for both possible assignments) applies only to the validity test; it is not a requirement of the invalidity test.

What has been explained for pedagogical reasons as two brief-truth-table techniques may also be viewed as one method summarized in this way:

Make a goal assignment of T to each premise and F to the conclusion. If the remaining assignments are completed without contradiction, the sequent is invalid. If the goal assignment forces a contradictory assignment, the sequent is valid.

EXERCISES

14. Use the brief-truth-table procedure to establish the invalidity of these arguments in the exercise set following Section 10.1.

    (a) Exercise 2
    *(b) Exercise 3

---

[13]Principle 2 and entry 1 entail entries 4 and 5.
  P4 and entry 3 entail 6 and 7.
  P4 and entries 2 and 6 entail 8 (top entry).
  P3 and entry 7 entail 9 and 10.
  P4 and entries 4 and 9 entail 11.
  P4 and entries 5 and 10 entail 12.
  P3 and entries 11 and 12 entail 8 (bottom entry).

(c) Exercise 4
(d) Exercise 6

15. Use the brief-truth-table procedure to establish the validity of these arguments in the exercise sets for Chapter Nine:

(a) Exercise 13
*(b) Exercise 3
(c) Exercise 2
(d) Exercise 12

Instructions for exercises 16 through 24: Symbolize and test by the brief-truth-table method. Indicate whether the sequent is valid or invalid.

16. Some lyrics from "King Herod's Song" in the rock opera *Jesus Christ Superstar:*

> *So you are the Christ, you're the great Jesus Christ*
> *Prove to me that you're divine—change my water into wine*
> *That's all you need do and I'll know it's all true*
> *. . .*
> *Or has something gone wrong? Why do you take so long?*
> *C'mon King of the Jews*
> *. . .*
> *You're a joke, you're not the Lord—*
> *   you are nothing but a fraud*
> *Take him away—he's got nothing to say!*[14]

Herod reasons:

> If Jesus changes my water into WINE, then he's DIVINE. Therefore, he is not divine because he did not change my water to wine.

*17. The doctor in the "Wizard of Id" strip presents an argument with this unstated conclusion: 'He pollutes the WATER or the AIR'. (B = He washes)

September 15, 1971. By permission of Johnny Hart and Creators Syndicate, Inc.

---

[14]"King Herod's Song" from *Jesus Christ Superstar: A Rock Opera* by Andrew Lloyd Webber and Tim Rice. © 1970 by Leeds Music Ltd., London, England. Sole selling agent, Leeds Music Corporation, 445 Park Ave., New York, N.Y., for North, Central, and South America. Used by permission. All rights reserved.

18. A letter to "Dear Abby" includes this paragraph:

    > ... *One woman who tried to call her husband at his place of business and found his line busy, then attempted to call a lady she knew, and when HER line was also busy, this wife assumed that her husband and this lady were talking to each other! She then began to call this lady on the phone and harass her with all sorts of vile accusations.*[15]

    Perhaps the jealous wife used this argument:

    > My HUSBAND'S phone is busy. SO-AND-SO's telephone is also busy. If they are TALKING with each other on the phone, then, of course, both phones are busy. Therefore, my husband and so-and-so are conversing over the phone.

19. The "Far Side" cartoon suggests these arguments:

    (a) You're DAMNED if you do, and damned if you don't. So, you're damned.

    (b) If you enter the FIRST door, you're DAMNED. If you enter the SECOND door, you're also damned. You will enter either the first or the second door. So, you're damned.

    (B = You do)

"C'mon, c'mon—it's either one or the other."

THE FAR SIDE © 1985 FARWORKS, INC.

[15]Abigail Van Buren, "Dear Abby" (Chicago Tribune–New York News Syndicate, Inc.), *Miami News* (January 7, 1972), p. 8C.

20. A student advanced the following argument as evidence for the spuriousness of Christianity:

> If [the Christian] God loves ALL people, then he doesn't love only ONE. And if he loves only one person, then he doesn't love all people. Thus, he does not love all people.

*21. This passage occurred in a term paper on the philosophy of science:

> *The instrumentalist interpretation of quantum theory is implied by positivism; positivism is false; hence, we must interpret quantum theory in a realistic fashion.*

I believe the student was reasoning as follows:

> Either INSTRUMENTALISM or REALISM is correct. If POSITIVISM is true, instrumentalism is correct. But positivism is false. Hence, realism is correct.

22. A sports story on a high-school baseball tournament includes the following:

> *Columbus (9–9 in conference)–lost yesterday: definitely will participate in the playoffs. . . .*
>
> *If Beach loses tonight, Columbus and Gables will be third- and fourth-place representatives from the GMAC Southern Division. . . .*
>
> *If Beach wins, Beach and Columbus will qualify.*[16]

The conclusion of the argument contained in this passage is asserted in the first paragraph. Ties in baseball are rare; for simplicity, let's equate *not winning* with *losing*. (C = Columbus will qualify, W = Beach wins tonight, G = Gables will qualify, B = Beach will qualify)

23. Ray is in a jam expressed by this argument:

> I take Maxine to the CONCERT iff I WIN this pool game. If I win this game I will be beaten UP. If I don't take Maxine to the concert, BERNARD will take her. Therefore, either I get beaten up or Maxine goes to the concert with Bernard.

LOOKIN' FINE © 1981 United Feature Syndicate. Reprinted by permission.

[16]"District Baseball: It's Loaded with 'Ifs'," *Miami News* (April 17, 1971), p. 2B.

24. The manuscript for a logic text I reviewed contained the following argument:

> Sequent S is formally UNSOUND iff it is VALID and has at least one FALSE premise. S has one or more false premises only if the CONJUNCTION of its premises is logically absurd. So, S is formally unsound if the conjunction of its premises is logically absurd.

(U = S is formally unsound)

25. (SEMICHALLENGE) Use the brief-truth-table procedure to establish the validity of these arguments:
    (a) Exercise 20 in Chapter Seven
    (b) Exercise 13 in Chapter Eight

11

Truth Trees

11.1 Constructing Trees

In this chapter we introduce one more procedure for checking argument validity: the truth-tree test.[1] This technique has many attractive features: Like formal proofs, it can be employed in other branches of logic; like full truth tables, it is an effective procedure (for propositional logic); and like proofs and brief truth tables, it is a practical test for complex arguments. The results it provides are consistent with the techniques previously studied.

A truth tree is a logic diagram that looks like a stick-figure tree turned upside down:

Every line connecting the root of the tree with a tip is called a "branch"; so the tree above has three branches. We call the top vertical line segment the "trunk" of the tree.

---

[1] The method is also known as the "semantic tableau" test. It was conceived independently by E. W. Beth and Jaakko Hintikka in the 1950s. Several truth-tree formats have been developed. The one employed in this chapter was devised by Gerald Massey. Another format is discussed in Appendix Four.

We will write wffs along the vertical segments of branches. Placing a wff on the left side of a branch represents the wff as true, while putting a wff on the right side represents it as false. Here's a good way to remember which side of a branch is the "truth" side. The method of truth trees can be seen as avenging millennia of discrimination practiced against left-handers. Two of the definitions for the adjective 'sinister', for example, are "suggesting or threatening evil" and "on the left side." In truth trees, however, the left side of the diagram represents truth, beauty, and goodness—well, at least truth.

The idea behind truth trees is to unpack the contents of wffs by decomposing or analyzing them into smaller and smaller parts, and to represent the whole process graphically. We'll need ten decomposition rules, two for each of our connectives. These rules are based on the five principles displayed on page 152.

Let's start by considering three of the left-hand (or truth-side) rules:

Dash Left (−L)	**Ampersand Left (&L)**	**Wedge Left (vL)**

We "check" a wff to show that it has been decomposed. The −L Rule makes perfect sense; if a negative wff is true, then its component is false. The &L Rule is very like the &O Rule (from Chapter Three). The vL Rule represents disjunction by dividing a branch into two sub-branches. I'll illustrate the use of the first three rules with this tree (in which 'C & −D' and 'E v F' are assumed as truths):

Let's draw a short horizontal line across the trunk beneath the initial assumptions. Several comments on tree construction: (1) The main connective in the wff determines what rule is to be applied. It would be a mistake to apply the −L Rule to the first wff since the dash is not the main connective in that wff. (2) Each wff added to a branch is written below the wffs already on that branch.

Wffs on different branches may be written on the same horizontal line. (3) You save yourself work by postponing branching as long as possible. If I had not followed that plan, the tree would look like this (with ten wffs instead of seven):

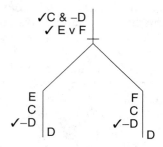

(4) Note that a move made after a line has split must be made on every branch (on which the wff being decomposed appears).

These are the two remaining left-hand rules:

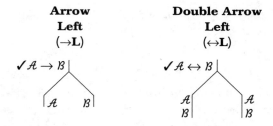

They rely on the following equivalences:

$$A \rightarrow B \quad = \quad -A \vee B$$
$$A \leftrightarrow B \quad = \quad (A \,\&\, B) \vee (-A \,\&\, -B)$$

The tree below illustrates the application of these two rules:

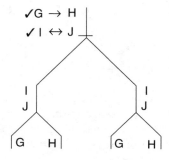

(I shorten the tree slightly by decomposing the biconditional first.)

Here are the five right-hand rules and the logical equivalences that make four of them more understandable:

Dash
Right
(−R)

Ampersand
Right
(&R)

$\mathcal{A}$ & $\mathcal{B}$✓

$$-(\mathcal{A} \,\&\, \mathcal{B}) = -\mathcal{A} \vee -\mathcal{B}$$

$\mathcal{A}$ $\mathcal{B}$

Wedge
Right
(vR)

$\mathcal{A}$ v $\mathcal{B}$✓
$\mathcal{A}$ $-(\mathcal{A} \vee \mathcal{B}) = -\mathcal{A} \,\&\, -\mathcal{B}$
$\mathcal{B}$

Arrow
Right
(→R)

$\mathcal{A} \to \mathcal{B}$✓ $-(\mathcal{A} \to \mathcal{B}) = \mathcal{A} \,\&\, -\mathcal{B}$
$\mathcal{A}$
$\mathcal{B}$

Double Arrow
Right
(↔R)

$\mathcal{A} \leftrightarrow \mathcal{B}$✓

$$-(\mathcal{A} \leftrightarrow \mathcal{B}) = (\mathcal{A} \,\&\, -\mathcal{B}) \vee (-\mathcal{A} \,\&\, \mathcal{B})$$

This tree illustrates the use of all five right-hand rules:

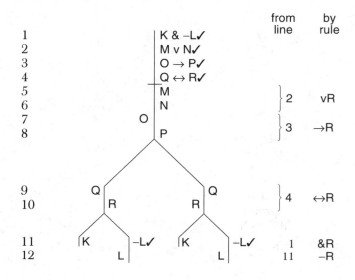

(The columns on the left and the right are instructional devices and not part of the tree diagram.) I attend to lines 2 and 3 first so as to postpone branching as long as possible.

All ten rules are displayed together at the back of the book.

11.2   Testing Arguments

The truth-tree test of validity is simple in concept, but to explain it I need to provide a few definitions:

> **A "closed" branch is a branch on which some wff appears on both the left and right sides. (We will mark closed branches with an asterisk at the tip.)**
>
> **An "open" branch is a branch that isn't closed.**
>
> **A "closed" tree is a tree all of whose branches are closed.**
>
> **An "open" tree is a tree some of whose branches are open.**

When a branch closes you add no more wffs to the branch.

An open branch (of a completed truth tree) reveals an assignment of truth-values to the capitals occurring on that branch that is consistent with the assumptions made on the trunk of the tree. Consider this tree, for example:

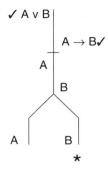

The open left branch shows that the assignment of truth to *A* (the wff *A* appears on the left side of that branch) and falsity to *B* (*B* occurs on the right) is compatible with the initial assumption that 'A ∨ B' is true and 'A → B' false. (And if all the capitals in the problem occur on that open branch, the assignment of truth-values indicated for them is not merely *compatible with* the values assigned to the initial wffs, but it *entails* those values. The tree above is an example.)

Every assignment of truth-values to all the capitals that is consistent with the assumptions made on the trunk of the tree will be represented by some open branch (and possibly more than one). And that means that if all the branches on a truth tree are closed, that is, if the tree itself closes, then *no* assignment of truth-values to all the capital letters is consistent with the assumptions made on the trunk. That provides the key to the truth-tree test for validity. Recall that a sequent is valid iff it is impossible for its premises to be true while its conclusion is false. So we set the test up by writing the premise wffs on the truth side of the trunk and the conclusion wff on the falsity side. The sequent is valid iff the tree closes.

I'll illustrate by testing four arguments (sequents). A newspaper columnist writes:

> *Mas states that "it is not true there have not been public hearings" on the proposed transfer of Radio Marti to Miami. . . . The fact is that there were no congressional hearings prior to lawmakers' sudden approval of the move last month.*[2]

The columnist's argument:

> There have been no HEARINGS. Hence the claim [made by Mas] that it is not true that there have not been hearings is itself not true.
>
> –H ⊢ – – –H

[2]Christopher Marquis, "'Truth-Telling' and Jorge Mas," *Miami Herald* (January 15, 1996), p. 13A.

The truth tree for this simple sequent:

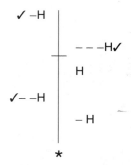

The tree has only one branch and that branch is closed because '−H' appears on both of its sides. The fact that the tree is closed shows the sequent to be valid. The premise cannot be true at the same time that the conclusion is false.

The second argument undergirds a joke that I will tell in a stripped-down version. The philosopher Réné Descartes is sitting in a bar when the bartender announces that it is closing time. When he asks Descartes whether he wants one for the road, Descartes answers, "I think not," and promptly vanishes. (Look, it's a philosopher's joke; it doesn't have to be that funny.)

Of course, the joke capitalizes on Descartes' famous *cogito ergo sum* argument ("I think; therefore I am"). The argument behind the joke, then, goes like this:

> If Descartes THINKS, then he EXISTS. But he thinks not [i.e., doesn't think]. So, he doesn't exist.
>
> $T \rightarrow E, -T \vdash -E$

(We ignore the equivocation in the second premise.) The tree:

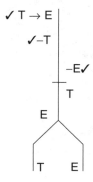

The tree is open; this shows that the sequent is invalid. The tree even tells you the invalidating assignment of truth-values. If *T* is false and *E* true, then the premises of the argument are true and the conclusion false.

In the animated musical "Aladdin," the hero sings, "Gotta eat to live, gotta steal to eat," suggesting this argument:

> My EATING is necessary for my continuing to LIVE. I eat only if I STEAL. Thus, stealing is necessary for my survival.

$$L \rightarrow E, E \rightarrow S \vdash L \rightarrow S$$

The tree:

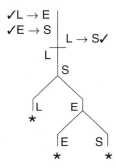

Every branch closes, so the sequent (and argument) is valid (which we knew anyway, since it is a chain argument).

The last example concerns an argument suggested by the "Sally Forth" comic strip.

Reprinted with special permission of King Features Syndicate.

> If Mom got her hair CUT and I don't say anything, I'm in trouble. But if she didn't get it cut and I do SAY something, I'm in just as much trouble. Therefore, I'm in trouble.

$$(C \ \& \ {-}S) \rightarrow T, ({-}C \ \& \ S) \rightarrow T \vdash T$$

This argument is invalid. Why?[3] The tree:

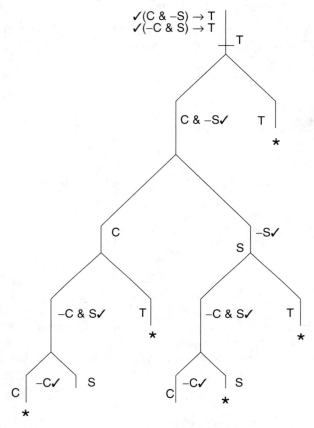

Two of the branches remain open, establishing the invalidity of the sequent.

Answers to some pertinent questions about the truth-tree test: (1) Q: When is a truth tree complete? A: When every compound wff has been decomposed or when every branch of the tree has closed. Note that these are independent conditions. (2) Q: Is it ever safe to stop constructing a tree before it is complete? A: Yes. If all the compound wffs on one branch have been decomposed and that branch remains open, then construction can stop. The tree will be open; no further construction will change that fact. (3) Q: Aside from postponing branching, does it matter in what order you decompose wffs? A: Sometimes you can simplify a tree by the order in which you decompose wffs, as these trees for the same sequent illustrate:

---

[3]Because it considers only two of four possible states of affairs. If Mom got her hair cut and Dad says something, for example, then he is not necessarily in trouble.

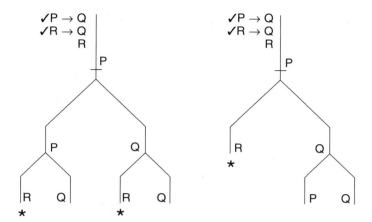

Compare the truth-tree and full-truth-table techniques. In one respect the two methods are mirror images of each other. In full truth tables you do truth-value calculations beginning with the smallest wff components. In truth trees you are in effect calculating truth-values in the opposite direction. Think about a truth table and a truth tree for a given set of wffs. Every row on the truth table on which the initial wffs have the truth-values indicated on the tree correlates with at least one open tree branch (and every open branch correlates with at least one such row). A truth table on which there is no row where the initial wffs have the indicated truth-values corresponds to a truth tree on which every branch closes.

The truth-tree and brief-truth-table methods also have something in common. In both techniques you assume the premises of a sequent to be true and the conclusion to be false, and then determine whether a contradiction follows from this assumption.

EXERCISES

1. Complete the following truth trees. Remember to place a check mark by each decomposed wff, and to mark each closed branch with an asterisk. Identify each tree as "open" or "closed."

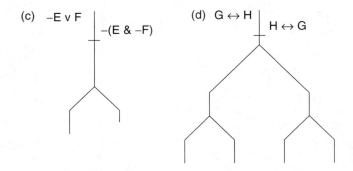

(c) −E v F

−(E & −F)

(d) G ↔ H

H ↔ G

2. Construct truth trees for each of these invalid arguments from Chapter Ten:
   (a) Exercise 18
   *(b) Exercise 16
   (c) Exercise 7

3. Construct truth trees for each of these valid arguments:
   (a) Exercise 5 in Chapter Six
   *(b) Exercise 17 in Chapter Ten
   (c) Exercise 22 in Chapter Ten

Instructions for exercises 4 through 14: Symbolize and test by the truth-tree method. Indicate whether the sequents are valid or invalid.

4. The seventeenth-century French mathematician–philosopher Blaise Pascal considers this argument (not approvingly):

   "Why do you kill me?" "What! Do you not live on the other side of the water? If you lived on this side, my friend, I should be a murderer, and it would be unjust to kill you. But since you live on the other side, it is just, and I am a hero." [4]

   (W = You live on this side of the water, J = It is just to kill you)

5. From Chapter Ten:
   (a) Exercise 21
   *(b) Exercise 10
   (c) Exercise 20
   (d) Exercise 23

The next four arguments relate to the "B.C." comic strip. The first three arguments are advanced by one man (the blond) and the fourth by the other.

---

[4]Norbert Guterman, ed., *The Anchor Book of French Quotations* (New York: Doubleday, 1990), p. 123.

By permission of Johnny Hart and Creators Syndicate, Inc.

6. The bird doing the bluebird call is a BLUEBIRD only if bluebirds are INDIGE-NOUS to these parts, which they aren't. So, it is not a bluebird.

*7. The bird doing the bluebird call is not a bluebird. It is either a BLUEBIRD or a MOCKINGBIRD imitating a bluebird. Therefore, it is a mockingbird imitating a bluebird.

8. The bird doing the bluebird call is a MOCKINGBIRD imitating a bluebird. Hence, the bird doing the bluebird call is a mockingbird imitating a bluebird, and the bird doing the CHICKADEE call is a mockingbird imitating a chickadee.

9. The bird doing the bluebird call is either a BLUEBIRD or it is a MOCKINGBIRD imitating a bluebird. If it is a bluebird, then bluebirds are INDIGENOUS to these parts; and if it is a mockingbird imitating a bluebird, then bluebirds are indigenous. It follows that bluebirds are indigenous.

10. A newspaper article on the O.J. Simpson civil trial discusses the inconsistencies between O.J.'s testimony and the testimony of several witnesses. The reporters note:

> *. . . Inconsistencies are especially tough on Simpson because they allow lawyers for the plaintiffs to argue that he is a liar, and showing that a defendant is a liar often is as powerful as showing that he committed the crime itself.*
>
> *People tell lies, the argument usually goes, to hide something. And why hide something unless you're guilty?* [5]

[5]Jim Newton and Henry Weinstein (Los Angeles Times Service), "Simpson's Cool Demeanor Can't Mask Inconsistencies," *Miami Herald* (November 28, 1996), p. 7A.

The argument formalized:

> Simpson's testimony is inconsistent with the testimony of others. If so, then Simpson is LYING. If Simpson is lying, then he is HIDING something. If Simpson is not guilty, then he will not be hiding things. This shows that he is GUILTY.

Note that the second and fourth premises are dubious. (C = Simpson's testimony is consistent with the testimony of others)

*11. We discussed this statement (a premise in the argument from evil against the existence of God) in Introduction to Philosophy:

> (S1) If God WANTS to eliminate all evil, KNOWS how to do this, and has the POWER to do it, then God will ELIMINATE all evil.

A student criticized S1 as follows:

> God does not want to eliminate all evil. Therefore, S1 is false.

12. From Chapter Ten:
   (a) Exercise 9
   *(b) Exercise 5
   (c) Exercise 24
   (d) Exercise 8

13. In an episode of the television series "Homicide" two policemen are accused of taking bribes. They both pass polygraph tests even though their statements made during the tests conflicted. A third party observed, "One of you beat the polygraph. You can't both be telling the truth." Here is one way to formalize this argument:

> Both officers passed the test. They did not both tell the truth. If the first officer passed the test but did not tell the truth, then he beat the test. The same is true of the second officer. So, at least one of them beat the test.

   A = Officer 1 passed the test
   B = Officer 2 passed the test
   C = Officer 1 beat the test
   D = Officer 2 beat the test
   E = Officer 1 told the truth
   F = Officer 2 told the truth

14. (CHALLENGE) I can construct a truth tree for exercise 20 in Chapter Seven that has only six branches. Can you?

12

$\mathscr{Statements}$

12.1 Logical Truths

Up to this point in the book our focus has been on assessing arguments (and sequents). In this chapter and the next we will turn our attention to *statements* (and wffs), examining their logical properties and relations.

Suppose a weather forecaster issued this "prediction":

(S1) Either it will RAIN today in Smallville or it won't.
(F1) R v −R

S1 has a major virtue and a major defect. The virtue is that it cannot be falsified no matter what the weather does. The defect of S1 is that it provides no information about the weather (or anything else). Statements such as S1 (and wffs like F1) whose falsity is logically impossible are called logical truths.[1] Sports announcer John Madden uttered the following logical truth during an NFL telecast (January 5, 1997): "When you take your last timeout you don't have any left." Two more examples of statements that express logical truths (when taken literally): the advertising slogan "Nothing else is a Pepsi," and Yogi Berra's now famous maxim, "It ain't over till it's over." Of course, these examples do not belong to propositional logic.

---

[1]Logical truths belonging to propositional logic are often called *tautologies*.

Here are some logically true propositional wffs:

    A v –A
    B → B
    C ↔ C
    –(D & –D)
    E ↔ – –E
    (F & G) → F
    H → (H v I)

We can use (1) full truth tables, (2) truth trees, or (3) formal proofs to show that a wff belonging to propositional logic is a logical truth.[2] I will explain and illustrate these methods in turn.

(1) The full-truth-table test:

A wff is logically true iff the column under its principal symbol is composed exclusively of *T*'s.

This truth table shows that F1 (S1) is a logical truth:

R	R v –R
T	T F
F	T T
	*

The table shows that F1 cannot be false.

(2) The truth-tree test:

To test a wff by truth tree place it on the right side of the trunk. The wff is logically true iff the tree closes.

This tree for F1 illustrates:

Writing F1 on the right side of the tree represents it as false. The tree shows that that assumption leads to contradiction; so F1's falsity is logically impossible.

(3) The formal-proof test:

If you derive a wff free of assumptions, then it is logically true.

---

[2]There is also a brief-truth-table test; exercise 12 invites you to devise it.

Note that the proof must contain an assumption-dependence column. This Dash Out proof shows that F1 is logically true:

```
1  (1)  –(R v –R)     PA
1  (2)  –R & – –R     1 DM
   (3)  R v –R        1-2 –O
```

The absence of an entry in the assumption-dependence column on line 3 signifies that line 3 is free of assumptions. Only a logical truth can be derived free of assumptions. Obviously a proof of logical truth will utilize one of the assumption-dependence-reducing rules (Dash Out, Dash In, and Arrow In). Here is a second example: This proof shows that 'T → [W → (W & T)]' is logically true:

```
1     (1)  T                     PA
2     (2)  W                     PA
1, 2  (3)  W & T                 2,1 &I
1     (4)  W → (W & T)           2-3 →I
      (5)  T → [W → (W & T)]     1-4 →I
```

For a given sequent, a *corresponding conditional* can be formulated by employing this recipe:

Make the conclusion of the sequent the consequent of the conditional. The antecedent of the conditional will be the premise (or the conjunction of the premises) of the sequent.

Two examples:

Sequent	Corresponding Conditional
L ↔ M ⊢ M ↔ L	(L ↔ M) → (M ↔ L)
N → O, N ⊢ O	[(N → O) & N] → O

Every sequent has a corresponding conditional, and every conditional corresponds to some sequent. This logical principle emerges:

A sequent is valid iff its corresponding conditional is a logical truth.

Thus, it is possible to test arguments by examining conditionals and vice versa.

Some arguments contain premises that are logically true; exercise 10 following Section 10.1 is such an argument. Because logical truths are without content, a logically true premise may be dropped from an argument without affecting the argument's validity (or invalidity). Can you construct a formal proof for exercise 10 that ignores its logically true premise?

12.2 Contradictions

A newspaper article included this sentence:

   (S1) Ralph was not white but he attended an all-white school.

If we interpret the expression 'all-white' strictly, so that it means "100 percent white," we must judge S1 false. We need not know Ralph's race or the racial composition of his school to know that S1 is false. S1 is false as a matter of logic; its truth is impossible. Statements (and wffs) whose truth is logically impossible are called *contradictions*.[3] While on the witness stand in his civil trial, O.J. Simpson told the court that he was 1000% sure that his former wife, Nicole, had pursued him after their divorce. People frequently claim to give 110% effort or commitment or whatever. Understood literally, all such claims are logically impossible; absolute certainty is just 100%; total effort is only 100%. Yogi Berra could utter contradictions as well as logical truths; he had this to say about a restaurant: "Nobody goes there anymore; it's too crowded." None of these examples belong to propositional logic. Here are some logically contradictory propositional wffs:

   P & –P
   –Q & – –Q
   R ↔ –R
   –(S → S)
   (T → U) & (T & –U)

The negation of any logical truth is a contradiction, and the negation of any contradiction is a logical truth.
   Since Chapter Five we have been using the concept of "standard contradiction." How does this concept relate to the just-introduced notion of "contradiction"? A standard contradiction is a special kind of contradiction–namely a conjunctive contradiction whose right conjunct is the negation of its left conjunct. Standard contradictions are useful because they are easily identified by their form.
   We can use (1) full truth tables, (2) truth trees, or (3) formal proofs to show that a propositional-logic wff is a contradiction.
   (1) The full-truth-table test:

A wff is a contradiction iff the column under its principal symbol is composed exclusively of *F*'s.

I'll illustrate with F2.

---

[3]Other labels: *logical contradictions, self-contradictions,* and *logically false statements.*

(S2) It is RAINING, but neither raining nor SNOWING.
(F2) R & –(R v S)

R	S	R & –(R v S)
T	T	F F T
F	T	F F T
T	F	F F T
F	F	F T F
		*

The table shows that F2 (and S2) cannot be true.

(2) The truth-tree test:

To test a wff by truth tree place it on the left side of the trunk. The wff is a contradiction iff the tree closes.

This tree for F2 illustrates:

Writing F2 on the left side of the tree represents it as true. The tree shows that that assumption leads to contradiction; so F2's truth is logically impossible.

(3) The formal-proof test:

If a standard contradiction depends on just one assumption, then that wff is a contradiction.

The justification for this method will be set forth in Section 13.1. This formal proof shows that F2 is a contradiction:

(1)	R & –(R v S)	A
(2)	R	1 &O
(3)	–(R v S)	1 &O
(4)	–R & –S	3 DM
(5)	–R	4 &O
(6)	R & –R	2,5 &I

As line 1 is the sole assumption in the proof, it is clear that the standard contradiction on line 6 depends only upon it.

A more complicated proof is required to demonstrate that F3 is a contra-diction.

(S3) It is RAINING iff it is not raining.
(F3) R ↔ –R

The proof:

1	(1)	R ↔ –R	A
1	(2)	R → –R	1 ↔O
1	(3)	–R → R	1 ↔O
4	(4)	R	PA
1,4	(5)	–R	2,4 →O
1,4	(6)	R & –R	4,5 &I
1	(7)	–R	4-6 –I
1	(8)	R	3,7 →O
1	(9)	R & –R	8,7 &I

An assumption-dependence column is required because the proof involves a provisional assumption. The proof could not be concluded on line 6 even though a standard contradiction was reached, for line 6 depends (partly) on an assumption other than line 1.

12.3   Contingent Statements

Statements (and wffs) that are neither logical truths nor contradictions are called *contingent*.[4] Contingent statements are statements whose truth (or falsity) is not a matter of logic but is dependent or contingent on the way the world is actually structured. Consider S1 as an example.

(S1) Al Gore is a Democrat.

S1 is true, but it is not logically true. It is true because it asserts to be the case something that happens to be the case. Most of the statements we encounter are contingent.

There are full-truth-table and truth-tree methods for establishing contingency, but no convenient formal-proof procedure for doing so.

---

[4]Other labels: *synthetic, factual.*

(1) The full-truth-table test:

A wff is contingent iff the column under its principal symbol contains at least one *T* and at least one *F*.

I'll illustrate with F2.

(S2) Gwendolyn Brooks is an AMERICAN, and she is also a POET.
(F2) A & P

A	P		A & P
T	T		T
F	T		F
T	F		F
F	F		F

The presence of both *T*'s and *F*'s in the third column indicates that F2 is contingent.

(2) The truth-tree test:

Construct two trees. In one tree place the wff on the left side of the trunk. In the other place it on the right side of the trunk. The wff is contingent iff both trees remain open.

These two trees show that F2 is contingent:

Every English statement symbolized by a logically true wff is a logical truth, and every statement symbolized by a contradictory wff is a contradiction, but not every statement symbolized by a contingent wff is contingent. Consider three examples:

(S3) All DOGS are dogs.
(F3) D
(S4) Some dogs are GRAY.
(F4) G
(S5) Not all dogs are dogs.
(F5) −D

All three of these wffs are contingent, but of the three statements only S4 is contingent; S3 is logically true and S5 contradictory. The explanation, of course, is that S3 and S5 have logical features that escape detection in propositional logic. So, when you reason from the contingency of a propositional wff to the contingency of the sentence it symbolizes, you need to make sure that the statement is appropriate for analysis in propositional logic.

The three full-truth-table tests explained in the chapter can be re-described as one test:

> **Construct a full truth table for the wff to be tested. If the column under its principal symbol consists of _T_'s only, the wff is logically true; if it consists of _F_'s only, it is contradictory; and if it consists of both _T_'s and _F_'s, it is contingent.**

The three truth-tree tests may also be redescribed as one test:

> **Construct a truth tree with the wff to be tested on the left side of the trunk. If the tree closes, the wff is a contradiction. If it remains open, construct a second tree with the wff on the right side of the trunk. If the second tree closes, the wff is a logical truth. If the second tree remains open, the wff is contingent.**

It should be clear from the definitions provided in this chapter that every statement is either a logical truth, a contradiction, or a contingent statement, and that no statement falls into two (or all three) of these categories. In logical terminology, the categories are _exhaustive_ and _exclusive_.

EXERCISES

Instructions for exercises 1 through 10: Symbolize each statement. Test by truth table and truth tree. Indicate for each statement whether it is logically true, contradictory, or contingent. Construct formal proofs for the logically true and contradictory statements.

*1. When the head of the Longshoreman's Union was asked whether his union would boycott shipments to England if that country did not give autonomy to Northern Ireland, he answered:

> _I don't think we'll have to go that far unless we have to._

(H = We have to go that far)

2. Book advertisement blurb:

> _Scepticism and realism are each true, and mutually contradictory._

This may be paraphrased:

> SCEPTICISM and REALISM are each true, but it is not the case that they are both true.

3. If at least one of the children (MARK and AMY) is telling the truth, then both of them are.

(M = Mark is telling the truth, A = Amy is telling the truth)

4. If both of the children (MARK and AMY) are telling the truth, then at least one of them is.

*5. Both of the children (MARK and AMY) are telling the truth although at least one of them isn't.

6. $-[A \to (B \lor A)]$

7. $[(C \to D) \to C] \to C$

8. A television reporter describing a dilemma facing government officials said:

> *They're damned if they do or damned if they don't.*

(A = They are damned, B = They do [take the action in question])

*9. The philosopher G. E. Moore[5] regards this statement as a contradiction:

> *If A had not had P, it would not have been true that A did not have P.*

Is Moore correct? Let *H* abbreviate 'A has P' in this exercise and the next.

10. A does not have P iff it is not true that A does not have P.

11. (CHALLENGE)
   (a) Think of a monadic English statement connective that will produce a logical truth when prefixed to any statement.
   (b) Think of a monadic English statement connective that will produce a contradiction when prefixed to any statement.
   (c) Think of a dyadic English statement connective that will produce a logical truth when placed between any two statements.
   (d) Think of a dyadic English statement connective that will produce a contradiction when placed between any two statements.

12. (CHALLENGE) Devise a brief-truth-table test that will demonstrate that a wff is a logical truth, another for contradictions, and a third for contingent wffs. Describe each technique and illustrate its use with an example.

---

[5]See *Philosophical Studies* (Totowa, N.J.: Littlefield, Adams, 1965), p. 283.

13

Logical Relations

13.1 Entailment

In this chapter we examine closely two logical relations that can obtain between statements (and wffs): entailment and logical equivalence. These relations were introduced in Section 3.3 and have been mentioned frequently in succeeding chapters. *Entailment* is the more fundamental relation; its definition:

> **One statement or wff entails a second iff it is logically impossible for the first to be true and the second false.**

The concepts of "entailment" and "validity" are tightly related. The premise of a one-premised argument entails its conclusion when and only when the argument is valid.

Two properties of entailment should be noted:

1. Every statement entails itself.
2. Whenever one statement entails a second and the second entails a third, the first entails the third.

In logicians' terminology the relation of entailment is (1) *reflexive* and (2) *transitive*.

When we combine the concept of "entailment" with the concepts of "logical truth" and "contradiction," four more logical principles emerge:

3. Any statement entails a logical truth.
4. A logical truth entails only logical truths.
5. A contradiction entails any statement.
6. Only contradictions entail a contradiction.

Principles 3 and 4 conform to the observation made in Chapter Twelve that a logical truth lacks informative content. The last two principles correspond to the observation that a contradiction has maximum content; it claims more than can possibly be true.

Principle 5 is captured in the familiar aphorism, "Anything follows from a contradiction." The other three principles, though not part of our heritage of common sense, are equally sound. I will defend principles 3 and 4; you can argue for 5 and 6.

A defense of principle 3:

Let *L* be some logical truth and *A* a statement selected at random. It is logically impossible for L to be false. So, clearly, it is logically impossible for A to be true and L false. Therefore (by the definition of *entailment*), A entails L.

The following sequent, which has a logically true conclusion, is an instance of principle 3:

A ⊢ B ∨ –B

It might be instructive to establish its validity by truth table, truth tree, or formal proof.

A justification of principle 4:

Let *L* be some logical truth and *A* a randomly selected statement that is not a logical truth. Then, it is logically possible for A to be false. So (as L is true no matter what), it is logically possible for L to be true and A false. Therefore (by the definition of *entailment*), L does not entail A.

Exercise 21 in Chapter Five concerned this sequent:

A & –A ⊢ B

Its validity is an instance of principle 5. You may want to demonstrate its validity by one of the methods we have studied.

In Section 12.2, I explained a method for proving that a statement is a contradiction by showing that the statement entails a standard contradiction. Principle 6 provides the rationale for this procedure. As only contradictions entail a contradiction, any statement that entails a standard contradiction must itself be a contradiction.

13.2   Logical Equivalence

Logical equivalence may be defined in terms of "entailment":

One statement or wff is logically equivalent to a second iff each entails the other.

So logical equivalence is mutual entailment. If one statement is logically equivalent to another, the two statements have the same content–they make the same claim. Examples may be useful. Each wff in the following lists is logically equivalent to the other wff(s) on the same row:

A	A & A	A v A	−A → A
B & C	C & B		
D v E	E v D		
F ↔ G	G ↔ F		
F ↔ G	−F ↔ −G		
H ↔ −I	−(H ↔ I)	−H ↔ I	
J & (K & L)	(J & K) & L		
M v (N v O)	(M v N) v O		
P ↔ (Q ↔ R)	(P ↔ Q) ↔ R		
S → (T → U)	(S & T) → U	T → (S → U)	

Many of these examples are old friends from earlier chapters (where the issue was entailment rather than logical equivalence). The derived inference rules of Double Negation, De Morgan's Law, Arrow, and Contraposition suggest 12 additional examples of pairs of logically equivalent wffs.

There is no special formal-proof, brief-truth-table, or truth-tree technique for demonstrating logical equivalence. You just use two proofs, brief truth tables, or truth trees to show mutual entailment. You can demonstrate nonequivalence by brief truth table or truth tree by showing that entailment fails in one direction.

On the other hand, there *is* a full-truth-table test for logical equivalence; it employs this principle:

One wff is logically equivalent to another iff the two columns of truth-values are identical.

I promised in Section 7.1 to demonstrate that F1 is logically equivalent to F2.

(F1) (C v M) & −(C & M)
(F2) C ↔ −M

I satisfy that promise now with this full truth table:

C M	(C v M) & –(C & M)	C ↔ –M
T T	T FF T	F F
F T	T TT F	T F
T F	T TT F	T T
F F	F FT F	F T
	*		*

On no row does one starred column contain a *T* and the other column an *F*; so, each wff is logically equivalent to the other.

In Section 2.2, I claimed that F3 is not logically equivalent to F4.

(F3) A → (B → C)
(F4) (A → B) → C

We can support that claim with this truth table:

A B C	A → (B → C)	(A → B) → C
T T T	T T	T T
F T T	T T	T T
T F T	T T	F T
F F T	T T	T T
T T F	F F	T F
✓ F T F	T F	T F
T F F	T T	F T
✓ F F F	T T	T F
	*	*

We place check marks beside the rows where the wffs have opposite truth-values. Either checked row is sufficient to establish that F3 is not logically equivalent to F4.

Some of the properties of logical equivalence:

1. Every statement is logically equivalent to itself.
2. Whenever one statement is logically equivalent to a second and the second is logically equivalent to a third, the first is logically equivalent to the third.
3. Whenever one statement is logically equivalent to a second, the second is logically equivalent to the first.

That is, the relation of logical equivalence is (1) reflexive, (2) transitive, and (3) *symmetrical*. (Note that entailment is *not* symmetrical.) Because logical equivalence is symmetrical, an alternative way of claiming that one statement *is logi-*

cally equivalent to another is to say that the two statements *are logically equivalent*. This latter phrase was used regularly in preceding chapters.

When we combine the concept of "logical equivalence" with the concepts of "logical truth" and "contradiction," two more principles result:

4. Any two logical truths are logically equivalent.
5. Any two contradictions are logically equivalent.

Principle 4 is a consequence of the fact that any statement entails a logical truth, taken together with the definition of *logical equivalence*. Principle 5 follows from the fact that a contradiction entails any statement, in conjunction with the definition. You should study these two claims until you understand them.

For any pair of wffs a *corresponding biconditional* can be formed by placing a double arrow between them. This logical principle holds:

Two wffs are logically equivalent iff the biconditional formed from them is logically true.

So, it is possible to test for logical equivalence by examining a biconditional.

EXERCISES

Instructions for exercises 1 through 9: Symbolize where required. Test each pair of statements or wffs for logical equivalence by full truth table and truth trees.

1. In Section 3.3, I asked whether the arrow is a *commutative* connective. That amounts to asking whether F1 and F2 are logically equivalent. Are they?

    (F1) A → B
    (F2) B → A

*2. A GRE preparation book[1] displays this principle in a box:

    "If p, then q" is equivalent to "If not-p, then not-q."

    Then it provides an example:

    Thus, the sentence "If John is selected for the committee, then Mary is also selected" is equivalent to "If Mary is not selected for the committee, then John is not selected."

    But the example is not an instance of the stated principle! Presumably either the principle or the example is incorrect. Check them both. (J, M)

3. In his article "Ifs, Cans and Causes,"[2] philosopher Keith Lehrer is anxious to show that the statement 'I can' is not properly analyzed as 'I shall,

---

[1]Thomas H. Martinson, *GRE: Graduate Record Examination General Test* (3rd ed., New York: Simon & Schuster, 1990), p. 88.

[2]*Analysis,* XX (1960), 122–24.

if I choose'. In the middle of an extended argument he makes the claim that the following two statements are logically equivalent:

(S1) I SHALL, if I CHOOSE.

(S2) I shall if I choose, if I choose.

His argument depends on the logical equivalence of S1 and S2. Are they equivalent?

4. (a) Exercise 15(c) in Chapter Seven involves symbolizing this sentence:

A 'no' from one of us (MOTHER and FATHER) means a 'no' from both of us.

Here are two symbolizations:

$(M \vee F) \rightarrow (M \& F)$
$M \leftrightarrow F$

Are they equivalent?

*(b) Two possible symbolizations for exercise 1(m) in Chapter Four:

The only way the BILLS and the CHARGERS can get to the playoffs is if JACKSONVILLE loses.

$(B \& C) \rightarrow J$
$(B \rightarrow J) \& (C \rightarrow J)$

Are they equivalent?

(c) Two possible symbolizations for exercise 1(p) in Chapter Seven:

If the BRAVES and GIANTS both win or both lose today, they will play a one-game PLAYOFF Monday night in San Francisco.

$[(B \& G) \vee (-B \& -G)] \rightarrow P$
$(B \leftrightarrow G) \rightarrow P$

Are they equivalent?

5. A husband debates about which of the following statements to address to his wife:

I'M happy only if YOU'RE happy.

I'm happy iff we are both happy.

What is the difference in content (if any) between these statements?

6. The University of Miami *Faculty Manual* proclaims:

The decision [to use faculty-produced teaching material] shall be made by the instructor or by the department and approved by the department chairman.[3]

This ambiguous sentence could be understood in either of the following ways (the author doubtless intended S1).

---

[3] *Faculty Manual 1980–81*, p. 53.

(S1) The decision shall be made by the INSTRUCTOR or the DE-PARTMENT, and it shall be APPROVED by the department chairman.

(S2) Either the decision shall be made by the instructor, or it shall be made by the department and approved by the department chairman.

Are S1 and S2 logically equivalent?

*7. A news story carries this headline:

   Teachers could EXPEL, SPANK only if law were CHANGED[4]

   F1 is one correct symbolization of this headline.

   (F1) (E → C) & (S → C)

   The first paragraph of the story begins:

   Changes in the law would be required to allow teachers to expel students or paddle them.

   This sentence may be symbolized by F2.

   (F2) (E v S) → C

   Do the headline and the lead sentence make the same claim? Find out by determining whether F1 and F2 are logically equivalent.

8. Bertrand Russell writes:

   . . . State ownership of land . . . was no advance unless the State was democratic, and even then only if methods were devised for curbing the power of officials.[5]

   This wff is one correct symbolization of Russell's claim:

   (−D → −A) & [D → (A → C)]

   Is Russell's statement logically equivalent to the following simpler statement?

   State ownership of land is an ADVANCE only if the state is DEMOCRATIC and methods are devised for CURBING the power of officials.

9. Philosopher Ramon Lemos concludes an argument with this assertion:

   . . . Both [the teleological and the deontological] forms of egoism are false if either [the teleological or the deontological] form of non-egoism is true, and both forms of non-egoism are false if either form of egoism is true.[6]

   Is there a difference in content between the two conjuncts in this statement, or are the conjuncts logically equivalent? Solve this problem by formal proof or truth tree (so as to avoid constructing a 16-row full truth table). (A = Teleological egoism is true, B = Deontological egoism is true,

---

[4] *Miami News* (April 8, 1971), p. 6A.

[5] *The Autobiography of Bertrand Russell* (Boston: Little, Brown, 1968), II: 277.

[6] "Egoism and Non-egoism in Ethics," *Southern Journal of Philosophy,* IX (Winter 1971), 382.

C = Teleological non-egoism is true, D = Deontological non-egoism is true)

Instructions for exercises 10 and 11: Test for equivalence by full truth table. If the wffs are equivalent, redemonstrate this with two formal proofs.

10. (CHALLENGE) On a logic test I asked my students to symbolize this statement:

    At least two of these three will come: AL, BILL, and CHARLIE.

    I expected them to employ F1, but one student offered F2.

    (F1) [(A & B) v (A & C)] v (B & C)
    (F2) [–A → (B & C)] & [A → (B v C)]

    Are these wffs equivalent?

11. (CHALLENGE) This sentence appeared on another logic exam:

    Exactly two of these people will participate: TINA, JOAN, and NANCY.

    I expected F1, but one student used F2.

    (F1) {[(T & J) v (T & N)] v (J & N)} & –[(T & J) & N]
    (F2) {[(T & J) & –N] v [(T & N) & –J]} v [(J & N) & –T]

    Are these wffs equivalent?

12. (CHALLENGE) In exercise 3 at the end of Chapter Four I note that

    ... every *statement is logically equivalent to some—perhaps quite involved—conditional.*

    Formulate three conditionals that are logically equivalent to S1.

    (S1) It is raining.

13. (CHALLENGE) A bumper sticker proclaims:

    (S1) If you ain't country, you ain't shit.

    This seems to be logically equivalent to S2:

    (S2) If you're shit, you're country.

    Yet while S1 is *pro*country, S2 is obviously *anti*country. Resolve this puzzle.

14. (CHALLENGE) Solve the puzzle on page 202.

1	2	3	■	4	5	6
7			■	8		
9			■	10		
■		11			■	■
12	13		■	14	15	16
17			■	18		
19			■	20		

Across

1. Is 'P → Q' true if 'Q' is true?
4. What you do if you try to apply a primitive rule to part of a line.
7. Logically equivalent to '−(−E v −R)'.
8. Inconsistent with '−A & U'.
9. Digit.
10. Sea terror.
11. Female relative.
12. Paris pal.
14. A wff full of arrows.
17. Entailed by 'S & Y'.
18. From 'E' by vI.
19. French summer.
20. Conjunction words (Fr.).

Down

1. Conjunction word.
2. Logically equivalent to 'E & O'.
3. Assumption.
4. Assumption.
5. A is a *sine qua non* for I.
6. Does '−(L & M)' entail '−(L v M)'?
12. Is '−(K & S)' false if 'K' is true and '−S' is false?
13. We'll see a MOVIE this week exactly if we receive our TAX refund.
15. Entailed by 'T ↔ −F'.
16. Is logical equivalence symmetrical?

14

Natural Arguments

14.1   Argument Identification

Deductive arguments occur in every medium involving language. They crop up in conversations, editorials, lectures, comic strips, novels, television programs, poems, scriptures, films, posters, and so on. Such sources constitute the natural habitat of arguments. Let's call arguments occurring in these sources *natural arguments.* Natural arguments differ in significant ways from *artificial arguments,* which have been invented by logicians to illustrate various logical forms or to provide practice in employing logical methods. The major difference between a natural argument and an artificial one is that the former was actually advanced by someone as an argument while the latter was not. This fact adds to the interest of natural arguments. Natural arguments often differ in other ways from their artificial cousins. Artificial arguments are usually stated in "standard form." Every essential element is explicitly expressed; no extraneous material is present; the conclusion is written after the premises. Natural arguments are almost never in standard form. Important parts may be missing, and material that is irrelevant from the standpoint of logic is probably included; the conclusion may appear before, after, or in the midst of the premises.

The main aim of a course in applied logic is to enhance the student's skill in assessing natural arguments. But natural arguments cannot be assessed unless they are identified as arguments. Familiarity with artificial arguments does not guarantee the ability to spot arguments in the "wild." In writing this text, I have done two things designed to help you apply propositional logic to natural arguments. First, I have in the exercises and examples of preceding chapters frequently presented natural arguments by using direct quotations. Often, these natural arguments were followed by my reformulations. I hoped by doing this to familiarize you with the style of natural arguments and to emphasize the differences between natural arguments and their purified reformulations. The second effort I have made to help you apply propositional logic is to include (in the present chapter) suggestions for identifying, formalizing, and assessing natural arguments.

The task of assessing a natural argument may be broken down for pedagogical purposes into four subtasks:

1. identification
2. formalization
3. evaluation of form
4. evaluation of content

The first three jobs fall within the scope of logic; to each of these I devote one section of this chapter. The fourth task involves judging the truth-value of the premises of the argument. As natural arguments cover all conceivable topics, skill in this area cannot be taught in one course or one book. Your total education (not just formal schooling) contributes to your ability to assess the content of natural arguments accurately.

How does one determine that a section of discourse contains an argument? In the main, one recognizes that a passage is argumentative by (a) having a grasp of the nature of argument and (b) understanding the passage in question. There are no foolproof clues—no certain indicators—of the presence of an argument. Nevertheless, the premise-introducing terms (such as 'since') and conclusion-introducing words (like 'therefore') are fairly reliable indicators. They are not foolproof clues for two reasons: (1) many argumentative passages contain none of these terms; and (2) some passages that contain one or more of these words do not express arguments.

Some dialogue from the film *Star Wars*[1] provides an example of argumentative discourse that lacks these indicator terms. Darth Vader and his storm troopers board Princess Leia's rebel starship and confront members of the crew.

> DARTH VADER: *Where are those transmissions you intercepted?* [*Vader grips the rebel by the throat.*]
>
> REBEL: *We intercepted no transmissions. This is a consular ship. We're on a diplomatic mission.*
>
> VADER: *If this is a consular ship, where is the ambassador?* [*Vader chokes the rebel to death.*]

[1]Written and directed by George Lucas. A Lucasfilm Ltd. Production. A Twentieth-Century-Fox Release.

How do we recognize that an argument is being employed here? In following the dialogue we realize that Vader is rejecting a claim made by the rebel and that he is giving a reason supporting the rejection. Of course, giving a reason involves advancing an argument. I discuss the structure of this argument in the next section.

An example of a passage that employs a conclusion-introducing word ('so') but does not present an argument comes from a children's book:

> *The sun was very hot and Harry had walked a long way from the main beach. He was tired, so he sat down at the water's edge.*[2]

Even though these clues are fallible, they are definitely worth bearing in mind.

A second group of indicator words is composed of statement connectives such as 'if . . . then', 'and', and so on. This set of clues is less reliable than the indicators just discussed. Quite often, compound statements occur in nonargumentive discourse. Nevertheless, because virtually every propositional argument contains one or more of these statement connectives, they provide useful clues. Note that Darth Vader's remark contained an 'if'.

In Chapter One we defined an *argument* as a set of statements, one of which (the conclusion) supposedly follows from the others (the premises). The most common use of an argument is to support the statement that occurs as the argument's conclusion—to provide a reason for thinking the conclusion true. The person advancing the argument hopes that the premises will be recognized as true and that this recognition will lead to an acceptance of the conclusion. If you determine that in a given block of discourse the author (speaker) aims to convince the reader (listener) of the truth of something, then this piece of discourse probably contains one or more arguments.

Providing support for statements is the primary use to which arguments are put, but it is not their sole use. Sometimes we employ arguments to provide *explanations* of already granted facts. The purpose in such an instance is not to establish some statement as true but (assuming that it is true) to explain *why* it is true. The statement being explained appears as the conclusion of the argument; the premises constitute the explanation.

Consider, as an example, part of the spiel of a tour guide at Thomas Edison's winter estate in Fort Myers, Florida (paraphrased):

> *Edison transplanted this rubber tree hoping that it would produce latex. However, two things are essential for the production of latex: high humidity and extended periods with temperatures above 105 degrees [Fahrenheit]. Southwest Florida has the former, but not the latter.*

---

[2]Gene Zion, *Harry by the Sea* (New York: Harper & Row, Pub., 1965), no pagination.

We can pick out this argument:

> The rubber tree produces latex only if there is high humidity and temperatures above 105 degrees. There is high humidity, but not temperatures above 105. Hence, the tree does not produce latex.

Notice that the point of the guide's remarks was not to *prove* that the tree did not produce latex, but to *explain* the nonproduction. Passages that convey explanations are likely to contain arguments.

14.2 Formalization

Having determined that some piece of discourse contains an argument, the next task is to *formalize* that argument–that is, to abstract from the passage a purified or regularized version of the argument. The first step in formalizing an argument is identifying the premises and conclusion. In addition, formalizing may involve any or all of the following operations:

- placing the conclusion last
- rephrasing so as to make apparent the connections between statements
- eliminating extraneous material
- expressing elements that, although not stated in the original, are essential parts of the argument.

When an argument has been adequately formalized, it is ordinarily easy to symbolize.

I will illustrate this process of formalization with several examples. While walking through Long Pine Key Campground in Everglades National Park, my son Mike (aged five) pointed to a travel trailer and said:

> *That one has TV because it has an antenna.*

He was giving a reason for believing that a certain travel trailer (call it *A*) sports a television set. A little effort results in this incomplete formalization:

> A has an antenna.
> So A has a TV.

It is clear that this version of the argument lacks a crucial premise–one that notes a connection between being equipped with an antenna and possessing a TV. Although no premise of this sort was overtly asserted by Mike, it is reasonable to suppose that he took some such premise for granted. What is the suppressed premise? Two candidates:

(P1) If A has an antenna, then it has a TV.
(P2) If A has a TV, then it has an antenna.

How do we choose between these statements? The ideal course would be to quiz Mike on the spot about his reasoning, but that opportunity passed 25 years ago, so we fall back on another consideration. If we select P1, the resulting argument will be an instance of *modus ponens;* if we select P2, the argument will commit the fallacy of affirming the consequent. In view of the fact that people use valid deductive arguments much more often than invalid ones, and in the absence of any indication that Mike was committing a logical error, we adopt P1. We thereby settle on formulation A1:

> (A1) A has an antenna.
> If A has an antenna, then it has a TV.
> So A has a TV.

(The order of the premises is unimportant.)

Mike's argument could also be formulated in a rather different way:

> (A2) A has an antenna.
> A is a travel trailer.
> All travel trailers that have antennas have TVs.
> So A has a TV.

A2 is a valid deductive argument that falls outside the scope of propositional logic. (Notice that it does not contain a single compound statement.) Both A1 and A2 are plausible formalizations of Mike's argument. At this point it is impossible to determine which better represents his inference. Because we are studying propositional logic, we naturally prefer A1.

Most natural arguments have one or more missing elements; we call such arguments "enthymemes." The missing parts may be premises or the conclusion or both. In the original version of the "Antenna" argument a premise was suppressed. Darth Vader's argument has an unstated premise and an unstated conclusion. Vader asks the question, 'If this is a consular ship, where is the ambassador?' He is refuting the rebel's claim that the cruiser is a consular ship, citing as evidence the absence of an ambassador. Vader's inference is *modus tollens*:

> If this is a consular ship, there is an ambassador on board.
> There is no ambassador on board.
> Therefore, this is not a consular ship.

One could also give a more complex interpretation of Vader's reasoning with an argument whose conclusion is reflected in Vader's act of killing the rebel.

> If you are telling the truth, this is a consular ship.
> If this is a consular ship, there is an ambassador on board.
> There is no ambassador on board.
> If you are not telling the truth, you are a rebel.
> Therefore, you are a rebel.

A final example of an enthymematic argument derives from a conversation with a colleague concerning a mutual acquaintance. My colleague said:

Royer's degree must not be in philosophy because Arizona State does not give the Ph.D. in philosophy.

A first attempt at formalization yields the following:

Arizona State does not give the Ph.D. in philosophy.
Royer's Ph.D. is from Arizona State.
Thus, Royer's Ph.D. is not in philosophy.

Notice that no simple statement occurs more than once in this formalization. An additional premise joining the parts of the argument is required for satisfactory treatment by propositional logic. A little thought suggests this premise:

If Royer's Ph.D. is in philosophy and from Arizona State, then Arizona State does give the Ph.D. in philosophy.

When we add this obviously true premise, the resulting argument is assessed as valid by the methods of propositional logic.

I conclude this discussion by comparing the process of formalization with the translation of a passage from one natural language (say, English) to another (German). It is not true that there is just one correct German translation of a given English passage; there can be several. But, on the other hand, it is not the case that *any* translation is as good as any other; some will definitely be defective. In the same way there will ordinarily be several distinct satisfactory formalizations of the argument contained in some passage; yet, some formalizations will obviously be incorrect. A further analogy between formalization and translation should be noted: In both activities, skill is gained largely through practice. The passages at the end of this chapter will provide practice in the art of formalizing arguments.

14.3 Evaluation

Having formalized an argument, you should be able to judge whether it falls within the scope of propositional logic. If the argument is not propositional, then (at this stage in your study of logic) you are forced to fall back upon your native logical intuition. The chances are that this intuitive assessment will be correct. If this approach leaves you unsatisfied, you will want to explore additional branches of logic. One area of logic that is built upon propositional logic and that can adequately treat many arguments beyond the capacity of propositional logic is called *predicate logic* or *quantificational logic*.

If the formalized argument in question is propositional, it should be symbolized. The sequent may exhibit a familiar pattern whose validity (or invalidity) you have established; in this case further testing is unnecessary. Although there is an infinite variety of forms of valid propositional arguments, most of the valid propositional arguments one encounters can be sorted out among a small group of argument patterns. Likewise, although there exists an infinite variety of forms of invalid propositional arguments, most of the invalid propositional arguments one actually encounters exhibit one or another of a few basic forms. The most common valid and invalid patterns are listed in the table below. Each pattern was discussed in some earlier chapter.

Common Argument Patterns

Valid		Invalid	
Name	Pattern	Pattern	Name
modus ponens	$P \rightarrow Q, P \vdash Q$	$P \rightarrow Q, Q \vdash P$	affirming the consequent
modus tollens	$P \rightarrow Q, -Q \vdash -P$	$P \rightarrow Q, -P \vdash -Q$	denying the antecedent
disjunctive argument	$P \vee Q, -P \vdash Q$ $P \vee Q, -Q \vdash P$	$P \vee Q, P \vdash -Q$ $P \vee Q, Q \vdash -P$	affirming a disjunct
conjunctive argument	$-(P \& Q), P \vdash -Q$ $-(P \& Q), Q \vdash -P$	$-(P \& Q), -P \vdash Q$ $-(P \& Q), -Q \vdash P$	denying a conjunct
chain argument	$P \rightarrow Q, Q \rightarrow R \vdash P \rightarrow R$		
dilemma	$P \rightarrow Q, R \rightarrow Q, P \vee R \vdash Q$ $P \rightarrow Q, R \rightarrow S, P \vee R \vdash Q \vee S$		

If the argument under examination is propositional but exhibits an unfamiliar logical form, you can evaluate it with one of the methods that we have examined in the preceding chapters.

EXERCISES

Instructions for exercises 1 through 26: For each passage determine whether it contains an argument. Label nonargumentive passages 'No Argument'. For argumentative passages follow steps (1) through (3). (1) Formalize the argument taking care to supply any suppressed elements. (2) Symbolize the argument, indicating for each capital employed the statement it abbreviates. (3) Demonstrate validity or invalidity using one of the techniques explained in the book.

1. "[Coach] Kevin Loughery is gone unless the Heat moves deep into the postseason. That's not going to happen, so Loughery is gone."

–Edwin Pope, "It's a Shame–
Only a Miracle Will Save Kevin,"
Miami Herald (March 23, 1994), p. 1D.

*2. "If the stock market never fluctuated, then stock would have no market risk. Of course, the market does fluctuate, so market risk is present."

—Eugene F. Brigham, *Fundamentals of Financial Management*
(Hinsdale, Ill.: Dryden Press, 1978), p. 116.

3. Garrick Utley reported for "ABC World News Tonight" (program of November 21, 1996) on the failure of authorities to arrest Bosnian war criminals: "A year ago President Clinton and others warned that there would be no peace in Bosnia without justice. Today there is still no justice."

4. "Had M. de Saint Alard been the criminal, he would never have kept an incriminating bottle. Finding it was a proof of his innocence."

—Agatha Christie, "Poirot Investigates" in *Triple Threat*
(Binghamton, N.Y.: Vail-Ballou Press, 1923), p. 282.

5. "He discovered that he had a scorching thirst. His face was so dry and grimy that he thought he could feel his skin crackle. Each bone of his body had an ache in it, and seemingly threatened to break with each movement. His feet were like two sores. Also, his body was calling for food. It was more powerful than a direct hunger. There was a dull, weightlike feeling in his stomach, and, when he tried to walk, his head swayed and he tottered."

—Stephen Crane, *The Red Badge of Courage and Selected Stories*
(New York: New American Library, 1980), p. 70.

*6. "But of course mice are famous for something," [Maximilian said].

"Don't be so sure," said the monkey as Maximilian turned to go. "If you're famous, why aren't you in the zoo?" called the monkey as Maximilian scampered away.

". . . They're right," he decided. "If mice were famous for anything, they'd have one in the zoo. And they don't."

—Florence Heide, *Maximilian Becomes Famous*
(New York: Funk & Wagnalls, 1969), no pagination.

7. ". . . This time she found a little bottle . . . , and tied around the neck of the bottle was a paper label, with the word 'DRINK ME' beautifully printed on it in large letters.

"It was all very well to say 'Drink me,' but the wise little Alice was not going to do *that* in a hurry. 'No, I'll look first,' she said, 'and see whether it's marked "*poison*" or not'; for . . . she had never forgotten that, if you drink much from a bottle marked 'poison,' it is almost certain to disagree with you, sooner or later.

"However, this bottle was *not* marked 'poison,' so Alice ventured to taste it. . . . "

—Lewis Carroll, *Alice's Adventures in
Wonderland, Through the Looking-glass,*
and *The Hunting of the Snark*
(New York: The Modern Library, n.d.), pp. 30–31.

8. "[Martina] Navratilova said she had flirted with the idea of vegetarianism for years. 'Someone always talked me out of it,' she said. 'It was definitely a gradual decision, something that I thought about for a long time.'

"An animal lover whose dog K.D. (Killer Dog) travels with her, she said a pheasant hunting trip with a friend was the catalyst.

"'The first year I went, it didn't bother me,' she said. 'The second year it did. I figured that if I was not willing to shoot it myself, why should I be willing to eat it? There were choices there and I thought I didn't have to be killing anything in order to eat dinner.'"

–Pam Smith O'Hara,
"Vegetarianism a Smashing Success for Navratilova,"
Miami Herald (December 5, 1996), p. 4E.

9.

Reprinted with special permission of King Features Syndicate.

10. "... (i) If the thing b has the disposition D_{SR} and the condition S is fulfilled for b, then ... the result R holds for b.

"Therefore:

"(ii) If S holds for b, but R does not, then b cannot have the disposition D_{SR}."

–Rudolf Carnap, "The Methodological Character of Theoretical Concepts," in *Minnesota Studies in the Philosophy of Science*, ed. Herbert Feigl and Michael Scriven (Minneapolis: University of Minnesota Press, 1956), I: 67.

*11. Conversation overheard at Coffman Memorial Union on the campus of the University of Minnesota:

SECURITY GUARD: *There's a really strong smoke smell in here. Think I should check out the penthouse?*

NIGHT MANAGER: *No, forget it. I just heard on the news that the biggest fire in ten years is burning down the street.*

12. "And when they drew near to Jerusalem and came to Bethphage, to the Mount of Olives, then Jesus sent two disciples, saying to them, 'Go into the village opposite you, and immediately you will find an ass tied, and a colt with her; untie them and bring them to me. If anyone says anything

to you, you shall say, 'The Lord has need of them,' and he will send them immediately.'"

–Matthew 21:1–3, Revised Standard Version
(New York: Thomas Nelson & Sons, 1952).

13. "So, if utilitarianism is true, . . . then it is better that people should not believe in utilitarianism. If, on the other hand, it is false, then it is certainly better that people should not believe in it. So, either way, it is better that people should not believe in it."

–Bernard Williams, *Morality: An Introduction to Ethics*
(New York: Harper & Row, Pub., 1972), p. 107.

*14.

15. "Hayden oil coolers–If you've got money to burn, you don't need one."

–Radio commercial.

16. "Finally, if stress and cancer are linked, wouldn't people subjected to unusual degrees of stress–prisoners of war, for instance–show higher rates of cancer later on in their lives? Robert J. Keehn of the Medical Follow-up Agency of the National Academy of Sciences National Research Council recently looked at this particular phenomenon. After studying former World War II and Korean War prisoners, Keehn found their cancer death rates were no different from cancer death rates in the population at large."

–M. Scarf, "Images That Heal,"
Psychology Today, XIV (September, 1980), 43.

17. Dialogue between Bruce Ennis of the American Civil Liberties Union and Chief Justice William Rehnquist in oral argument of the Communications Decency Act case before the Supreme Court on May 19, 1997:

ENNIS: *If you are not a commercial speaker,[3] most credit card companies will not verify the credit card at all, period, for any cost.*

REHNQUIST: *So if you're a commercial speaker, they will?*

---

[3]Mr. Ennis defined a "commercial speaker" as a speaker who charges for access to his or her speech.

*18. "DENVER–(AP)–Police hunting for the driver in the 100-mph hit-and-run death of a newspaper columnist tracked down the suspect through a piece of the car–a "cosmos black" $56,000 BMW so rare there are only three of them in Colorado. . . .

" . . . Two of them were accounted for and could not have been involved in the accident, police said."

–"A Second Sad Twist to Hit-and-run; Suspect
in Fatal Accident Dies, an Apparent Suicide,"
Miami Herald (March 21, 1996), p. 3A.

19. "A woman accompanied her husband to the doctor's office. After the checkup, the doctor told the wife, 'If you don't do the following, your husband will surely die:

"'1. Each morning, fix him a healthy breakfast and send him off to work in a good mood.

"'2. At lunchtime, make him a warm nutritious meal and put him in a good frame of mind before he goes back to work.

"'3. For dinner, fix an especially nice meal, and don't burden him with household chores.

"'4. Have sex with him several times a week and satisfy his every whim.'

"On the way home, the husband asked his wife what the doctor had said. 'You're going to die,' she replied."

"Nancy Carlisle, Blackfoot, Idaho"
–"Health Jokes," *American Health*
(March, 1992), p. 73.

20.

By permission of Johnny Hart and Creators Syndicate, Inc.

21. Newton Davis (Steve Martin) explains to his parents why they cannot invite the parents of the woman pretending to be his fiancée, Gwen (Goldie Hawn), to a reception: "Well, Gwen's parents are divorced. And what's more they hate each other, and you can't invite one and not the other, and if you get the two of them in the same room at the same time, it's bedlam."

–*Housesitter* (MCA Universal, 1992).

*22. "I was particularly anxious to learn . . . why the Nile, at the commencement of the summer solstice, begins to rise, and continues to increase for a hundred days—and why, as soon as that number is past, it forthwith retires and contracts its stream, continuing low during the whole of the winter until the summer solstice comes round again. On none of these points could I obtain any explanation from the inhabitants. . . .

"Some of the Greeks, however, wishing to get a reputation for cleverness, have offered explanations of the phenomena of the river. . . .One pretends that the Etesian winds cause the rise of the river by preventing the Nile-water from running off into the sea. But . . . if the Etesian winds produced the effect, the other rivers which flow in a direction opposite to those winds ought to present the same phenomena as the Nile, and the more so as they are all smaller streams, and have a weaker current. But these rivers, of which there are many both in Syria and Libya, are entirely unlike the Nile in this respect."

—Herodotus, *History,* trans. George Rawlinson
(New York: Dutton, 1910), Vol. I, Book II, Chapters 19–20.

23. A film about the French Foreign Legion, *Desert Sands* (United Artists), includes this dialogue:

CAPTAIN: *Well, Lieutenant, I guess we'd better turn in.*

LIEUTENANT: *Sir, I thought we'd wait up for the [relief] column.*

CAPTAIN: *Oh, sitting up all night may sound more romantic, Lieutenant, but it's not going to help them much. If everything is all right, then we've lost a lot of sleep for nothing. If it isn't—I'd rather we got some sleep now. Good night, Lieutenant.*

24.

PEANUTS. © United Feature Syndicate. Reprinted by permission.

25. (CHALLENGE) "Many theories . . . have been advanced to explain the origin of the cuckoo laying its eggs in other birds' nests. M. Prévost alone, I think, has thrown light by his observations on this puzzle: he finds that the female cuckoo, which, according to most observers, lays at least from four to six eggs, must pair with the male each time after laying only one or two eggs. Now, if the cuckoo was obliged to sit on her own eggs, she would either have to sit on all together, and therefore leave those first laid so long, that they probably would become addled; or she would have to hatch separately each egg or two eggs, as soon as laid: but as the cuckoo stays a shorter time in this country than any other migratory bird, she certainly would not have time enough for the successive hatchings. Hence we can perceive in the fact of the cuckoo pairing several times, and laying her eggs at intervals, the cause of her depositing her eggs in other birds' nests, and leaving them to the care of foster-parents."

> —Charles Darwin, *The Voyage of the Beagle*
> (London: Dent, 1959), pp. 50–51.

26. (CHALLENGE) "Let me summarize . . . [my formulation of St. Anselm's second ontological] proof. If God, a being a greater than which cannot be conceived, does not exist then He cannot *come* into existence. For if He did He would either have been *caused* to come into existence or have *happened* to come into existence, and in either case He would be a limited being, which by our conception of Him He is not. Since He cannot come into existence, if He does not exist His existence is impossible. If He does exist He cannot have come into existence (for the reasons given), nor can He cease to exist, for nothing could cause Him to cease to exist nor could it just happen that He ceased to exist. So if God exists His existence is necessary. Thus God's existence is either impossible or necessary. It can be the former only if the concept of such a being is self-contradictory or in some way logically absurd. Assuming that this is not so, it follows that He necessarily exists."

> —Norman Malcolm, "Anselm's Ontological Arguments,"
> *Philosophical Review,* LXIX (1960), 49–50.

27. (CHALLENGE) Locate in newspapers, magazines, books (other than logic texts), films, television broadcasts, or radio broadcasts five natural arguments that fall within the scope of propositional logic. For each argument provide (1) an accurate quotation of the argument in its original form,[4] (2) a reference to the source (including title, date, and page number); (3) your formalization of the argument (with needed suppressed elements supplied); (4) a symbolization of your formalization (including a dictionary that indicates for each capital the statement it abbreviates); and (5) an assessment of the argument that employs some technique explained in this book.

---

[4] Consider clipping or photocopying long passages.

Metatheory: Soundness and Completeness of the System PL

William G. Lycan

In this book we began by considering particular arguments stated in English. Then we abstracted their logical forms, representing them by means of sequent expressions. Then we considered sequents that did not result from translation of any particular English arguments, but represented logical forms only. Then we introduced script metavariables, any of which can stand for any formula of our logical system, simple or compound. Well, now we are going to jump up yet another level of abstraction. This new ascent will be of little use in the analysis and evaluation of arguments given in everyday language, but it is of crucial importance to logicians. Namely: Having learned Professor Pospesel's system of formal proof, which consists of his inference rules and instructions for applying them, we will now look at the system itself and examine some of its features. Until now, we have been *using* the system to prove various sequents. But now we shall step back and upward, to look at the system as a whole, and, in a more abstract language, prove things *about* it; this sort of activity is called "metatheory." To get used to the idea, let's give the system a nice, romantic name: "**PL**," for *propositional logic* or *Pospesel's logic* as you prefer.

PL, then, includes: (i) The formation rules (provided in Section 8.3) that define what officially counts as a well-formed formula of Pospeselese; (ii) the primitive rules of inference: →O, &I, &O, →I, –I, –O, ↔I, ↔O, vI and vO; and, not very importantly, (iii) the derived rules presented in Chapter Nine.

For our metatheoretical investigation, we shall require that every proof have an assumption-dependence column. That is because every rule has its official assumption-dependence principle as an essential component, whether or not assumption-dependence is explicitly recorded in every proof. In fact, let's slightly reconceive the applying of a rule.

It is easy to think of applying a rule as *deriving a formula,* either from one or more previous formulas or on the basis of a completed subderivation. But as was pointed out in Chapter Four, each line of a proof constitutes the validation of a whole sequent–namely that sequent which has the formula on that line as conclusion and has as premises the assumptions listed in the line's assumption-dependence column. When we apply a rule, we establish the resulting sequent on the basis of the set of sequents associated with the relevant earlier lines of the proof. For example: In the proof

1	(1)	A & B	A
2	(2)	A → C	A
1	(3)	A	1 &O
1,2	(4)	C	2,3 →O

the application of Arrow Out at line 4 takes us from the sequents A → C ⊢ A → C and A & B ⊢ A to the new sequent A & B, A → C ⊢ C. And in the proof

1	(1)	A & B	A
2	(2)	C	PA
1	(3)	A	1 &O
1,2	(4)	A & C	3,2 &I
1	(5)	C → (A & C)	2-4 →I

the application of Arrow In at line 5 takes us from the sequent A & B, C ⊢ A & C to the sequent A & B ⊢ C → (A &C). (Line 4 records the needed sub-derivation of A & C, from C with the aid of the assumption A & B.) From now on we shall think of rules as proving sequents from other sequents, and I shall talk of a given rule's "input" sequent(s) and "output" sequent.

With these preliminaries behind us, what do we want to know, and show, about **PL**? Two things, mainly. To explain them will take a little review.

A concept of *validity* was introduced in Section 1.2. But now we can and must distinguish three separate concepts of validity:

- *Intuitive* validity is what some arguments and argument forms are felt to have by competent speakers of English; an argument is intuitively valid if, without special training in symbolic logic, such speakers judge that its conclusion follows from its premises.
- We award a verdict of "valid" to a sequent when we prove that sequent formally. Validity in this second sense is *provability* in **PL** itself.
- *Truth-table* validity is what is shown when a sequent is given a truth table's seal of approval.

Though they are supposed to be closely related, those three notions are defined differently; on their face, they are not exactly the same.[1] If any two of them are thought to coincide, that will have to be argued, because it isn't at all obvious.

We already have ample evidence that provability does not coincide with intuitive validity: There are intuitively valid arguments stated in English that

---

[1]Of course, there is a fourth notion, corresponding to Chapter 11's method of truth trees, but in the interest of brevity I shall set it aside.

cannot be translated into provable sequents of **PL**, and there are sequents provable in **PL** that are not intuitively valid (see Appendix 2). Philosophers, and we users of **PL**, may make of that what we like, but our purpose here is instead to look at the relation between provability and truth-table validity.

On page 158, it was asserted that provability and truth-table validity coincide—that *every provable sequent is truth-table valid* and that *every truth-table-valid sequent is provable*. But those are two highly substantive, daring claims. They are (as a matter of fact) true, but they need to be demonstrated.

The relation is a little one-sided: I would argue[2] that as between provability and truth-table validity, the latter is "real" validity: A truth table is a graphic display of *all the possibilities there are* with respect to a given propositional argument, and its great virtue is that it allows us simply to list those possibilities and (literally) see whether there is any possibility of the argument's conclusion being false while its premises are true. In this sense, the notion of truth-table validity flows directly from our original definition of "valid." So we want our inference rules and our whole system **PL** to be adequate to *it,* not vice versa. We want every provable sequent to be truth-table valid; otherwise there is something wrong with the system. And we want every truth-table-valid sequent to be provable in the system; otherwise there is something wrong with the system. The first property is called *soundness* (or sometimes "consistency"). The second is called *completeness*. Let's begin with soundness.

PL is sound, then, iff every sequent provable in **PL** is truth-table valid. (A shorter word for truth-table validity is "tautologous"; I shall use it from now on.) How might we show that every sequent provable in **PL** is tautologous?

The first problem here is that *infinitely many* sequents are provable in **PL**.[3] So we cannot examine all the provable sequents one at a time and check whether each one is tautologous. We have to find a way of dealing with an infinite class of items.

In mathematics, that way is called *proof by induction,* though we needn't worry about the specifically mathematical applications here. The method works when one's infinite class has the shape of a *one-ended chain* reaching off indefinitely in one direction. That is, it has a first link, and then a second, and then a third, and so on, without limit. The idea is that there is a unique first element, and every element (the first and every other) has exactly one successor.[4] Fortunately for us, every proof in **PL**, in particular, has that very shape. The

---

[2]This claim is *a little* controversial among philosophers, but not very.

[3]This is true for several reasons. First, there is no limit on the length of **PL** formulas; a formula can be arbitrarily long and complicated. Second, there is no limit on the number of premises an argument may have. Third, for every provable sequent, every *substitution-instance* of that sequent is also provable. (A sequent S1 is a "substitution-instance" of a sequent S2 just in case S1 results from uniformly replacing each of S2's sentence letters by a wff.) And, fourth, since (again) there is no limit on the length of **PL** formulas, every sequent has infinitely many substitution-instances. If you find this confusing, relax and take my word for it.

key things to see are (a) that every correct proof begins in the same way, by one or more applications of the Assumption Rule A, and (b) that after that standard beginning they proceed in stages, by the application of one rule at a time. Now: Suppose we can show (a) that *the Assumption Rule cannot be used to prove a nontautologous sequent,* and (b) that *every other inference rule of* **PL** *is "safe," in that it cannot possibly take us from a set of tautologous sequents to a nontautologous one.* Then, since a whole proof in **PL** is nothing but a stepwise sequence of individual rule applications, it would follow that no proof could result in a nontautologous sequent, which is to say that every provable sequent is tautologous, which is to say that **PL** is sound.

Happily, we can establish both (a) and (b); (a) is entirely obvious: No application of the Assumption Rule ever does anything but prove a sequent of the form $\mathcal{A} \vdash \mathcal{A}$. And no sequent of that form could fail to be tautologous, since its conclusion is the very same formula as its premise and so can't very well be false while the premise is true. All we need to do, then, is show (b).

To do that, we need to examine each of our primitive rules in turn, and show that it is incapable of taking us from a set of tautologous sequents to a nontautologous one. Let's start right in with Arrow Out.

→O

First we need a bit of notation. If we're going to talk abstractly and generally about a given rule, without reference to any particular sequent or proof, we'll need a generic way of representing the rule and its assumption-dependence routine. I'll represent Arrow Out in this way:

$$[\alpha] \vdash \mathcal{A} \to \mathcal{B}$$
$$\underline{[\beta] \vdash \mathcal{A}}$$
$$[\alpha],[\beta] \vdash \mathcal{B}$$

What that means is: The rule applies to two lines of a proof, each line representing a sequent from some set of assumptions to a formula of a certain form (respectively, a conditional and the conditional's antecedent). The bracketed Greek letters stand for the assumption sets.[5] What is below the line shows both

---

[4]Example for the curious: There are infinitely many natural numbers (the integers 0, 1, 2, . . .). How could we prove that each and every one of them has some property P? Suppose we can show (a) that 0 has P, and we can also show (b) that for any natural number that has P, its successor has P also. Then we would know that since 0 has P and 1 is 0's successor, 1 has P as well, and since 2 is 1's successor, 2 must have P as well, and so on through the whole infinite list. Therefore, the proofs of (a) and (b) taken together amount to a proof that every natural number has P.

[5]As we have seen more than once, a line of a proof may rest on no assumptions at all, so the "set" [α] or [β] might be empty or null.

the nature of the conclusion (it's the conditional's consequent) and the assumptions that the conclusion rests on, viz., the accumulated sum of all the assumptions from the two lines to which Arrow Out was applied. So the above diagram is to be read as saying that when you have a conditional resting on assumptions so-and-so, and you also have that conditional's antecedent resting on assumptions such-and-such, you can infer the conditional's consequent, resting on the sum of the two original bodies of assumptions.

Now, how do we show that Arrow Out cannot lead from a pair of tautologous sequents to a nontautologous one? Let's try an informal *reductio ad absurdum,* reminiscent of the brief-truth-table method.

Hypothetically suppose that the two input sequents are tautologous but the output sequent is not. Then since the output sequent is not tautologous, there must be at least one assignment of truth-values to the atomic sentence letters occurring in the formulas $A \rightarrow B$ and A that makes all the assumptions in $[\alpha]$ and $[\beta]$ true but B false. But then the same assignment makes all of $[\alpha]$ and $[\beta]$ true where they occurred at the two original lines as well, and since we're supposing that the two original sequents are tautologous, that means the formulas $A \rightarrow B$ and A must be true under the assignment in question. But then, by elementary truth-table reasoning, the conclusion B must be true after all on the same assignment, which contradicts our claim that B is false. Our original hypothesis (that the two input sequents are tautologous but the output sequent is not) has led to contradiction and so cannot be true; thus, Arrow Out cannot take us from a pair of tautologous sequents to a nontautologous one, which is to say it is a "safe" or sound rule.

&I

Ampersand In is:

$$[\alpha] \vdash A$$
$$\underline{[\beta] \vdash B}$$
$$[\alpha],[\beta] \vdash A \ \& \ B$$

Reasoning exactly parallel to our argument about Arrow Out succeeds here too: Suppose the two input sequents are tautologous but the output sequent isn't. Then there is at least one row of a truth table that makes all the assumptions in $[\alpha]$ and $[\beta]$ true but the conjunction $A \ \& \ B$ false. But, since the input sequents are stipulated to be tautologous, that means each of A and B must be true at the row in question—in which case their conjunction $A \ \& \ B$ would have to be true at that row also, contradicting our hypothesis. So, as before, it cannot be that the two input sequents are tautologous but the output sequent is not; &I is sound.

(Actually, &I is so simple that we needn't have used the indirect *reductio* style, but could have put it this way: If the two input sequents are tautologous, then any assignment of truth-values to atomic sentence letters that makes both the assumption sets [α] and [β] true will also make the formulas A and B true. But by truth table, when A and B are both true, so is A & B, so there is no assignment that makes [α] and [β] true but A & B false—which is to say that the output sequent must be tautologous also.)

Similar reasoning holds for every other rule that goes by the standard cumulative assumption-dependence routine: &O, ↔I, ↔O, vI and vO. (It would be a good exercise to write out a few of those arguments.) But the other rules have the more complicated assumption-dependence patterns, involving subproofs.

→I

In our metatheoretic notation, Arrow In will be represented in this way:

$$\frac{[\alpha], PA_n(A) \vdash B}{[\alpha] \vdash A \to B}$$

The idea is that when we have a subproof of B resting on a provisional assumption A plus (perhaps) some other assumptions [α], we get to infer $A \to B$ on the basis of the remaining assumptions [α] if any. (The new notation "$PA_n(A)$" represents the provisional assumption A that was made at line n.)

Now, for the argument that Arrow In is sound: Suppose the input sequent is tautologous but the output sequent isn't. Then there is a truth-table row at which the assumptions in [α] are true but $A \to B$ is false, and at that row A must be true and B must be false. But that very row invalidates the input sequent, contrary to our supposition, because it makes [α] and A true but B false. (Contradiction; out supposition cannot be true; if the input sequent is tautologous the output sequent must be also; Arrow In is sound.)

−I

Dash In is represented as:

$$\frac{[\alpha], PA_n(A) \vdash B \& -B}{[\alpha] \vdash -A}$$

Try to suppose the input sequent is tautologous and the output sequent isn't. Then there must be a truth-table row that makes the assumption set [α] all true but $-A$ false. At that row, accordingly, A is true. But then our input sequent would have all true assumptions, and if it is to be tautologous, its conclusion

B & −*B* would be true also. Yet *B* & −*B* cannot be true; its truth table goes "F, F." So there is no such truth-table row as we tried to hypothesize. If the output sequent is not tautologous, the input sequent can't be either; Dash In is sound.

Almost exactly similar reasoning shows that Dash Out is sound.

The Derived Rules

MT, DA, CA, and the rest all obey the standard assumption-dependence principle, and could be shown sound by reasoning like that which we employed for Arrow Out and Ampersand In. But there is no need to do that: Derived rules merely abbreviate segments of proofs that have been accomplished using the primitive rules. Therefore, since the primitive rules are sound, the derived ones will be also.

We have established the soundness of **PL**. (Let's call this Metatheorem (1).) Completeness is a good deal harder, and space is limited, so I am not going to do the entire proof. Instead, I'll just indicate in outline how it would go.[6]

We need to show that for every tautologous sequent, **PL** affords at least one correct proof of that sequent. The best way of showing that (some philosophers contend, the only legitimate way) is to provide a *general recipe* for proof construction, as well as a compelling argument that the recipe is guaranteed to succeed every time. That is, we should come up with a set of instructions so general and so powerful that, when they are applied to any arbitrarily chosen tautologous sequent whatever, they reliably generate a correct **PL**-proof of that sequent. At this point in our progress, it's an open question whether we (or anyone) will be able to do that. We don't yet know whether we have enough rules.

In math and in computer science, a demonstrably guaranteed recipe for constructing some particular kind of derivation (or other mathematical item) is called an *algorithm*. An algorithm starts with a task to be performed given certain materials, and consists of a recipe for completing that task given those materials, plus a demonstration that the recipe is sure-fire and cannot fail. In our completeness proof for **PL**, what we are seeking is an algorithm that, given any tautologous sequent whatever, turns out a correct **PL**-proof of that sequent.

Big complicated algorithms can be made out of smaller, less ambitious algorithms (just as a complicated recipe in cooking can be composed of several subrecipes for the various main components of the finished product), and that will be the case for our completeness proof.

Here is a simple little algorithm regarding **PL**. (It's *really* simple, nearly trivial. I offer it, at this point, just to illustrate the general form or format of an

---

[6]My overall strategy, like **PL** itself, is based on E. J. Lemmon's *Beginning Logic*.

algorithm.) *Task*: Given that a sequent $\mathcal{A} \vdash \mathcal{B}$ is provable, show that one can also prove the premiseless sequent[7] $\vdash \mathcal{A} \to \mathcal{B}$.

Recipe: Take the proof of $\mathcal{A} \vdash \mathcal{B}$ (however it may go). Add a step of Arrow In, conditionalizing $\mathcal{A}$ onto $\mathcal{B}$–and you're done.

Demonstration: Obvious, if we know how Arrow In works. (Since $\mathcal{A}$ is the original sequent's only assumption, none will be left behind after it is discharged and removed by $\to$I.)

Here's another algorithmic argument, again for illustration, though it will also figure in our completeness proof. Given a sequent $\mathcal{A}_1, \mathcal{A}_2, \dots \mathcal{A}_n \vdash \mathcal{B}$, call the corresponding single formula $\mathcal{A}_1 \to (\mathcal{A}_2 \to (\dots (\mathcal{A}_n \to \mathcal{B}) \dots))$ that sequent's *associated conditional*.[8] Then we can show that, if a sequent's associated conditional is provable in **PL**, the sequent itself is also provable in **PL**.

So (*task*:) we are given some correct proof of the associated conditional $\mathcal{A}_1 \to (\mathcal{A}_2 \to (\dots (\mathcal{A}_n \to \mathcal{B}) \dots))$, and instructed to produce a proof of the original sequent $\mathcal{A}_1, \mathcal{A}_2, \dots \mathcal{A}_n \vdash \mathcal{B}$.

Recipe: Take the associated conditional and, using the Assumption Rule, assume its *n* embedded conditional antecedents one after the other, thus:

```
1   (1)   𝒜₁   A
2   (2)   𝒜₂   A
         .
         .
         .
n   (n)   𝒜ₙ   A
```

Then append the proof of the associated conditional (however it may go, and renumbering its step (1) as step (n + 1) and so on down). Then perform n successive steps of Arrow Out, using premises (1), (2), ... (n) in order. The result will be a correct proof of the sequent $\mathcal{A}_1, \mathcal{A}_2, \dots \mathcal{A}_n \vdash \mathcal{B}$.

Demonstration: Obvious, given the way Arrow Out works. (If you don't find it so obvious, try it for yourself.) And so we have established that if a sequent's associated conditional is provable in **PL**, the sequent itself is also provable in **PL**; let's call this result "Metatheorem (2)."

Now I'll outline a completeness proof for **PL**. The "demonstrations" for the various subalgorithms will continue to be nearly trivial given knowledge of the way **PL**'s rules work; that is a virtue, not a defect.

---

[7]Remember that in Chapter 4 the notion of a "sequent" was broadened to include sequents whose premise sets are null. Logicians sometimes call such sequents "theorems."

[8]This concept of an "associated conditional" should be distinguished from the concept of a "corresponding conditional" that was introduced in Section 12.1.

My general strategy will be to show that there are complicated patterns of **PL** proof that *imitate* the truth tables. Thus, if all our usual proof strategies were to fail, one of these more complicated patterns—however unintuitive and ugly—would eventually succeed by mimicking a truth-table test itself.[9]

Stage 1

To show: (**3**) That for any formula A and for any assignment of truth-values to A's atomic sentence letters L_1, L_2, ... (that is, any row of A's truth table), we can in **PL** prove either the sequent $L_1/-L_1$, $L_2/-L_2$, ... $\vdash A$ or the sequent $L_1/-L_1$, $L_2/-L_2$, ... $\vdash -A$, depending on whether the various sentence letters and the formula A are true or false on the assignment (at the row) in question. The notation "$L_n/-L_n$" means the atomic letter L_n or its negation, depending on whether the given assignment gives that letter the value T or the value F.

Example: Take this one row of the truth table for the formula (A & B) v C.

A	B	C		(A & B) v C
T	F	F		F

Then, according to Metatheorem (**3**), there is in **PL** a correct proof of the sequent A, −B, −C ⊢ −[(A & B) v C]. Informally, the idea is that for any formula and any row of that formula's truth table, a certain sequent corresponding to that row can be proved in **PL**.

Recipe: Again we follow the pattern of mathematical induction, though over the step-by-step structure of formulas themselves rather than (as in the soundness argument) the step-by-step nature of **PL**-proof. Though it is not immediately apparent that individual **PL** formulas have "step-by-step structure," in fact the grammatical composition of any well-formed formula itself has the desirable one-ended-chain shape: Remember that, as was shown in Section 8.3, every formula of **PL** is the result of starting with some atomic sentence letter(s) and applying the connectives, *one by one,* in some order or other as marked by grouping symbols.

The idea is to demonstrate, first that (**3**) is true of atomic formulas, and then that (**3**) is true of any formula made by applying − to any formula, or →, &, v, or ↔ to any pair of formulas.

The first of those two claims is easily shown to be true. If A is an atomic formula, its truth table is just

---

[9]You may wonder: If the rules are going to be used merely to mimic the truth tables, what's the point? The point is to show that the rules of **PL** are indeed collectively powerful enough to do what truth tables do—which is anything but obvious.

$$\begin{array}{c|c} \mathcal{A} & \mathcal{A} \\ \hline T & T \\ F & F \end{array}$$

So the two sequents to be proved are $\mathcal{A} \vdash \mathcal{A}$ and $-\mathcal{A} \vdash -\mathcal{A}$. And each of those is proved in one step by the Assumption Rule. (The simplest imaginable algorithm!)

But then we must also address each connective of **PL** and show that, for every formula made by applying that connective to one or more simpler formulas that obey Metatheorem (**3**), that formula also obeys Metatheorem (**3**). For example, if $\mathcal{A}$ and $\mathcal{B}$ each obey Metatheorem (**3**), then $\mathcal{A}$ & $\mathcal{B}$ obeys Metatheorem (**3**)–and so on for every other connective in **PL**.

Let's stick with $\mathcal{A}$ & $\mathcal{B}$. By hypothesis, (**3**) holds of the two conjunct formulas $\mathcal{A}$ and $\mathcal{B}$ themselves; we are to show that if that is true, then (**3**) also holds of their conjunction.

If (**3**) holds of $\mathcal{A}$ and $\mathcal{B}$ themselves, then for any row of their common truth table, where $L_1, L_2, \ldots L_n$ are the atomic sentence letters occurring in $\mathcal{A}$, and $M_1, M_2, \ldots M_o$ are those occurring in $\mathcal{B}$, there exist proofs of two sequents:

(a) Either $L_1/-L_1, L_2/-L_2, \ldots L_n/-L_n \vdash \mathcal{A}$
or $L_1/-L_1, L_2/-L_2, \ldots L_n/-L_n \vdash -\mathcal{A}$,

depending on whether $\mathcal{A}$ is true or false at the given row, and

(b) Either $M_1/-M_1, M_2/-M_2, \ldots M_o/-M_o \vdash \mathcal{B}$
or $M_1/-M_1, M_2/-M_2, \ldots M_o/-M_o \vdash -\mathcal{B}$,

ditto for $\mathcal{B}$.

Now, there are four possible truth-value combinations for the two conjunct formulas $\mathcal{A}$ and $\mathcal{B}$; let's take each case in the usual order.

(i) Suppose $\mathcal{A}$ and $\mathcal{B}$ are both true. Then there are proofs of

$$L_1/-L_1, L_2/-L_2, \ldots L_n/-L_n \vdash \mathcal{A}$$

and

$$M_1/-M_1, M_2/-M_2, \ldots M_o/-M_o \vdash \mathcal{B}.$$

To (*task:*) convert those two proofs into a single proof of $\mathcal{A}$ & $\mathcal{B}$, (*recipe:*) simply graft one onto the other, renumbering appropriately, and add a single step of &I; that will yield

$L_1/-L_1, L_2/-L_2, \ldots L_n/-L_n, M_1/-M_1, M_2/-M_2, \ldots M_o/-M_o \vdash \mathcal{A} \& \mathcal{B}.$

(ii) Suppose $\mathcal{A}$ is false and $\mathcal{B}$ is true. Then there are proofs of

$L_1/-L_1, L_2/-L_2, \ldots L_n/-L_n \vdash -\mathcal{A}$

and

$M_1/-M_1, M_2/-M_2, \ldots M_o/-M_o \vdash \mathcal{B}.$

So the step-by-step structure (*recipe.*) by reasoning parallel to that offered in (i), there is a proof of

$L_1/-L_1, L_2/-L_2, \ldots L_n/-L_n, M_1/-M_1, M_2/-M_2, \ldots M_o/-M_o \vdash -\mathcal{A} \& \mathcal{B}.$

Now, produce a proof of the sequent $-\mathcal{A} \& \mathcal{B} \vdash -(\mathcal{A} \& \mathcal{B})$,[10] and simply graft it onto the proof you've got (renumbering appropriately); *voilă*.

(iii) Suppose $\mathcal{A}$ is true and $\mathcal{B}$ is false. Then there are proofs of

$L_1/-L_1, L_2/-L_2, \ldots L_n/-L_n \vdash \mathcal{A}$

and

$M_1/-M_1, M_2/-M_2, \ldots M_o/-M_o \vdash -\mathcal{B}.$

Proceed just as in (ii), except that the proof you will need to produce at the end is of the sequent $\mathcal{A} \& -\mathcal{B} \vdash -(\mathcal{A} \& \mathcal{B})$.

(iv) Suppose $\mathcal{A}$ and $\mathcal{B}$ are both false. Ditto, ditto, except that the proof you will need to produce at the end is of the sequent $-\mathcal{A} \& -\mathcal{B} \vdash -(\mathcal{A} \& \mathcal{B})$.

That concludes the argument for the claim that if $\mathcal{A}$ and $\mathcal{B}$ each obey Metatheorem (**3**), then $\mathcal{A} \& \mathcal{B}$ obeys Metatheorem (**3**).

Similar arguments will work for each of the other connectives. Now, since every well-formed formula of **PL** is built up out of one-at-a-time applications of single connectives to shorter formulas, it follows that Metatheorem (**3**) holds of every formula whatever, no matter how long and complicated the formula may be.

---

[10]Trifling:

1	(1)	−A & B	A
2	(2)	A & B	PA
1	(3)	−A	1 &O
2	(4)	A	2 &O
1,2	(5)	A & −A	4,3 &I
1	(6)	−(A & B)	2-5 −I

Stage 2

Now, let's consider only *tautologous* formulas. (A tautologous *formula,* as opposed to a tautologous sequent, is a formula that has no F's in its truth table; it takes the value T at every row.)

To show: (4) That for any tautologous formula $\mathcal{A}$, the sequent $\vdash \mathcal{A}$ (the premiseless sequent whose conclusion is $\mathcal{A}$) is provable.

Recipe: Suppose $\mathcal{A}$ is tautologous; then, since it takes the value T for every assignment of truth-values to its atomic sentence letters, we will be able to prove *every* sequent of the form $L_1/-L_1, L_2/-L_2, \ldots L_n/-L_n \vdash \mathcal{A}$. For example, the formula $(A \,\&\, B) \rightarrow B$ is tautologous (as you can easily check by truth table), so Metatheorem (3) guarantees that each of the following four sequents is provable:

$$A, B \vdash (A \,\&\, B) \rightarrow B$$
$$-A, B \vdash (A \,\&\, B) \rightarrow B$$
$$A, -B \vdash (A \,\&\, B) \rightarrow B$$
$$-A, -B \vdash (A \,\&\, B) \rightarrow B$$

Now, in **PL** we can also prove each of the sequents $\vdash L_1 \vee -L_1$ through $\vdash L_n \vee -L_n.$[11] If we amalgamate the proofs of those sequents with all the proofs of the 2^n sequents that have the form $L_1/-L_1, L_2/-L_2, \ldots L_n/-L_n \vdash \mathcal{A}$, renumbering like mad, then a long series of Arrow Ins and Wedge Outs will eventually eliminate all the assumptions and prove $\vdash \mathcal{A}$ alone. (Try this as an exercise, using $(A \,\&\, B) \rightarrow B$ as an example; it's perfectly feasible.)

Demonstration: Here as usual, if you know $\vee$O and the other rules of **PL**, you will see that this will work, because you will see how the amalgamated proof goes and that it is a correct one. Thus, Metatheorem (4) is established—or would be, once we had actually written out the proof.

Stage 3

Let $\mathcal{A}_1, \mathcal{A}_2, \ldots \mathcal{A}_n \vdash \mathcal{B}$ be any tautologous sequent. Then its associated conditional, $\mathcal{A}_1 \rightarrow (\mathcal{A}_2 \rightarrow (\ldots (\mathcal{A}_n \rightarrow \mathcal{B}) \ldots))$ is a tautologous formula, as can readily be checked using the truth definition of the arrow. Since the conditional is tautologous, Metatheorem (4) guarantees that it is provable. And because Metatheorem (2) says that, if a sequent's associated conditional is provable, the sequent itself is also provable, it follows that our original sequent $\mathcal{A}_1, \mathcal{A}_2, \ldots \mathcal{A}_n \vdash \mathcal{B}$ is provable.

But that sequent-schema represented any arbitrarily chosen tautologous sequent. So the argument of the previous paragraph amounts to a general proof that: (5) Any tautologous sequent of **PL** is provable in **PL**—which is precisely to say that **PL** is complete. Our completeness proof is finished.

[11]The proofs are, of course, exactly parallel. Try one.

Summary: At **Stage 1** it is shown that for any formula $\mathcal{A}$ and for any assignment of truth-values to $\mathcal{A}$'s atomic sentence letters L_1, L_2, ..., we can prove either the sequent $L_1/-L_1$, $L_2/-L_2$, ... $\vdash \mathcal{A}$ or the sequent $L_1/-L_1$, $L_2/-L_2$, ... $\vdash -\mathcal{A}$, depending on whether the various sentence letters and the formula $\mathcal{A}$ are true or false on the assignment in question. (That's Metatheorem (**3**).)

At **Stage 2** it is shown, assuming Metatheorem (**3**), that for any tautologous formula $\mathcal{A}$, the sequent $\vdash \mathcal{A}$ is provable. (That's Metatheorem (**4**).)

At **Stage 3** it is shown, assuming Metatheorems (**4**) and (**2**), that any and every tautologous sequent is provable. (That's Metatheorem (**5**), completeness itself.)

PL is *OK,* at least in being both sound and complete.

APPENDIX 2

Is Propositional Logic Reliable?

Consider this argument:[1]

> If I will have ETERNAL life if I BELIEVE in God, then GOD must exist. I do not believe in God. Therefore, God exists.

It is possible for this argument to have true premises and a false conclusion; hence, it is invalid. The inference's symbolization:

$$(B \to E) \to G, -B \vdash G$$

You can establish by formal proof, truth table, or truth tree that this sequent is valid! We have here an invalid English argument whose symbolization is valid.

Consider again exercise 19 from Chapter Four and exercise 22 from Chapter Five, the so-called paradoxes of material implication:

> 19. Tipper Gore is MONOGAMOUS. Hence, if she has TWO husbands she is monogamous.
>
> $$M \vdash T \to M$$
>
> 22. Tipper Gore does not have two husbands. Hence, if she has two husbands she is monogamous.
>
> $$-T \vdash T \to M$$

The English arguments have true premises and false conclusions, so they are invalid; but the sequents that symbolize them are demonstrably valid! How are these anomalies to be explained?

The basic explanation in each case is that the sequent is not a wholly satisfactory translation of the natural-language argument. The major symbols in propositional logic are the five statement connectives. How do these symbols acquire their meanings? Are they simply assigned the meanings of the English connective expressions they translate? English connective expressions exhibit the vagueness characteristic of most natural-language words. Because logicians require precision in the symbols they employ, they are not content to let their logical symbols absorb the somewhat vague meanings of natural-language expressions; hence, they stipulate the meanings of their connectives. In propositional logic this stipulation commonly occurs through stating inference or truth-tree rules governing the connectives, or by providing a basic truth table.

[1]This is an adaptation of an example given me by Charles L. Stevenson.

All three methods have been employed in this book. Fortunately, the set of inference rules we adopted in Chapters Two through Seven completely conforms to the basic truth table presented in Chapter Ten and the truth-tree rules given in Chapter Eleven. Had these methods not conformed, we would have been assigning distinct meanings to some or all of our connective symbols.

Now the question arises as to how closely the meanings of the connective symbols correspond to the meanings of the English expressions they translate. For example, how nearly synonymous are the logic symbol '&' and the English word 'and'? The answer is that '&' and 'and' are as nearly synonymous as could be expected. The meaning of '–' is nearly the same as the meaning of 'not', and the meaning of 'v' is similar to the inclusive meaning of 'or', but there is a greater disparity between the meanings of '→' and 'if . . . then', and there is a similar disparity between the meanings of '↔' and 'if and only if'.

Let's concentrate on the case of the arrow. Consider statement S1 and its translation into propositional notation F1:

(S1) If Carmen is a PRIEST, then Carmen is a MAN.
(F1) P → M

We will regard S1 as a true statement only if we believe that there is some connection between the situation described by its antecedent and the one described by its consequent. One obvious connection would be this: Carmen's religion excludes women from the priesthood.

The case is different with F1. We may ascribe truth to F1 in the absence of knowledge of a connection between the antecedent and the consequent. As a result of adopting the basic truth table of Chapter Ten, we are prepared to attribute truth to F1 if its antecedent is false or if its consequent is true. In fact, the presence or absence of some connection between antecedent and consequent (other than a connection of truth-values) is irrelevant to the truth-value of F1. If the consequent of F1 is true but there is no nontruth-functional connection between the parts of S1, F1 will be true and S1 false. Therefore F1 does not entail S1. On the other hand, if F1 is false (having a true antecedent and false consequent) necessarily S1 will also be false. So the falsity of F1 entails the falsity of S1; but that means that S1 entails F1. The meaning of 'if . . . then' in S1 is logically stronger than the meaning of the arrow in F1.

Let's return to the "God" argument discussed at the beginning of this appendix. The analysis of this argument that is provided by propositional logic fails because of a difference in meaning between the first premise of the English argument and its symbolization. Specifically, the problem is this: The second premise of the argument, S2, does not entail S3, the antecedent of the first premise. But S2 does entail F3, the symbolization of S3.

(S2) I do not believe in God.
(S3) I will have eternal life if I believe in God.
(F3) B → E

Consider again the first "Tipper Gore" example:

(S4) Tipper Gore is monogamous.
(S5) If Tipper Gore has two husbands she is monogamous.

(F4) M
(F5) T → M

Wff F5 is logically weaker than S5, and that explains why F5 can follow from F4 even though S5 does not follow from S4.

As the above discussion reveals, propositional logic sometimes gives incorrect results even with arguments that appear to fall within the scope of propositional logic. In view of this fact, should we scrap the propositional logic developed in this book, attempt to modify it, or retain it in its present form? I believe it should be retained. Here are five reasons in support of my view: (1) Anomalous arguments such as the "God" inference are extremely rare. (2) Every such argument I have ever encountered was invented by some logician to illustrate a defect in propositional logic. In my experience propositional logic never "misfires" on natural arguments.[2] (3) Logic can be a workable science only if it abstracts from the complexities of natural language. The English expression 'if . . . then' has different meanings in different contexts. A logic that had a different symbol for each meaning would be too complicated to learn or use. (4) Although the meaning of the arrow is an abstraction from the meaning of 'if . . . then', it captures that part of the meaning that is crucial for logical purposes. (5) There are English conditional sentences that are perfectly translated by propositional logic. Statement S6 (uttered by sportscaster Sonny Hirsch) is an example.

(S6) If the BALL is on the one-foot line, I'm an ADMIRAL in the Swiss Navy.[3]

The only connection between the antecedent and consequent of S6 has to do with truth-values; so, it is exactly translated by F6:

(F6) B → A

The meaning that 'if . . . then' has in S6 (which is the meaning of the arrow) is the common denominator of the various senses of this English connective.

---

[2] I exclude from consideration natural arguments falling within the scope of some advanced branch of logic (like predicate logic).

[3] S6 is an enthymematic *modus tollens*. It amounts to a denial of the claim that the ball rests on the one-foot line.

APPENDIX 3

Alternative Symbols

Unfortunately, symbolic logic has not reached a stage of maturity where scholars agree about the notation to be used. Hence, if you read material that treats or employs symbolic logic, you are quite likely to encounter statement connective symbols other than the ones used in this book. The following dictionary may prove useful.

English Connectives	Symbols Used in This Book	Other Symbols	Polish Notation
not	−	~ ¬	N
and	&	· ∧	K
or	v		A
if	→	⊃	C
iff	↔	≡	E

In Polish notation (developed by the Warsaw school of logicians) statement letters are written in lower case to distinguish them from connectives. Also, dyadic connective symbols precede the wffs they "connect," rather than appearing between them. Thus, for example, F1 symbolizes S1.

(S1) If PAUL attends, then RALPH will attend.
(F1) Cpr

One unusual feature of Polish notation is that it employs no groupers.

One-Sided Truth Trees

The truth trees employed in Chapter Eleven have two sides; one side represents truth and the other side falsity. Some logicians prefer a different style of tree, one that has just one side (representing truth).[1] In this appendix I briefly describe that technique and list the rules it employs. I will assume that you have studied Chapter Eleven. A fuller presentation of the material, which is Chapter 11 rewritten as an introduction to one-sided truth trees, is available either on the Internet or from the *PropLogic* CD packaged with this book. (1) The Internet site is **www.miami.edu/phi/one-sided-trees**. (2) You may use a word processor to view or print the DOS text file, **ch11a.txt**, contained on the CD. (For proper formatting of this document, select a fixed-width font such as Courier New and set the point size to 12.)

The one-sided-tree technique involves nine decomposition rules.

Rules for One-Sided Truth Trees

Ampersand (&)	Dash Ampersand (−&)
✓ 𝓐 & 𝓑 𝓐 𝓑	✓ −(𝓐 & 𝓑)

For Dash Ampersand, a branch:
$$-\mathcal{A} \qquad -\mathcal{B}$$

Wedge (v)	Dash Wedge (−v)
✓ 𝓐 v 𝓑	✓ −(𝓐 v 𝓑) −𝓐 −𝓑

For Wedge, a branch:
$$\mathcal{A} \qquad \mathcal{B}$$

Arrow (→)	Dash Arrow (−→)
✓ 𝓐 → 𝓑	✓ −(𝓐 → 𝓑) 𝓐 −𝓑

For Arrow, a branch:
$$-\mathcal{A} \qquad \mathcal{B}$$

[1]This format was developed by Richard Jeffrey.

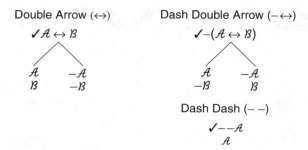

This system dispenses with representing a wff as false by representing its negation as true.

Capital letters and their negations cannot be decomposed. Any other wff will exhibit one of the nine forms covered by the rules above. On each branch of the tree you decompose formulas until you can decompose no further or until the branch has closed. A branch closes when it includes some wff and also its negation. You show that you have decomposed a wff by affixing a check mark to it, and you indicate that a branch has closed by placing an asterisk beneath it. Because these trees are one-sided, there is no need for vertical lines; only diagonal branching lines are used.

To test a sequent you begin the tree by listing all of the premise wffs followed by the negation of the conclusion wff. (We can separate these initial assumptions from the rest of the tree by drawing a short horizontal line below them.) The sequent is valid iff the tree closes (that is, every branch closes). I illustrate the method by evaluating this sequent:

$$(P \;\&\; Q) \to R \vdash [Q \to (P \to R)]$$

		from line	by rule
1	✓$(P \;\&\; Q) \to R$		
2	✓$-[Q \to (P \to R)]$		
	$\underline{Q}$		
4	✓ $-(P \to R)$	2	$-\to$
	P		
	$-R$	4	$-\to$
7	✓$-(P \;\&\; Q)$ \qquad R	1	$\to$
	\qquad\qquad\qquad ∗		
	$-P$ \qquad $-Q$	7	$-\&$
	∗ \qquad ∗		

(The columns on the left and right are instructional devices and not part of the tree diagram.) Every branch closes, so the sequent is valid.

APPENDIX 5

Using PropLogic

You can dive straight into *PropLogic* and learn how to use it as you go, or, if you prefer, read about the program first in this appendix.

Getting Started

PropLogic is a tutorial program designed to help you master the material presented in *Propositional Logic*, 3rd ed. It will assist you as you learn to symbolize sentences and arguments, construct proofs of validity, build full and brief truth tables, and create truth trees. The program will assess your work, enabling you to catch errors as you make them, and it will offer hints for solving problems. The program also includes four games that let you build your logic skills as you have some fun. System requirements are Windows 95 or 98, a color monitor, and a mouse.

PropLogic can be run directly from the CD-ROM disk or from the hard drive of your computer. It is better to run the program from your hard drive for several reasons, including faster and smoother operation. You should run the program from the CD-ROM disk only if you are prevented from loading it on the hard drive. (This will likely be the case if you use a computer in a college computer lab.)

Installing *PropLogic* on Your Hard Drive

1. Click the *Start* button on the taskbar.
2. Click *Run.*
3. Type: D:setup *(Here I assume that "D:" names your CD-ROM drive. If your CD-ROM drive is identified with a different letter, use that letter in place of "D".)*
4. Click *OK.*
5. Follow the instructions displayed on-screen.

Running *PropLogic* from Your Hard Drive (after Installation)

1. Click the *Start* button on the taskbar.
2. Highlight *Programs.*

3. Highlight *Logic.*
4. Click *PropLogic.*

Of course, if you place the *Shortcut to PropLogic* icon on the desktop, you can run the program by double-clicking that icon. (Instructions for placing the shortcut on the desktop are provided in the section on "Trouble Shooting.")

Running *PropLogic* from the CD-ROM Disk

1. Click the *Start* button on the taskbar.
2. Click *Run.*
3. Type: D:PropLogic *(Here I assume that "D:" names the CD-ROM drive. Make appropriate adjustments if necessary.)*
4. Click *OK.*

Using *PropLogic*

I'll start by explaining features found throughout the program, and then provide explanations for each of the six sections of *PropLogic.*

Special logic symbols may be entered by pressing buttons at the bottom of the screen or by typing characters or pressing certain *F*-keys:

For this symbol	... Type this character	... Or press this *F*-key
↔	<	F7
→	>	F8
v	@	F9
&	&	F10
–	–	F11
⊢	+	F12

The symbol buttons at the bottom of the screen can be removed by invoking a command on the *View* drop-down menu (on the toolbar).

There are three main ways to navigate between the sections of *PropLogic.*

1. You can use the menu on the initial screen. Click on a section name to move to that section.
2. You can use the drop-down menu under *Sections.*
3. You can use the first six *F*-keys. For example, pressing F1 takes you to the first section.

You can transfer sequents from one section of the program to another by moving to the new section by either the second or the third method described above. If you move via the first method, the sequent will be lost. (Note that in-valid sequents cannot be transported to the PROOFS section; the method of proofs establishes nothing about invalid sequents.)

Several buttons are common to most or all of the sections. Here is what they do:

NAME	GRAPHIC	FUNCTION
Help		Explains how the section operates.
Menu		Returns you to the main menu screen.
Save		Saves the problem. (If you run *PropLogic* from the CD-ROM disk, remember that you must save problems on another drive.)
Open		Retrieves a saved problem.
New		Erases the sequent *and* your work.
Clear		Erases your work but not the sequent.
Next		Sets the next practice problem.
Hint		Provides a hint.
Check		Checks your work.
Print		Prints the problem.

I'll mention some miscellaneous matters next. (You might want to skip on to the instructions for using the program section you are most interested in, and return to these points later.)

- Right-clicking often brings up a pop-up shortcut menu with common commands. Different sections have different shortcut menus.
- *PropLogic* installs some sample proof, truth table, and truth tree files. The files are located in *PropLogic*'s default working directory. Use the *Open* button (in the relevant section) to load one of these files.
- Sections three through five remember the four most recently used files. A list of these files may be found on the *File* drop-down menu.
- You may wish to print several problems on one sheet of paper. You can do this (in most sections) by saving the problems to be printed and then placing the file names on the printer manifest. (You can print multiple problems on one sheet only if the problems are of the same type, for example, all proofs.)

- Correct answers are often identified with a green check mark, and incorrect answers are marked with a red *X.* In some sections, a non-wff is labeled with a purple slashed circle.
- All of the program's help messages can be accessed by means of the *Help* drop-down menu on the toolbar.
- You can turn off sounds via the *Options* drop-down menu.

The Six Sections of *PropLogic*

Formulas.   Overview: In this section you learn to distinguish between formulas that are well-formed (wffs) and those that are not well-formed (non-wffs). The program explains why certain formulas are ill-formed.
Instructions for using this section:

- Enter a formula in the white window. It will be automatically checked as you type. If your formula is well-formed the *wff* box appears. If your formula is not well-formed the *not a wff* box appears.
- Use the *Hint* button to get an explanation for why a formula is not well-formed.
- Press the *About wffs* button to study the definition of a well-formed formula.

Symbolizations.   Overview: In this section you symbolize textbook exercises while the program checks your work. This is particularly useful because mis-symbolizing an exercise will adversely affect the rest of your work on that exercise. It is reassuring to know that you have symbolized a given problem correctly. The section also provides problems for further symbolization practice. The program catches your symbolization mistakes, and offers hints designed to help you reach the correct symbolization.
Instructions for using this section:

- Select a chapter (2–13) from the white box in the upper-left corner. Then select an exercise from either the *Book Exercises* or the *Practice Problems* box to the right of the *Chapter* box. (Note: Practice Problems are available for Chapters 2–7 only.)
- Enter your answer in the large white window. Each line is automatically checked as you type. An evaluation symbol will appear to the left of each line to indicate whether it is correct (check mark), incorrect/incomplete ("X"), or not well-formed (slashed circle).
- If a problem has you stumped, use the *Hint* button. The program will reveal the overall structure of the correct formula. To avoid giving away the entire answer, question marks replace sentence letters. If the problem involves several formulas, you can tell the program which formula you want a hint for by placing the cursor on that line.
- If the program evaluates your symbolization as well-formed but incorrect (by posting a red *X*), you may press the *Hint* button to obtain an expla-

nation of the problem. Typically the program will identify an assignment of truth values that makes your symbolization true and the sentence false or vice versa (or both). If your symbolization were correct, then it would have to have the same truth value as the sentence, no matter what.

- Note that to be correct a symbolization must have the same content as the sentence, and must also "track" the sentence satisfactorily. For more on "tracking" see page 30.
- A yellow smiley face will appear when the symbolization of a sequent is entirely correct. A correctly symbolized sequent may be saved, printed, and/or transported to other sections of the program.

Additional points:

- Exercises that are already symbolized in the book are included in the *Book Exercises* list as a convenience to the user. These exercises can be transported to other sections of the program without the user typing them in.
- Press the *Symbolization Guide* button for a list of English connective expressions and the symbols that translate them.

Proofs.   Overview: In this section, you construct formal proofs for valid sequents while the program checks your work and offers explanations of the mistakes you may make.

Instructions for using this section:

- Select a chapter (2–9, 12) from the white box in the upper-left corner. Then select an exercise from the white *Practice Problems* box. Or just create your own proof problem by typing premises and a conclusion in the proof box.
- Enter formulas and justifications in the appropriate columns. (The columns automatically expand as you type.) To move between columns, use the tab or arrow keys, or click on the columns or their headings. *PropLogic* creates line numbers for you, and renumbers lines automatically as you insert or delete lines. It makes the necessary adjustments to the line numbers occurring in the justification and assumption-dependence columns. The assumption-dependence column automatically appears when necessary.
- Use the *Check* button to check your proof.
- Use the *Hint* button for a more detailed explanation of an error in your justification column.

Additional points:

- To undo the most recent action, use the *Undo* button or the command on the *Edit* drop-down menu.

- To toggle between strict (default) and lenient line number checking, use the *Strict Checking* command on the *Options* drop-down menu. In strict checking, line numbers in justification entries are accepted in only one order: the order that corresponds to the statement of the rule.
- To toggle between wide and narrow columns, use the *Re-size Formula Column* button or the command on the *Edit* drop-down menu.
- Press the *Rules* button to see a list of the inference rules. Pressing on a rule name on this list provides an example of the rule in use in a proof.
- Press the *Font Size* button to change font size. You can keep a long or wide proof from extending beyond the screen by reducing font size.

Truth Tables.   Overview: In this section, you construct truth tables (full or brief) while the program checks your work.

Instructions for using this section:

- Select full truth tables or brief truth tables by clicking on the button beneath the *Help* button. (This button displays a large *F* when the program is in full-table mode, and a large *B* when it is in brief-table mode.)

FULL TRUTH TABLES

- Enter one or more formulas or a sequent in the white edit box at the top of the screen. Place commas between formulas and precede the conclusion of a sequent with the turnstile. If every formula is well-formed, the matrix for a full truth table will be constructed automatically. Or you can click on the down arrowhead to the right of the white edit box and select a practice problem from the list that appears.
- Empty truth table entries appear as red question marks. Click on them to alternate between *T* (True) and *F* (False). When a column is correct, the connective at the top of the column will turn green.
- When all the columns are complete, click on the blue question marks at the far left to make check marks appear or disappear. For sequents, a check mark signifies a critical row. For multiple formulas, a check mark signifies non-equivalence.
- When the table is correct, the program will ask what the full truth table demonstrates. Answer the question correctly and a yellow smiley face appears.

BRIEF TRUTH TABLES

- Enter a sequent in the white edit box at the top. (We do not use brief truth tables to evaluate formulas or pairs of formulas; we apply them to sequents only.) Place commas between the premise formulas and precede the conclusion with the turnstile. If every formula in the sequent is well-formed, the matrix for a brief truth table will be constructed automatically. Or you can click on the down arrowhead to the right of the white edit box and select a practice problem from the list that appears.

- Empty table entries appear as red question marks. Click on them to alternate between T (True) and F (False). For valid sequents, click below the entry where the contradiction occurs to place a T or F.
- When all columns are complete, click on the blue question mark at the far left to make a check mark appear or disappear. A check mark signifies invalidity.
- If the table is correct, the red letters and connectives at the top of the table will turn green and the program will ask what the brief truth table demonstrates. Answer correctly and a yellow smiley face appears.

Additional points:

- Press the *Principles* button to see a list of truth table principles and a sample basic truth table.   **P**
- When you create full truth tables you may elect to include or hide the columns of values that duplicate the guide columns; this option is selected on the *View* drop-down menu.
- Press the *Font Size* button to change font size. You can keep a deep or wide truth table from extending beyond the screen by reducing font size.
- You can stop the program from asking what a completed table shows via a command on the *Options* drop-down menu.

Truth Trees.   Overview: In this section you construct truth trees while the program checks your work. The program will locate errors that you may make.

Instructions for using this section:

- Enter a sequent or a single formula in the white edit box at the top. Place commas between premises of a sequent and precede the conclusion with the turnstile. If every formula is well-formed, the trunk of a truth tree will be constructed automatically. Or you can click on the down arrowhead and select a practice problem from the list that appears.
- Empty tree entries appear as red question marks. Left-click on the question mark (or subsequent red dot) until the correct rule has been applied to the wff indicated by the yellow arrow. Formulas that have not been decomposed appear in red. Formulas that have already been decomposed or single capitals are printed in black.

- *PropLogic* positions the yellow arrow to help minimize tree length. You may use the tab or arrow keys to move the yellow arrow to another red (not yet decomposed) formula.
- To mark a completed branch closed (*) or open (no *), left-click the red question mark at the tip. To close an incomplete branch, right-click the question mark.
- To check a truth tree press the *Check Truth Tree* button. If the tree is correct, the program will ask what the tree demonstrates. If the tree is incorrect, the program will draw a red *X* at the spot (or one of the spots) where the tree goes wrong. If you move the cursor to the *X*, the cursor will become an eraser. Left-click to remove the erroneous part of the tree, then make corrections in the usual fashion.

Additional points:

- To create a tree with a single wff on the right of the trunk, precede the wff by R and a period (.).
- When creating large truth trees, branches can overlap. Use the *Redraw Tree* button. To view more of a large tree, reduce font size with the *Change Font Size* button.
- Use the *Undo Move* button (repeatedly if necessary) to undo the most recent moves. To undo larger portions of a tree, move the cursor over the region in question. When the cursor becomes a pair of pruning shears, left-click to undo the tree to that point.
- Press the *Rules* button to see a list of truth tree rules.
- You can stop the program from asking what a completed truth tree shows via a command on the *Options* drop-down menu.

Games.   Select a game from the game menu screen. Choose a one- or two-player version of the game (using one of the buttons displayed on the right). Each one-player game has a game story, which can be turned off. For one-player games choose a skill level and decide whether you will play against the clock. (Highest scores are attained when playing the clock. There is no "pause" function for timed games, so come to the game prepared to play.) For a two-player game enter the names of the players.

Pressing the *Games Menu* button will terminate the game and return you to the games menu. Pressing either the *One-Player* or the *Two-Player* button will restart the game. Two additional buttons common to many of the games are the *Stop* and *Go* buttons.

If you attain a record high score in a one-player game, you may enter your name and a date or comment in the Hall of Fame for that game. To view the Hall of Fame, click the command on the *Games* drop-down menu.

ONE-PLAYER WOOF!

The game *Woof!* involves determining whether a formula is well-formed.

The program presents five formulas. Using the mouse mark each formula as well-formed or not well-formed. Transform each non-wff into a wff by adding or deleting a SINGLE character.

Game score is based on the correctness of your answers, the skill level selected, and the speed at which you work. The game ends when you complete six rounds of play, earn a score of −500 or lower, or allow the game clock to expire.

TWO-PLAYER WOOF!

One player creates five formulas for the other player to assess; they may be well-formed formulas (wffs) or not. Non-wffs must be capable of being changed into wffs in a single step (that is, by adding or deleting a single character). The player is penalized if the non-wff created cannot be changed into a wff in a single step. The other player marks each formula as a wff or a non-wff. If a non-wff can be changed into a wff in a single step, the player makes the needed change. If a non-wff cannot be changed into a wff in a single step, then the player does not edit it. Use the mouse, the tab key, the arrow keys, or the Enter key to move between problems.

Game score is based on the correctness of answers and the speed at which players work. The game ends when both players complete six rounds of play, or one player earns a score of −500 or lower.

ONE-PLAYER ELLIE

The game *Ellie* involves recognizing whether two formulas are logically equivalent.

The program presents wffs in five pairs. Using the mouse mark each pair as logically equivalent or not equivalent.

Game score is based on the correctness of your answers, the skill level selected, and the speed at which you work. The game ends when you complete six rounds of play, earn a score of −500 or lower, or allow the game clock to expire.

TWO-PLAYER ELLIE

One player creates five pairs of wffs for the other player to assess; the formulas in the pairs may be logically equivalent or not, but should be well-formed. Players take turns marking the pairs equivalent, not equivalent, or not well-formed. Use the mouse, the tab key, the arrow keys, or the Enter key to move between problems.

Game score is based on the correctness of answers and the speed at which players work. The game ends when both players complete six rounds of play, or one player earns a score of −500 or lower.

ONE-PLAYER AIR GO

The game *Air Go* involves devising a formula that follows from a set of formulas; in other words, creating a conclusion that follows validly from a set of premises.

The program presents several formulas which you are to view as the premises of a sequent. You provide a conclusion formula that must meet both of these conditions: (1) It is entailed by the premise set (that is, the sequent is valid); (2) it is not entailed by any (proper) subset of the premises (that is, if you eliminated any premise, the revised sequent would be invalid). For example, if the premises are:

$$P \& Q$$
$$Q \to R$$

the answer R satisfies both conditions, but the answer P fails the second condition (since it is entailed by the first premise alone). You should aim to provide the shortest formula that satisfies the two conditions. So, for the above premises, R is a better answer than $P \& R$.

Game score is based on the correctness and brevity of your answers, the skill level selected, and the speed at which you work. The game ends when you complete eight rounds of play, earn a score of −500 or lower, or allow the game clock to expire.

TWO-PLAYER AIR GO

One player presents from two to five premise formulas. (Of course, the formulas must be well-formed.) Players take turns providing conclusion formulas that are entailed by the complete premise set but not entailed by any (proper) subset of the premises. The second conclusion formula presented may not be identical to the first.

Game score is based on the correctness and brevity of answers and the speed at which players work. The game ends when both players complete eight rounds of play, or one player earns a score of −500 or lower.

Q.E.D.

The game *Q.E.D.* involves constructing proofs for valid sequents. (There is no two-player version of this game.) On the Tyro skill level (easiest), you may select the last chapter studied. The proofs you are asked to construct can be completed using only the proof rules and logic symbols already covered.

The program presents a valid sequent and you construct a proof for it. The game clock runs until you have completed the proof and had the program verify its correctness.

Game score is based on the skill level selected and the speed at which you work. Points are lost for computer checks of (or hints requested for) an incomplete or incorrect proof. The game ends when you complete four rounds of play, earn a score of −500 or lower, or allow the game clock to expire.

Trouble Shooting

Symptom: Logic symbols (specifically the arrow, double arrow, wedge, and turnstile) do not appear correctly on the monitor or printouts. For example: Typing the '@' symbol produces '@' on the screen, rather than the wedge (v).

Cause: "Logic" font is not installed correctly.

Solution: Exit *PropLogic.* Use *Windows Explorer* to open the Windows\Fonts folder on the hard drive. Look for font name *Logic* (filename: pl_fnt.ttf). If this font is not present, copy the file (pl_fnt.ttf) from the *PropLogic* CD-ROM disk into the Windows\Fonts folder. Restart *PropLogic.*

Note: The program uses two other fonts: *Clock* (filename: Clock.ttf) and *Computerfont* (filename: Computer.ttf). If either is missing from the Windows\Fonts folder it can be copied from the CD-ROM disk.

* * *

Symptom: The logic problem (proof, truth table, or truth tree) does not entirely fit on the monitor screen.

Various Solutions:

a. Reduce font size using the *Change Font Size* button.
b. Increase screen resolution (choose *Settings* from the Start menu, click on *Control Panel,* double-click on *Display,* and then choose the *Settings* tab).
c. Hide the Windows taskbar or other toolbars that occupy screen space. To hide the taskbar click the *Start* button, highlight *Settings,* click *Taskbar,* check *Auto hide,* and click *OK.*
d. Use the scrollbar that appears when the problem extends beyond the screen.

* * *

Symptom: The shortcut to *PropLogic* is not on the desktop.

Solution:

1. Run *Windows Explorer* (with part of the desktop exposed).
2. Locate the file *PropLogic.exe* in the folder Program Files\PropLogic
3. Using the left mouse button drag the filename to the desktop.
4. Exit *Windows Explorer.*

Uninstalling *PropLogic*

1. Click the *Start* button on the taskbar.
2. Highlight *Settings.*
3. Click *Control Panel.*
4. Double-click *Add/Remove Programs.*
5. Click *PropLogic.*
6. Click *Add/Remove.*
7. Click *Yes* (to confirm file deletion).
8. Click *OK* (to exit uninstaller).
9. Click *Cancel* (to exit Add/Remove Programs).
10. Click *X* (to exit Control Panel).

APPENDIX 6

Solutions to Starred Exercises

Chapter 2:   If

1. (b) O → W
   (f) Q → P
   (j) A → (D → T)

2. (b) If the manual is correct, then if salt is added to the solution it will boil sooner.

3. (b) (3) E
   (4) F

5.
(1)	N	A
(2)	N → M	A
(3)	M → R	A
(4)	M	2,1 →O
(5)	R	3,4 →O

The one-line symbolization of the argument is omitted; the symbolization can be read from the proof.

9.
(1)	P → (A → B)	A
(2)	P → A	A
(3)	P	A
(4)	A → B	1,3 →O
(5)	A	2,3 →O
(6)	B	4,5 →O

The proof for this exercise can also be completed as follows:

(4)	A	2,3 →O
(5)	A → B	1,3 →O
(6)	B	5,4 →O

In general only one proof will be provided for each argument, even though often there will be two or more correct proofs.

Chapter 3:   And

1. (b) P & T
   (f) (F & U) & D
   (j) (O → L) & (H → W)

2. (b) If Miami wins its last regular-season game and New York loses its last regular-season game, then Miami wins the division championship.

3. (b) (3) A
   (4) C
   (5) A & B
   (6)   5,4 &I

5.   (1) B & (B → A)   A
      (2) B   1 &O
      (3)   1 &O
      (4) A   3,2 →O

A formula has been omitted from the above proof; you should supply it. Such omissions will occur regularly in this appendix. The purpose is to encourage you to engage in proof construction, rather than passively observing the results of my work.

8.   (1) H & L   A   *The conjuncts in the an-*
      (2) C   A   *tecedent of the third premise*
      (3) [(H & C) & L] → R A   *may be grouped differently.*
      (4) H   1 &O
      (5)   1 &O
      (6)   4,2 &I
      (7)   6,5 &I
      (8) R   3,7 →O

13.   (1) D   A
      (2) D → S   A
      (3) C   A
      (4) (S & C) → W   A
      (5) W → V   A
      (6) V → L   A
      (7)   2,1 →O
      (8)   7,3 &I
      (9)   4,8 →O
      (10)   5,9 →O
      (11) L   6,10 →O

Chapter 4:   If (Again)

1. (b) Q → E
   (f) P → S   *Don't confuse 'if only' with 'only if'.*
   (j) S → E   *Could not survive without enticing = Enticing is*
                           necessary for survival
   (n) [(F & B) & (D & K)] → [(C & P) → E]

2. (b) Burke's maxim warns that whenever good people do nothing, evil
       will triumph; that is captured by S3.

The use of 'necessary' is potentially confusing. If you think the sentence de-picts "doing nothing" as a necessary condition, then you will choose S4. But notice that "only necessary condition" and "a necessary condition" are not equivalent.

3. (b)   yes (If you wear Tretorn tennis shoes, then you will be more com-fortable on the court.)

   (f)   yes (If you have a copy of our new book, then you can do a little sightseeing before you go on vacation.)

4. (b)   1   (1)
         2   (2)
         3   (3)
         1,3   (4)   D   1,3 →O
         2,3   (5)   2,3 →O
         1,2,3   (6)   D & E   4,5 &I

6.   1   (1)   L → P   A
         2   (2)   L & E   PA
         2   (3)   2 &O
         1,2   (4)   1,3 →O
         1   (5)   (L & E) → P   2-4 →I

10.   1   (1)   K → (A & B)   A
         2   (2)   [K & (A & B)] → W   A
         3   (3)   K   PA
         1,3   (4)   1,3 →O
         1,3   (5)   3,4 &I
         1,2,3   (6)   2,5 →O
         1,2   (7)   K → W   3-6 →I

14.   1   (1)   T → (L & M)   A
         2   (2)   T   PA
         1,2   (3)   1,2 →O
         1,2   (4)   L   3 &O
         1   (5)   2-4 →I
         1,2   (6)   3 &O
         1   (7)   2-6 →I
         1   (8)   (T → L) & (T → M)   5,7 &I

Chapter 5:   Not

1. (b)   − −B
   (f)   −C → −I
   (j)   (−R → T) & (R → F)

2. (b) Justice O'Connor is not a Democrat but she is a Republican.

3. (b)
(2)	1 &O
(3)	1 &O
(4)	
(5)	3,4 &I
(6)	4-5 −I
(7)	2,6 &I

5.
1	(1)	$G \rightarrow C$	A
2	(2)	R	A
3	(3)	$R \rightarrow -C$	A
4	(4)	G	PA
1,4	(5)		1,4 →O
2,3	(6)		3,2 →O
1,2,3,4	(7)		5,6 &I
1,2,3	(8)	−G	4-7 −I

9.
1	(1)	R	A
2	(2)	$R \rightarrow B$	A
3	(3)	$--M \rightarrow -B$	A
4	(4)	$--M$	PA
3,4	(5)		3,4 →O
1,2	(6)		2,1 →O
1,2,3,4	(7)		6,5 &I
1,2,3	(8)	−M	4-7 −O

13.
1	(1)	$P \rightarrow C$	A
2	(2)	−C	PA
3	(3)	P	PA
1,3	(4)		1,3 →O
1,2,3	(5)		4,2 &I
1,2	(6)		3-5 −I
1	(7)	$-C \rightarrow -P$	2-6 →I

Chapter 6: Iff

1. (b) $P \leftrightarrow A$ *or* $A \leftrightarrow P$
   (f) $(M \leftrightarrow -W) \& (-M \rightarrow S)$

2. (b) Smith wins the batting crown if, and only if, Smith gets a hit and Jones makes an out.

3. (b)
| 1 | (1) |
| 2 | (2) |

	3	(3)		
	1	(4)		1 ↔O
	1,2	(5)		2,4 →O
	1	(6)	D → E	1 ↔O
	1,3	(7)	F → G	3,6 →O
	1,2,3	(8)		7,5 ↔I
5.	1	(1)	C ↔ S	A
	2	(2)	–S	A
	3	(3)	C	PA
	1	(4)	C → S	1 ↔O
	1,3	(5)		4,3 →O
	1,2,3	(6)		5,2 &I
	1,2	(7)	–C	3-6 –I
9.	1	(1)	V ↔ C	A
	2	(2)	–C	PA
	3	(3)	V	PA
	1	(4)	V → C	1 ↔O
	1,3	(5)		4,3 →O
	1,2,3	(6)		5,2 &I
	1,2	(7)		3-6 –I
	1	(8)	–C → –V	2-7 →I
13.	1	(1)	C ↔ V	A
	1	(2)	V → C	1 ↔O
	3	(3)	–V	PA
	4	(4)	C	PA
	1	(5)		1 ↔O
	1,4	(6)		5,4 →O
	1,3,4	(7)		6,3 &I
	1,3	(8)		4-7 –I
	1	(9)		3-8 →I
	1	(10)	(V → C) & (–V → –C)	2,9 &I

Chapter 7:   Or

1. (b) –E v –N
   (f) –(C v U) → D
   (j) –(F v H) *or* –F & –H
   (n) (D v Y) → (S & C)
   (r) –(R v A) → H

2. (b) Zero is neither positive nor negative.

3. (b)

1	(1)		
1	(2)		1 &O
1	(3)	E → D	
4	(4)	C v E	
1,4	(5)	D	

6.

(1)	A & B	A
(2)	A	1 &O
(3)	C v A	2 vI
(4)	(C v A) v D	3 vI

10.

1	(1)	F → K	A
2	(2)	R → K	A
3	(3)	S → K	A
4	(4)	H → K	A
5	(5)	(F v R) v (S v H)	A
6	(6)	F v R	PA
1,2,6	(7)		6,1,2 vO
1,2	(8)		6-7 →I
9	(9)	S v H	PA
3,4,9	(10)		9,3,4 vO
3,4	(11)		9-10 →I
1,2,3,4,5	(12)	K	5,8,11 vO

14.

1	(1)	F → (L & A)	A
2	(2)	–L v –A	A
3	(3)	–L	PA
4	(4)	F	PA
1,4	(5)		1,4 →O
1,4	(6)	L	5 &O
1,3,4	(7)		6,3 &I
1,3	(8)		4-7 –I
1	(9)	–L → –F	3-8 →I
10	(10)	–A	PA
1,4	(11)		5 &O
1,4,10	(12)		11,10 &I
1,10	(13)		4-12 –I
1	(14)	–A → –F	10-13 →I
1,2	(15)	–F	2,9,14 vO

Chapter 8:   Résumé

1. (b) Wff.
   (f) Not a wff.

2. (b)
1	(1)		
2	(2)		
3	(3)		
2,3	(4)		3,2 &I
2,3	(5)		4 &O
2	(6)		3-5 →I
7	(7)		
8	(8)		
2,7	(9)		7,2 &I
2,7,8	(10)		9,8 &I
2,7,8	(11)		10 &O
2,7	(12)		8-11 –O
2	(13)		7-12 →I
	(14)		1,6,13 vO

4.
1	(1)	C → A	A
2	(2)	–A	A
3	(3)	–C → –P	A
4	(4)	C	PA
1,4	(5)		1,4 →O
1,2,4	(6)		5,2 &I
1,2	(7)		4-6 –I
1,2,3	(8)	–P	3,7 →O

8.
1	(1)	F ↔ –S	A
2	(2)	–F & –S	PA
1	(3)	–S → F	1 ↔O
2	(4)	–S	2 &O
1,2	(5)		3,4 →O
2	(6)		2 &O
1,2	(7)		5,6 &I
1	(8)	–(–F & –S)	2-7 –I

12.
1	(1)	A → (P → B)	A
2	(2)	–B	A
3	(3)	–A → –P	A
4	(4)	P	PA
5	(5)	A	PA
1,5	(6)		1,5 →O
1,4,5	(7)		6,4 →O
1,2,4,5	(8)		7,2 &I
1,2,4	(9)		5-8 –I
1,2,3,4	(10)		3,9 →O
1,2,3,4	(11)		4,10 &I
1,2,3	(12)	–P	4-11 –I

Chapter 9: Derived Rules

1. (b) (5)   1,4 →O
      (6)   2,3 CA
      (7)   5,6 DA
      (8)   4-7 →I

3. (1) F v R   A
   (2) F → S   A
   (3) –S   A
   (4) R → B   A
   (5)   2,3 MT
   (6)   1,5 DA
   (7) B   4,6 →O

5. (c) (1) T   A
      (2) (T & O) → M A
      (3) –M   A
      (4) –O → (C & R) A
      (5)   2,3 MT
      (6)   5,1 CA
      (7)   4,6 →O
      (8) –O & (C & R) 6,7 &I

7. 1   (1) (C → S) & (–C → S) A
  1   (2) C → S   1 &O
  1   (3)   1 &O
  4   (4) –S   PA
  1,4 (5)   2,4 MT
  1,4 (6)   3,4 MT
  1,4 (7)   5,6 &I
  1   (8) S   4-7 –O

8. (b) (3)   1,2 MT
      (4)   3 DN

9. (b) Line 3: CA is inapplicable to lines 1 and 2.
  (f) Line 2: DN is inapplicable.

10. (b) (1) R   A
      (2) R → B   A
      (3) – –M → –B A   *or more elegantly:*
      (4)   2,1 →O
      (5)   4 DN   (5)   3 CN
      (6)   3,5 MT   (6) –M   5,4 →O
      (7) –M   6 DN

12. (1) R → F   A
     (2) –R → E   A
     (3) (F v E) → P   A
     (4)   1 CN
     (5)   4,2 CH
     (6)   5 AR
     (7) P   3,6 →O

14. (b) (1) C → (A → S)   A
        (2) A & –S   A
        (3)   2 AR
        (4) –C   1,3 MT

16.   (1) U → –C   A
       (2) C   A
       (3) –U → (A v B)   A
       (4) B → –O   A
       (5) O   A
       (6)   1 CN
       (7)   6,2 →O
       (8)   3,7 →O
       (9)   4 CN
       (10)   9,5 →O
       (11) A   8,10 DA

Chapter 10:   Truth Tables

1. (b)

	B	C	B → C	⊢ B v –C	
	T	T	T	T	F
✔	F	T	T	F	F
	T	F	F	T	T
	F	F	T	T	T
				*	

invalid

3.

	S	C	S → C	–S	⊢ –C
	T	T	T	F	F
✔	F	T	T	T	F
	T	F	F	F	T
	F	F	T	T	T

invalid

7.

	S	M	R	S → M	R → M	R	⊢ S	
	T	T	T	T	T	T	T	invalid
✔	F	T	T	T	T	T	F	
	T	F	T	F	F	T	T	
	F	F	T	T	F	T	F	
	T	T	F	T	T	F	T	
	F	T	F	T	T	F	F	
	T	F	F	F	T	F	T	
	F	F	F	T	T	F	F	

14. (b)

	S	C	S → C	–S	⊢ –C
✔	F	T	T	T	F

15. (b)

	F	R	S	B	F v R	F → S	–S	R → B	⊢ B
	T	F	F	F	T	T	T	T	F
						F			

Note: There are alternative correct brief-truth-table solutions for this problem, and for every valid argument.

17.

B	W	A	B → W	–B → A	⊢ W v A	
F	F	F	T	T T	F	valid
				F		
				*		

21.

	I	R	P	I v R	P → I	–P	⊢ R	
✔	T	F	F	T	T	T	F	invalid

Chapter 11: Truth Trees

1. (b)

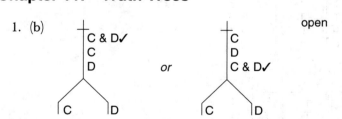

open

In the following, only one solution will be provided even though in many cases there are several correct solutions.

2. (b)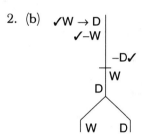

3. (b)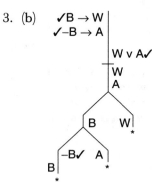

5. (b)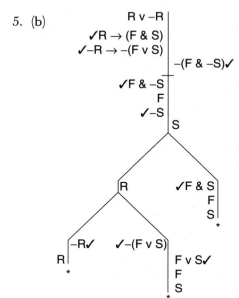

valid

Note that premise one is superfluous. Section 12.1 sheds light on this matter.

7. 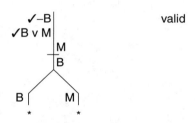   valid

11.   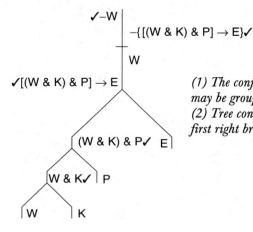   invalid

(1) The conjunction in the conclusion may be grouped differently.
(2) Tree construction can stop after the first right branch is complete.

12. (b)   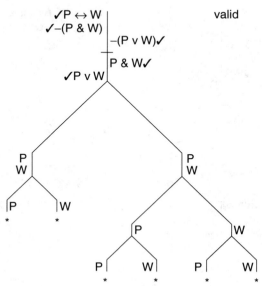   valid

Chapter 12: Statements

1.

H		−H	→	−H		logically true
T		F	T	F		
F		T	T	T		
			*			

```
        |−H → −H✓
        +
   −H   |
        |−H
        *
```

1	(1)	−H	PA
1	(2)		1 DN
1	(3)		2 DN
	(4)	−H → −H	1-3 →I

5.

M	A		(M & A)	&	(−M v −A)		contradictory
T	T		T	F	F FF		
F	T		F	F	T TF		
T	F		F	F	F TT		
F	F		F	F	T TT		
				*			

```
✓(M & A) & (−M v −A)  |
                      +
              ✓M & A  |
            ✓−M v −A  |
                   M  |
                   A  |
                      ↙ ↘
         ✓−M  |     ✓−A  |
            |M       |A
            *        *
```

(1)	(M & A) & (−M v −A)	A
(2)	M & A	1 &O
(3)		1 &O
(4)		3 DM
(5)	(M & A) & −(M & A)	2,4 &I

9.

H		−H	→	− −H		contingent
T		F	T	TF		
F		T	F	FT		
			*			

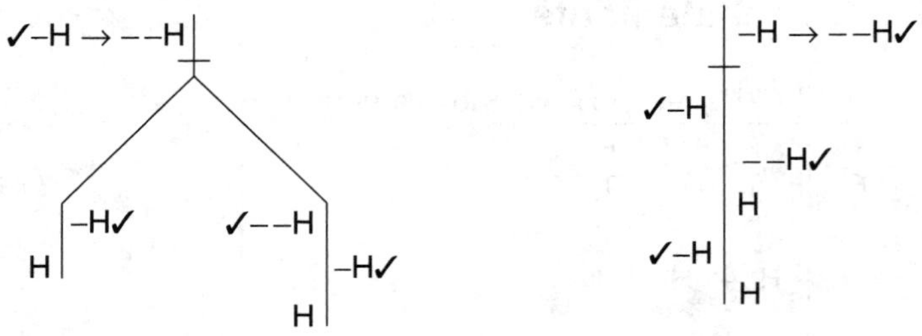

It is arguable that standard propositional logic is not applicable to Professor Moore's statement because it is expressed in the subjunctive mood.

Chapter 13: Logical Relations

2.

	P	Q	P → Q	–P	→	–Q
	T	T	T	F	T	F
✓	F	T	T	T	F	F
✓	T	F	F	F	T	T
	F	F	T	T	T	T
					*	

not logically equivalent

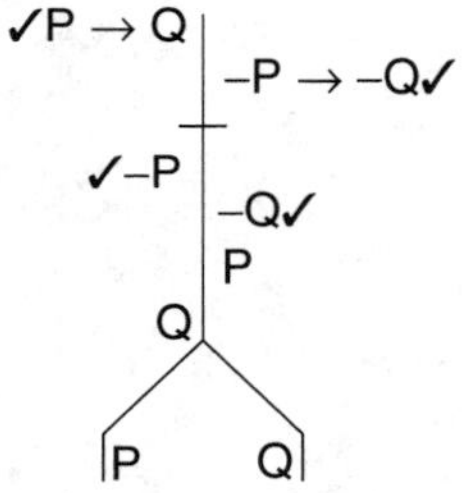

J	M	J → M	–M	→	–J
T	T	T	F	T	F
F	T	T	F	T	T
T	F	F	T	F	F
F	F	T	T	T	T
				*	

logically equivalent

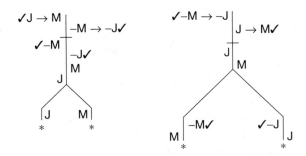

4. (b)

B	C	J	(B & C)	→ J	(B → J)	&	(C → J)	
T	T	T	T	T	T	T	T	
F	T	T	F	T	T	T	T	
T	F	T	F	T	T	T	T	
F	F	T	F	T	T	T	T	
T	T	F	T	F	F	F	F	
✔ F	T	F	F	T	T	F	F	
✔ T	F	F	F	T	F	F	T	
F	F	F	F	T	T	T	T	
				*		*		

not logically equivalent

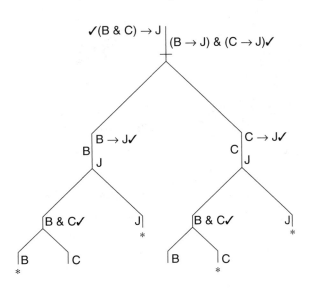

7.

E	C	S	(E → C)	&	(S → C)	(E v S)	→ C
T	T	T	T	T	T	T	T
F	T	T	T	T	T	T	T
T	F	T	F	F	F	T	F
F	F	T	T	F	F	T	F
T	T	F	T	T	T	T	T
F	T	F	T	T	T	F	T
T	F	F	F	F	T	T	F
F	F	F	T	T	T	F	T
				*			*

logically equivalent

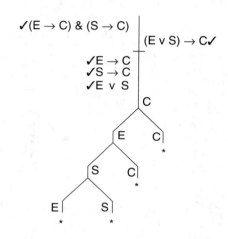

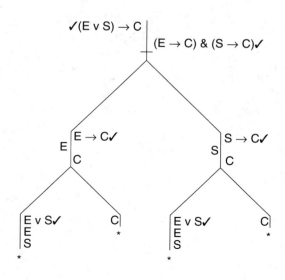

Chapter 14:   Natural Arguments

2. If the stock market does not FLUCTUATE, then stocks have no market RISK.
   The stock market does fluctuate.
   So, stocks have market risk.

F	R		−F	→	−R	F	⊢ R
---	---		----	---	----	---	------
✓ T	F		F	T	T	T	F

   invalid

   *

6. If mice are FAMOUS, then there is a mouse in the ZOO.
   There is no mouse in the zoo.
   So, mice are not famous.

   (1) F → Z   A
   (2) −Z   A
   (3) −F   1,2 MT

11. There is SMOKE in the building.
    If so, then there is a fire INSIDE the building or a fire OUTSIDE the building.
    There is a fire outside the building.
    So, there is no fire inside the building.

    | S | O | I || S | S → (I ∨ O) | O | ⊢ −I |
    |---|---|---||---|-------------|---|------|
    | ✓ T | T | T || T | T | T | F |

    invalid

    *

14. If it is not the case that I am disorganized, then I SAVE money on taxes.
    If I FEEL better about myself, then I am not disorganized.
    If I BUY the cute shoes, I will feel better about myself.
    So, if I buy the cute shoes, then I save money on taxes.

    I have employed the indicative (rather than the subjunctive) mood in my formalization because it is more suitable for treatment in standard propositional logic.

    O = I am organized

    | O | S | F | B || −−O → S | F → −−O | B → F | ⊢ B → S |
    |---|---|---|---||---------|---------|-------|---------|
    | T | F | T | T || TF F T | T TF | T | F |
    | | | | || F | | | |

    valid

    *   *

18. Either BMW A or B, or C was involved in the accident.
    BMWs A and B were not involved.
    So, BMW C was involved.

    (1) (A ∨ B) ∨ C   A
    (2) −A & −B   A

(3) –(A v B)   2 DM
(4) C   1,3 DA

22. If the Etesian WINDS cause the Nile to rise, then OTHER rivers flowing oppo-
    site to the winds will rise.
    But the other rivers do not rise.
    So, the Etesian winds do not cause the Nile to rise.

W	O	W → O	–O	⊢ –W	valid
T	F	T	T	F	
		F			

Index

Proof Rules
and
Truth Tree Rules

Proof Rules

Primitive Inference Rules		
	In	Out
→	From the derivation of B from assumption A (and perhaps other assumptions) derive $A \rightarrow B$.	From $A \rightarrow B$ and A derive B.
&	From A and B derive A & B.	From A & B derive either A or B.
v	From A derive either A v B or B v A.	From A v B, $A \rightarrow C$, and $B \rightarrow C$ derive C.
↔	From $A \rightarrow B$ and $B \rightarrow A$ derive $A \leftrightarrow B$.	From $A \leftrightarrow B$ derive either $A \rightarrow B$ or $B \rightarrow A$.
−	From the derivation of B & $-B$ from assumption A (and perhaps other assumptions) derive $-A$.	From the derivation of B & $-B$ from assumption $-A$ (and perhaps other assumptions) derive A.

Derived Inference Rules	
Modus Tollens (MT)	From $A \rightarrow B$ and $-B$ derive $-A$.
Disjunctive Argument (DA)	From A v B and $-A$ derive B. From A v B and $-B$ derive A.
Conjunctive Argument (CA)	From $-(A$ & $B)$ and A derive $-B$. From $-(A$ & $B)$ and B derive $-A$.
Chain Argument (CH)	From $A \rightarrow B$ and $B \rightarrow C$ derive $A \rightarrow C$.
Double Negation (DN)	From A derive $--A$ and vice versa.
De Morgan's Law (DM)	From $-(A$ & $B)$ derive $-A$ v $-B$ and vice versa. From $-(A$ v $B)$ derive $-A$ & $-B$ and vice versa. From $-(-A$ & $-B)$ derive A v B and vice versa. From $-(-A$ v $-B)$ derive A & B and vice versa.
Arrow (AR)	From $A \rightarrow B$ derive $-A$ v B and vice versa. From $-A \rightarrow B$ derive A v B and vice versa. From $A \rightarrow B$ derive $-(A$ & $-B)$ and vice versa. From $-(A \rightarrow B)$ derive A & $-B$ and vice versa.
Contraposition (CN)	From $A \rightarrow B$ derive $-B \rightarrow -A$ and vice versa. From $A \rightarrow -B$ derive $B \rightarrow -A$. From $-A \rightarrow B$ derive $-B \rightarrow A$.

Truth-Tree Rules

LEFT	RIGHT
✓ −𝒜 𝒜	𝒜 −𝒜✓

✓ 𝒜 & ℬ
  𝒜
  ℬ
	𝒜 & ℬ ✓
	⟋⟍
	𝒜 ℬ

✓ 𝒜 ∨ ℬ ⟋⟍ 𝒜 ℬ	𝒜 ∨ ℬ ✓ 𝒜 ℬ
✓ 𝒜 → ℬ ⟋⟍ 𝒜 ℬ	𝒜 → ℬ ✓ 𝒜 ℬ
✓ 𝒜 ↔ ℬ ⟋⟍ 𝒜 𝒜 ℬ ℬ	𝒜 ↔ ℬ ✓ ⟋⟍ 𝒜 𝒜 ℬ ℬ

273

SINGLE PC LICENSE AGREEMENT AND LIMITED WARRANTY

READ THIS LICENSE CAREFULLY BEFORE OPENING THIS PACKAGE. BY OPENING THIS PACKAGE, YOU ARE AGREEING TO THE TERMS AND CONDITIONS OF THIS LICENSE. IF YOU DO NOT AGREE, DO NOT OPEN THE PACKAGE. PROMPTLY RETURN THE UNOPENED PACKAGE AND ALL ACCOMPANYING ITEMS TO THE PLACE YOU OBTAINED THEM.

1. GRANT OF LICENSE and OWNERSHIP: The enclosed computer programs ("Software") are licensed, not sold, to you by Prentice-Hall, Inc. ("We" or the "Company") and in consideration of your purchase or adoption of the accompanying Company textbooks and/or other materials, and your agreement to these terms. We reserve any rights not granted to you. You own only the disk(s) but we and/or our licensors own the Software itself. This license allows you to use and display your copy of the Software on a single computer (i.e., with a single CPU) at a single location for academic use only, so long as you comply with the terms of this Agreement. You may make one copy for back up, or transfer your copy to another CPU, provided that the Software is usable on only one computer.

2. RESTRICTIONS: You may not transfer or distribute the Software or documentation to anyone else. Except for backup, you may not copy the documentation or the Software. You may not network the Software or otherwise use it on more than one computer or computer terminal at the same time. You may not reverse engineer, disassemble, decompile, modify, adapt, translate, or create derivative works based on the Software or the Documentation. You may be held legally responsible for any copying or copyright infringement which is caused by your failure to abide by the terms of these restrictions.

3. TERMINATION: This license is effective until terminated. This license will terminate automatically without notice from the Company if you fail to comply with any provisions or limitations of this license. Upon termination, you shall destroy the Documentation and all copies of the Software. All provisions of this Agreement as to limitation and disclaimer of warranties, limitation of liability, remedies or damages, and our ownership rights shall survive termination.

4. LIMITED WARRANTY AND DISCLAIMER OF WARRANTY: Company warrants that for a period of 60 days from the date you purchase this SOFTWARE (or purchase or adopt the accompanying textbook), the Software, when properly installed and used in accordance with the Documentation, will operate in substantial conformity with the description of the Software set forth in the Documentation, and that for a period of 30 days the disk(s) on which the Software is delivered shall be free from defects in materials and workmanship under normal use. The Company does not warrant that the Software will meet your requirements or that the operation of the Software will be uninterrupted or error-free. Your only remedy and the Company's only obligation under these limited warranties is, at the Company's option, return of the disk for a refund of any amounts paid for it by you or replacement of the disk. THIS LIMITED WARRANTY IS THE ONLY WARRANTY PROVIDED BY THE COMPANY AND ITS LICENSORS, AND THE COMPANY AND ITS LICENSORS DISCLAIM ALL OTHER WARRANTIES, EXPRESS OR IMPLIED, INCLUDING

WITHOUT LIMITATION, THE IMPLIED WARRANTIES OF MERCHANTABIL-
ITY AND FITNESS FOR A PARTICULAR PURPOSE. THE COMPANY DOES
NOT WARRANT, GUARANTEE OR MAKE ANY REPRESENTATION RE-
GARDING THE ACCURACY, RELIABILITY, CURRENTNESS, USE, OR RE-
SULTS OF USE, OF THE SOFTWARE.

5. LIMITATION OF REMEDIES AND DAMAGES: IN NO EVENT,
SHALL THE COMPANY OR ITS EMPLOYEES, AGENTS, LICENSORS, OR
CONTRACTORS BE LIABLE FOR ANY INCIDENTAL, INDIRECT, SPECIAL,
OR CONSEQUENTIAL DAMAGES ARISING OUT OF OR IN CONNECTION
WITH THIS LICENSE OR THE SOFTWARE, INCLUDING FOR LOSS OF USE,
LOSS OF DATA, LOSS OF INCOME OR PROFIT, OR OTHER LOSSES, SUS-
TAINED AS A RESULT OF INJURY TO ANY PERSON, OR LOSS OF OR DAM-
AGE TO PROPERTY, OR CLAIMS OF THIRD PARTIES, EVEN IF THE COM-
PANY OR AN AUTHORIZED REPRESENTATIVE OF THE COMPANY HAS
BEEN ADVISED OF THE POSSIBILITY OF SUCH DAMAGES. IN NO EVENT
SHALL THE LIABILITY OF THE COMPANY FOR DAMAGES WITH RESPECT
TO THE SOFTWARE EXCEED THE AMOUNTS ACTUALLY PAID BY YOU, IF
ANY, FOR THE SOFTWARE OR THE ACCOMPANYING TEXTBOOK. BE-
CAUSE SOME JURISDICTIONS DO NOT ALLOW THE LIMITATION OF LIA-
BILITY IN CERTAIN CIRCUMSTANCES, THE ABOVE LIMITATIONS MAY
NOT ALWAYS APPLY TO YOU.

6. GENERAL: THIS AGREEMENT SHALL BE CONSTRUED IN AC-
CORDANCE WITH THE LAWS OF THE UNITED STATES OF AMERICA AND
THE STATE OF NEW YORK, APPLICABLE TO CONTRACTS MADE IN NEW
YORK, AND SHALL BENEFIT THE COMPANY, ITS AFFILIATES AND AS-
SIGNEES. THIS AGREEMENT IS THE COMPLETE AND EXCLUSIVE STATE-
MENT OF THE AGREEMENT BETWEEN YOU AND THE COMPANY AND SU-
PERSEDES ALL PROPOSALS OR PRIOR AGREEMENTS, ORAL, OR
WRITTEN, AND ANY OTHER COMMUNICATIONS BETWEEN YOU AND
THE COMPANY OR ANY REPRESENTATIVE OF THE COMPANY RELATING
TO THE SUBJECT MATTER OF THIS AGREEMENT. If you are a U.S. Govern-
ment user, this Software is licensed with "restricted rights" as set forth in subparagraphs
(a)-(d) of the Commercial Computer-Restricted Rights clause at FAR 52.227-19 or in
subparagraphs (c)(1)(ii) of the Rights in Technical Data and Computer Software clause
at DFARS 252.227-7013, and similar clauses, as applicable.

Should you have any questions concerning this agreement or if you wish to contact the Company for any reason, please contact in writing: Executive Manager, Media
Technology, Prentice Hall, One Lake Street, Upper Saddle River, NJ 07458.